Erich Reinhardt
oo Laurine juloften 1984

From Cumberland to Cape Horn

The Complete History of the Sailing Fleet of Thomas & John Brocklebank of Whitehaven and Liverpool – 'The World's oldest Shipping Company'

—

And the early history of their associated Company Robert & Henry Jeffersons of Whitehaven, plantation owners, Merchants and Shipowners. Established 1734

by D. Hollett

The Brocklebank barque Sindia *outward bound, 1887.*
(Liverpool public libraries.)

Published and distributed by
Fairplay Publications Limited
52–54 Southwark Street
London SE1 1UJ

ISBN 0905045 62 9

Printed and bound in Great Britain by
Page Bros (Norwich) Ltd, Mile Cross Lane,
Norwich, Norfolk NR6 6SA

The Author

Dave Hollett – married and with two daughters – has lived all his life on Merseyside, and like many of his fellow citizens, feels his roots deeply embedded in the history of the port. In his case, this interest has been stirred to active research by having among his forebears a number of mariners who served and rose to command in Liverpool sailing vessels, and this study has occupied him for many years.

Although naturally saddened by the decline of the port of Liverpool, he feels that there is still much to be recorded of its past history, especially its links with Cumberland in general and Whitehaven in particular. These links seem to be better remembered in Whitehaven than they do in Liverpool, and he hopes that this book may encourage his fellow Merseysiders to renew the connection with Whitehaven, a town which he has visited a great deal in the course of his researches, and one for which he has developed a great admiration.

A member of the Liverpool Nautical Research Society, he is naturally also an enthusiastic supporter of the new Merseyside Maritime Museum, and looks forward to its continued rapid development.

He feels it particularly appropriate that his work should be published in the year when the Sail Training Association's 'Tall Ships' Races will – albeit briefly – bring square-sails back to the Mersey.

Contents

Preface

The long and romantic story of the famous Brocklebank Line of Whitehaven and Liverpool begins in the reign of Queen Anne, when the Reverend Daniel Brocklebank, father of the founder of the Line was born in Cumberland in 1705. The Line dates its inception from the year 1770, when the Reverend Daniel Brocklebank's younger son, Capt Daniel Brocklebank, first began to build ships at Sheepscutt, New England. Capt Daniel Brocklebank died in 1801, the business then being continued by his bachelor sons, Thomas & John Brocklebank at Whitehaven, and then, at a later date Liverpool.

The firm of Thomas & John Brocklebank continued to build ships at Whitehaven until the 1860s, until the yard was closed and they began to purchase their sailing vessels from other builders, notably Messrs Harland and Wolff of Belfast. Apart from building ships Thomas & John Brocklebank became even more well-known for the great fleet of sailing vessels which they developed during the last century. The firm in fact remained with sail until they obtained their last great windjammer from Harland & Wolff, this being the steel barque *Holkar*, which remained in Company service until 1901. During the first part of the 20th century the firm built up a large fleet of steamers before becoming an integral part of Cunard-Brocklebank. However, this work is confined to the history of the firm's 18th, and 19th century sailing fleet, and the history of their associated company, Messrs Robert & Henry Jeffersons, also of Whitehaven and Liverpool.

The oldest business house in Whitehaven today is that of Robert & Henry Jeffersons, of Lowther street. The history of this ancient company is inextricably linked with the history of the Brocklebank Line, the development of Whitehaven, and the island of Antigua, where the firm's great sugar plantations were once located. Primarily the Jeffersons were wine, sugar and rum merchants, but their interests tended to be widespread. In Cumberland they had interests in shipbuilding, and they were active in the development of the railway system. At Liverpool they once operated as cotton brokers.

In the year 1818 Robert & Henry Jefferson began to operate a small fleet of ships. These vessels were mainly employed in the West Indies trade, but they also made many other voyages to distant parts of the globe. Both the Brocklebanks and the Jeffersons held an interest in the shipbuilding firm of Lumley Kennedy and Company, which gentleman once served as manager of the Brocklebank yard before striking out on his own account. This firm in fact built several of the Jeffersons' best known ships, including the clipper-barque *Ehen*. In the early years of this century Henry Jefferson, descendant of the founder of the firm succeeded Capt William Ray as Marine Superintendent of the Brocklebank Line. Jeffersons' principal mariner was my maternal great grandfather, Capt Joseph Wise, commander and part owner of their best known vessels. Joseph Wise was in turn the son of Capt Abraham Vaux Wise of Brigham, once master of the Brocklebank vessels *Swallow* and *Maranham*.

Captain Abraham Vaux Wise was born at Cockermouth in the parish of Brigham in 1784. Early in the last century he married Miss Eleanor Braithwaite of Whitehaven, the couple had seven children, two girls and five boys, but alas Abraham Wise died at Drogheda in 1827 when my great grandfather Joseph was just six years old, and his younger brother Francis just one year old. Despite, or perhaps because of this setback all the sons of Capt Abraham Vaux Wise were apprenticed to a life at sea. Whilst Joseph was apprenticed to Robert and Henry Jefferson, his brothers, Abraham, George, and Francis served with Thomas & John Brocklebank, before becoming commanders of some of their best known ships. Understandably it is these factors which motivated me to research and write this book in the 1980s. In this work I have let the pattern of my ancestors' lives act as a connecting thread running through the general history of these two famous maritime enterprises.

D. Hollett, Bebington, Merseyside 1983.

8

Acknowledgements

Many records relating to individual mariners, 19th century shipping in general, and to Messrs Brocklebanks and Jeffersons in particular have survived. Unfortunately many more have also been lost. The records that have survived tend to be widely spread geographically, which factor made this work difficult and time consuming to research. Without the kind help and co-operation of many individuals and organisations it would not have been possible to complete this work.

First I would like to thank Mr B. N. Barlow, Secretary of Cunard for allowing me to quote from the records of Thomas & John Brocklebank held at Liverpool, and also for allowing me to obtain illustrations of early Brocklebank ships used in this work. Miss Constance, and Miss Elizabeth Jefferson also granted me permission to quote from the remaining records of their Company, Robert and Henry Jefferson, held on permanent loan by the Record Office, Carlisle, Cumbria. I am most grateful to them for this.

Mr Malcolm Barr-Hamilton of the National Maritime Museum, Greenwich, deserves much praise and credit for his help in locating Masters Certificates, and Claim forms, Letters, Crew Lists, etc. relating to the four Wise Brothers (and others), held by the National Maritime Museum. I would also like to thank him here for the help and advice he gave me on numerous occasions.

Mr B. C. Jones M.A., Cumbria County Archivist, and his colleagues at the Record Office, Carlisle, gave me much help and assistance on my many visits to their office, whilst on Merseyside I must thank Mr Mike Stammers, Keeper of Maritime History at Merseyside County Museum, and Miss Jill Sweatnam, Assistant Keeper of Maritime History at this Museum, who was assigned to assist me on this project. Their help in locating records held at the Museum was much appreciated.

Ships' Registers, and the majority of 19th century Crew Lists and Log Books are held at the Public Record Office, Kew. I would like to thank the hard-working staff at this busy office for the assistance that they gave me on numerous occasions. The staff at the Liverpool Record Office in particular, helped me on many occasions, as did the staff at the Picton Library, Liverpool.

Lloyd's Register of Shipping, London, granted me permission to make reference to their Registers etc. for which I am most grateful, and the Corporation of Lloyd's, London, allowed me to make use of their illustration of one of my ancestor's commands, the brig *Kitty* of Whitehaven; this was really appreciated. At Liverpool the 'Journal of Commerce' granted me permission to quote from early editions of their paper, for which I thank them. I would also like to thank Mr Craig Carter, Editor of 'Sea Breezes', for reading my manuscript, and helping me in various other ways. Messrs Brown, Son and Ferguson, of Glasgow granted me permission to use their illustration of the Brocklebank barque *Chinsura*, which was very much appreciated. Mr D. H. Deere of Marine Publications International, London, also read my manuscript, and helped me on a number of occasions.

To obtain the material I required for this book I was obliged to visit, or write to many Libraries, amongst them being the following, whom I would like to thank for their help – Whitehaven, Barrow, Workington, Cockermouth, Carlisle, Wallasey, Bebington, and Birkenhead. From Whitby Library, North Yorkshire, I obtained invaluable material related to the building of the Jefferson clipper-barque *Antigua*. In London I must give special thanks to the staff at the Guildhall Library, masters records being held at this place.

The late Daniel Hay, F.R.S.A., Senior Librarian at Whitehaven for many years deserves a special mention; he helped me on several occasions, and was always most kind and helpful. Mr L. Heath, Editor of the 'Whitby Gazette', allowed me to use material related to the maiden voyage of the Jefferson clipper *Antigua*, which appeared in his paper in June 1858. Rick Hogben, author and maritime expert, read my manuscript and made many helpful observations, for which I am grateful.

The help and co-operation of the 'Whitehaven News' was most welcome. I must thank Mr J. A. Clague, Head of the History Department and Acting Chairman of the Maritime History Group at the University of St. John's, Newfoundland, Canada, where Crew Lists for the British Commonwealth are also held. I received help from the World Ship Society, and in particular the Society's Mutual Interest Scheme Organiser, Captain Nelson, of Manchester, and Mr W. Martin Benn, whose notes on early Brocklebank ships were helpful. Captain William Ray's grandson, Mr Ray Snr., deserves particular thanks for helping me to re-locate his ancestor's memoirs, and I must also thank Mrs Ida Parrish of Whitehaven for her assistance. Mr Harry Fancy, Curator of Whitehaven Museum, and Mr Michael Moon, Publisher of Whitehaven, deserve particular thanks for allowing me to reproduce many of the illustrations that I have used in this work.

Last, but not least I would like to give particular thanks to my wife Vera, who gave me much help and assistance whilst working on this project, and my daughters Susan and Christine, whose encouragement was very welcome. I must also pay tribute here to my late parents, Frederick William Charles Hollett and Mabel Hollett, grand-daughter of Capt Joseph Wise of Whitehaven, and my maternal grandparents, Tom Alfred Wise, youngest son of Capt Joseph Wise, grandson of Capt Abraham Vaux Wise of Brigham, and Mary Maria Wise, whose fascinating recollections passed down to me via my parents, motivated me to research and write this book.

CHAPTER 1

Early History – The Brocklebank Line, and Jeffersons of Whitehaven

The histories of the famous Brocklebank Line, and Jeffersons of Whitehaven, both begin in the reign of Queen Anne near the small market town of Wigton, Cumberland, the Reverend Daniel Brocklebank, father of the founder of the Line being born near this small market town in the year 1705. In 1734 young Daniel Brocklebank married a Miss Sarah Slack at Ireby. The couple set up home at this village, and it was here that their first son John was born – a man whose descendants were destined to become mariners rather than merchants. Shortly after the birth of their first son the family moved to the adjacent parish of Torpenhow, where Daniel Brocklebank had been offered the post of curate-in-charge of Torpenhow Parish Church.

Daniel Brocklebank, and his wife, remained at Torpenhow until 1757, for this entire period being merely curate-in-charge of the parish, since the living at that time was held by absentee vicars with duties elsewhere. For almost twenty-three years Daniel Brocklebank was obliged to do the work of these absentee vicars – without much financial remuneration, but his reward for devotion to duty finally came in 1757 when he was instituted vicar of Moorland, in the county of Westmorland.

It was whilst the couple were at Torpenhow however that Sarah and Daniel had five more children, these being Thomas, Ralph, born in 1737, who was to follow in his father's footsteps by becoming a clergyman, Margaret, Daniel and Eleanor. Daniel junior, the founder of the firm was born in 1741, and at the tender age of 14, before the family moved to Moorland, he made his way to Whitehaven, at which port he was placed as an apprentice carpenter to a shipbuilder. Daniel remained at Whitehaven for the next fourteen years as a single man. Then at the age of 28 he married a Miss Anne Cuppage at Holy Trinity Church, Whitehaven, on the 7th March 1769. On the 19th August of the following year they returned to the same church to baptise their first child, whom they named Sarah, after her grandmother. The young couple were to remain at Whitehaven for another year, before seeking their fortune in the new world.

The history of the ancient house of Jefferson also begins at a village near Wigton, Aikton, a small scattered community which lies some three miles to the north of Wigton. It was here that the Jefferson family was recorded as landowners in 1696, and for some time previously. The family connection with Whitehaven began with Robert Jefferson who was born at Aikton in 1704. When he was still a young man he also made his way to Whitehaven where he lost no time in establishing himself as a wine merchant. Some time after the founding of his wine business he decided to combine this occupation with that of a sea captain – such a combination – merchant and mariner – being common practice at this time. At sea he occupied himself in the lucrative 'Virginia Trade', exporting a variety of goods to Virginia, bringing back to his home port valuable cargoes of Virginia tobacco.

The tobacco trade at Whitehaven owes its inception to Sir John Lowther, about whom much reference will be made later in this story. At this point however it is sufficient to state that he established this trade at the port in 1680. By the year 1740, when Capt Robert Jefferson became involved in the trade, no less than fifty Whitehaven ships were engaged in this work. On the outward passage the small Whitehaven vessels would carry a truly amazing variety of goods, ranging from coal and iron, often used to an extent as ballast, to saddles, whips, and other such items, then collectively known as 'Horse Furniture', whilst woven goods from places as far apart as Cockermouth, Kirkcudbright, and the Isle-of-Man, were much in demand by merchant-mariners such as Robert Jefferson.

Martha and Capt Robert Jefferson had four children, but whilst three of them died very young, Henry Jefferson, born in 1750, was destined to live to the ripe old age of 77, and it was this son who continued the business – working as a merchant and a mariner.

Captain Robert Jefferson, founder of the firm died in 1779. His obituary in the famous local paper, the 'Cumberland Pacquet', describing him as 'many years a captain in a ship in the Virginia Trade, and much respected as an honest man'. Prior to his father's death, Capt Henry Jefferson took up residence at 4 Cross Street, Whitehaven, and in 1775 became master of his own ship. The *Gale* was an interesting ship, having been built on the coast of Cumberland in 1758. She was a vessel of 200 tons register – quite a large craft for her day. There can be no doubt that she was named after the Gale family of Whitehaven, John Gale being a well known tobacco agent and merchant at the port.

Captain Henry Jefferson remained in command of this ship for several years, trading her from both Whitehaven and London to Quebec, Virginia, and the island of Antigua in the West Indies. It was on this island that he met a Miss Anne Tweedie, whom he married in 1780. Shortly after this date Capt Jefferson sold the snow *Gale* – the ship becoming the property of her new commander, Capt Parker of Whitehaven.

The marriage of Capt Henry Jefferson of Whitehaven, to Miss Anne Tweedie of Antigua took place on the 18th May 1780 at the island's capital, St. John's. Anne was very young at the time of her marriage, but the couple prospered, and according to Cumbrian historian Daniel Hay, they had four children. The sons were Robert (1785–1848) who appears to have been born at Antigua, and Henry (1800–77), baptised at Holy Trinity Church, Whitehaven. With this marriage of Henry Jefferson of Whitehaven to Anne Tweedie of Antigua, the firm of Robert and Henry Jefferson of Whitehaven began its long association with this beautiful island.

For several decades the development of the ancient port of Whitehaven was to be

12

influenced by the Brocklebanks and the Jeffersons. The lives of many, particularly the lives of many Cumberland mariners, were now to be shaped by the development of their respective enterprises. However, perhaps no individual family of master mariners was to relate more with the development of this port and these firms, than the Wise family of Holme Cultram, and Cockermouth, in the parish of Brigham. To trace their history here will therefore give one an insight into the life and times of many such families of 19th century mariners.

For generations the Wise family farmed near the river Wyse, at the ancient settlement of Abbey Town, Holme Cultram, near the shores of the Solway Firth. It was here, on the family estate, that Abraham Wise was born in September 1756 being the eldest son of Abraham and Esther Wise. Despite the fact that he was the eldest son, and thus heir to the Wise family's small estate, Abraham was not intent on becoming a yeoman farmer. Whilst still very young he was placed as an apprentice to a local surgeon. On the completion of his training he became one of three surgeons based at the famous 'Cockermouth Dispensary'.

On the 12th September 1782 my maternal ancestor, Abraham Wise, surgeon at Cockermouth, married Hannah Jones, also of Cockermouth. The couple were to have four children whilst resident there, the eldest being my great-great grandfather, Abraham Vaux Wise, born in 1784.

There can be little doubt that young Abraham Vaux Wise would have been educated at the famous Cockermouth Grammar School, the establishment founded in 1676 by Sir George Fletcher and others, the school responsible for educating the world famous descendant of the Fletcher and Christian families, the mutineer, Fletcher Christian.

About the year 1798 young Abraham Vaux Wise followed in the footsteps of Fletcher Christian, making his way to the town of Whitehaven – the port which clearly acted as a magnet to the adventurous young men of Cumberland in the 18th century. About my ancestors' early life at Whitehaven little can be said, for, to the best of my knowledge no records have survived which can enlighten us; however, I think we can safely assume that he was apprenticed to Capt Wilson Fisher, shipowner, and son-in-law of Capt Daniel Brocklebank – founder of the Brocklebank Line.

On the 26th September 1809 Capt Abraham Vaux Wise of Brigham was appointed master of Capt Fisher's armed brigantine *Swallow*. The Wise family's long association with the Brocklebank Line, as commanders of their famous ships had now begun, for Thomas Fisher (1814–1906), the son of Wilson Fisher, was later to assume the name Brocklebank, become head of the world famous enterprise, and in 1845, the 1st Baronet. Now we must turn our attention to the history of the port of Whitehaven itself, for without this knowledge the subsequent history of the Brocklebank Line, and the House of Jefferson, cannot be fully understood.

The ancient port of Whitehaven

In a survey taken in 1566, Whitehaven consisted of six isolated cottages, the homes of local fishermen, and the men who kept a nine-ton vessel there, used to supply the religious settlement of St. Bee's with its requirements. By the year 1633 there were still no more than about nine or ten thatched cottages, but things were soon to change, for soon after this

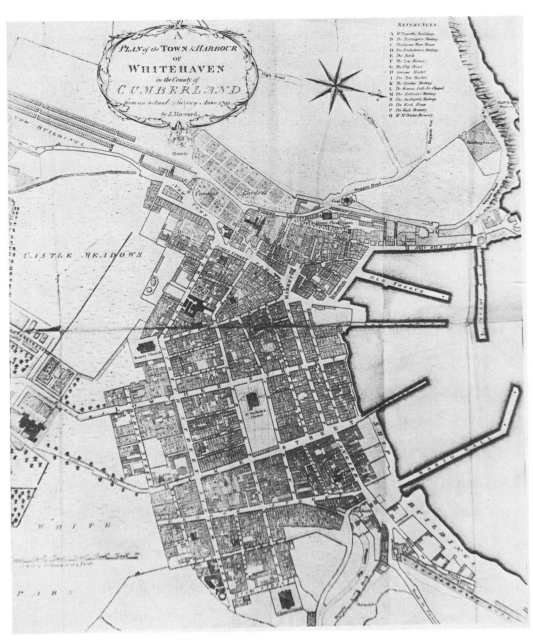

The town and harbour of Whitehaven, 1790

date Sir John Lowther, already mentioned in connection with the Virginia Trade, conceived the idea of working the large deposits of coal known to exist in the area. Thus inclined he obtained from King Charles II in 1666, a grant for all the ungranted lands near Whitehaven; and later, in 1678, he managed to obtain a further grant for all the lands for two miles northwards – between high and low water mark. With these moves the phenomenal development of Whitehaven had begun.

By the end of the 17th century the town's population had increased to 2,272; the port's vessels by 1685 numbered 46 – many, if not most of these engaged in the coal trade, now well developed by Lowther. By the year 1772 the number of vessels belonging to Whitehaven had risen to no less than 197, with similar proportional increases being made along the whole coast of Cumberland. In the 18th and the early 19th century the 'port' of Whitehaven comprised within its jurisdiction not only the harbour and town of Whitehaven itself, but also the smaller harbours at Workington, Harrington, Ravenglass, and until 1841 Maryport – to the north of Workington. Collectively, this 44-mile stretch of Cumbrian coastline, then known as the port of Whitehaven, became at one point in time one of the largest ports of registration in the United Kingdom.

Coal by the sea. Saltom pit photographed when derelict in 1880.

The export of coal, much of it to Ireland, remained the basic source of wealth for Whitehaven for many years; but the port's trade with Europe, Africa, America, and the West Indies in particular soon began to develop. Alongside the development of the mines, the port's shipbuilding industry also began to expand, and as ships built for the coal trade had to be built very strongly, there developed from this requirement the excellence in shipbuilding which was later to be employed to such advantage by firms such as Brocklebank, Lumley Kennedy, and other great Cumbrian shipbuilders.

The impressive seat of the Right Hon. the Earl of Lonsdale was Whitehaven Castle, which was a very large stone building pleasantly situated at the south end of the town. This great mansion, which occupied the site of the original manor house built by Sir John Lowther, was surrounded by fine lawns, ornamental gardens, and woody pleasure grounds. The Lowthers were well able to afford the luxury of this magnificent establishment, for by the end of the 18th century Sir John Lowther, descendant of the founder of the port's coal industry, was obtaining an annual income of no less than £16,000 from his mines – a truly astronomical figure by the monetary standards of the day.

The mines at Whitehaven, first developed by the Lowthers, were amongst the most extraordinary in the world, being at the time among the deepest in existence; they also ran for a great distance beneath the waters of the Solway Firth, thus making them susceptible to flooding! A writer of the period described these remarkable pits in the following terms:

'The mines are sunk to a depth of an hundred and thirty fathoms, and are extended under the sea to places where there is sufficient depth of water for ships of large burthen. These are the deepest coal mines that have hitherto been wrought; and perhaps the miners have not, in any other part of the globe penetrated to so great a depth below the surface of the sea . . .'

In order to improve the mines at Whitehaven Sir James Lowther (who died in 1755) sent his famous engineer, Carlyle Spedding, to Newcastle – 'In order to establish and pursue the same methods at Whitehaven.' At Newcastle Carlyle Spedding got himself employed as a hewer of coals in the pits under a fictitious name, from which it would seem 'industrial espionage', much in the news today, has a long and interesting history. Spedding worked in the Newcastle pits for some time, keeping his eyes and ears open, obtaining all the information he could for his Whitehaven master. Unfortunately Spedding was burnt by a fire in the pits before he had completed his work there, and when this happened a message was sent to Newcastle to obtain the best medical assistance possible for Lowther's injured industrial spy.

Alas, the extraordinary attention paid to an apparent humble hewer of coal by Newcastle's most eminent medical practitioners led to the discovery of Mr Spedding's real intentions. On recovery the engineer had no option other than to return to Whitehaven, but not before he had in great measure accomplished his mission. Back at Whitehaven he did much to improve the state of the mining industry. He invented the wheel and flint device, but later lost his own life in an explosion whilst surveying one of the mines.

Another great name linked with the development of mining at Whitehaven was that of John Peile, under whose direction the Whitehaven mines made much progress. The

Whitehaven harbour in the 1790s.

importance of these Whitehaven Collieries may be judged by the fact that in 1816 no less than 900 persons were employed there, and during Mr Peile's term of office output of the Whitehaven mines reached almost 250,000 tons per annum.

The method of loading the numerous vessels in the port, even in the year 1811 was surprisingly modern, for on the west side of the Harbour was situated the coal staith, where five vessels of 300 tons burthen could be loaded from the hurries at one time. 'By an easy and gentle descent, the loaden waggon runs by its own weight on the frame of the way, with above two tons of coal therein, from the pit to the staith, without any horse to draw it. Where the descent is so great, that the motion of the waggon becomes too rapid, a man who is mounted behind the waggon, by pressing down upon one of the wheels a piece of wood called the convoy, fixed to the waggon for the purpose, can restrain the motion, so as to moderate it sufficiently. The only use for a horse is to draw the empty waggon back again, to the pit along another road, laid at a small distance from the side of the road, down which the loaden waggons descend. By this contrivance, the loaden & empty waggons never interrupt or interfere with each other; and by this kind of waggon and road, one horse does as much work as twenty four pack horses used to.' – so wrote a local historian some years before 1811.

Apart from Daniel Brocklebank's Ropery at Bransty, the town boasted two other such establishments, both at Cortickle, one belonging to Mr John Hartley, the other to John

St. Nicholas Parish Church, Whitehaven as it was at the end of the 18th century.

Sargeant. The town had two good Butchers' Markets, three public Breweries and a poor house. The local newspaper, the 'Cumberland Pacquet', had already been in existence for 37 years.

The postal service to and from the port seems to have been exceptionally good for the period, the London Post arriving promptly at seven each evening, and departing the same evening at a quarter past ten. The Isle of Man Packet boat was timed to leave Whitehaven the first tide after the arrival of the Saturday's post from London.

It is quite clear that by 1810 the town of Whitehaven was already very well developed, the streets had been laid out on a regular plan; the shops were considered by one writer at the time to be 'genteel', and on a par with the shops of even London or Paris. The houses of the town were in general roofed with blue slate, which gave the town a most beautiful appearance from the sea or the adjoining heights, and the approach from the north side was by a fine portico of red freestone, with a rich entablature, ornamented with the arms of the family of Lowther. This edifice had not been constructed by Lowther for mere show, for it served the useful purpose of continuing the course of the gallery, by which the waggons, laden with coals, were designed to pass to the harbour.

The harbour at Whitehaven, even at the end of the 18th and the beginning of the 19th century was considered to be perhaps the largest and most convenient pier harbour in the kingdom, a pier first being erected here by Sir John Lowther some time before 1687. After this construction the harbour was rendered so commodious by it as to be capable of containing a fleet of 100 sail. In 1767 the New Quay was lengthened; and in 1784, the North Wall was finished: the Old Quay was made longer in 1792, and many other improvements were effected about the year 1809. So far as mariners using the harbour were concerned, it was considered secure, rather than easy of access, masters of sailing vessels being advised to keep up full sail until well into the harbour and past the pier heads. In the year 1810 no less than 188 vessels were registered at Whitehaven, the majority of the masters of these craft living in or near the town.

On the 4th September 1811 young Capt Abraham Vaux Wise from Brigham, now master of the larger Fisher/Brocklebank vessel *Maranham*, married Miss Eleanor Braithewaite at St. Nicholas parish church, Whitehaven – the bride's father – Mr John Braithewaite, being a stocking manufacturer, and it would seem assistant overseer of the township of Whitehaven.

In the near future the bride was to have the honour of having the family's own ship the *Eleanor* of Whitehaven named after her; in the meantime the young couple set up home in King Street, Whitehaven before moving to the village of Sandwith, on St. Bees Head, overlooking the town and harbour of Whitehaven. Abraham and Eleanor Wise were to have seven children – five boys and two girls.

19

CHAPTER 2

With Daniel Brocklebank
1770–1801

It was in the year 1770 that Daniel and Anne Brocklebank decided to leave Whitehaven to seek their fortune in the new world. The move seems to have been a particularly well planned one, for he left Whitehaven with a very definite objective in mind, and that was to establish a small shipbuilding yard in New England. How did the younger son of a country clergyman raise the capital for such a venture, and why establish his first enterprise in America rather than England?

To such questions no documentary material remains to enlighten us, but circumstantial indications can provide us with some clues. In the 18th, and early 19th centuries, shipbuilding was very much a collective venture – capital being raised by subscription, from relatives, friends, neighbours, farmers, merchants, the local clergy, and landowners. One must assume that Daniel Brocklebank raised money in this manner for his shipbuilding venture – no doubt obtaining the support of his father, the Reverend Daniel Brocklebank in these endeavours. To this we must note the fact that much of the timber used in the construction of Cumberland vessels was, even in the 18th century, imported from the new world – an obviously expensive operation. Daniel, we must assume, decided to cut costs by taking his men to the cheap and readily available American timber, rather than bring the timber across the Atlantic to his men! A shrewd move.

Shortly after his arrival in America Daniel established his yard at a place called Sheepscutt, New England, where over the course of the next five years he built five ships. It is thought that he named the first four vessels the *Minerva*, *Hector*, *Nestor*, and *Jane* – but there is no certain evidence to support this – what we do know for certain however is that he named his fifth vessel the *Castor*.

The timing of Daniel Brocklebank's move to America was intriguing, for as he must have been aware, events in America were drifting inevitably towards war, owing to the resentment on the part of the colonists against the taxes imposed on them by the British Government. The situation worsened; in 1770 the citizens of Boston attacked British soldiers in the street; in 1772 a British vessel was burned at Providence. The famous 'Boston Tea Party' occurred in 1773, and in 1775 hostilities broke out at Lexington.

Opinion over the issue was divided in America and Britain. Feeling was running high, with the situation causing a crisis in the lives of each resident of America; each had to choose which side to support. Daniel Brocklebank made his decision – it was to make the long voyage back to Whitehaven.

On the 8th May 1775, Daniel Brocklebank assumed command of the near completed *Castor* and set sail for Whitehaven. In the report of the event which has survived no mention is made of Anne Brocklebank, or of the couple's two young children, Sarah born at Whitehaven before they left Cumberland, or of Daniel, born in 1773 whilst they were living at Sheepscutt, and we do not know whether they returned with Daniel in the *Castor*, or were sent on ahead. Before setting sail for Whitehaven, Daniel made all efforts to purchase provisions for the long voyage home, but these it would seem were not available, or perhaps not being made available to departing Englishmen. Under these conditions Daniel felt he had no option than to sail with a poorly provisioned ship. His departure and voyage home were later described in considerable detail in the columns of the 'Cumberland Pacquet' on the 15th June:

> 'Captain Brocklebank left Sheepscutt with a vessel he had built there, on board of which he had only one barrel of beef and some bread, provisions could not be purchased there. He therefore gave his seamen the choice of running for Nova Scotia or the Banks of New Foundland, to try whether they could procure a sufficiency of fish to support them on their passage to Europe. They chose the latter, and in a few hours caught an amazing great quantity.
>
> They had some salt, but not enough to preserve the fish they had taken. This dificiency they however soon supplied by scraping up the salt which had been laid between the timbers (a custom used for preserving ships) whenever they could get it, and by these means got as much as cured a quantity which served them plentifully on the passage. After twenty days sail they were in St. Georges Channel, and the 11th from that came safe into Whitehaven to the great joy and astonishment of their friends who did not expect them so soon, as the Captain had purposed building another vessel but from the disturbed state of the Province thought it prudent to quit it and a considerable part of his cargo which he had purchased and had ready for shipping.'

And so it was that Daniel Brocklebank returned to his home town of Whitehaven. For the next four years he remained in command of the famous brig *Castor*, whilst his brother John, now also a ship's master, sailed out of Liverpool to the waters close to Greenland, for this elder brother was now actively engaged in the whaling trade. The war with America continued, and despite all efforts Daniel Brocklebank seemed unable to steer clear of the conflict, as the following article, taken from the 'Cumberland Pacquet' of the 8th February 1776, will indicate:

> 'On passage of the *Castor* Captain Brocklebank from Newfoundland to Halifax, a Man-of-War bore down upon her supposing her to be an American Privateer, one *Jerry O'Brian*, who had taken many vessels and who the Man-of-War was in quest of. On the captain of the *Castor* not readily showing his colours, the matches were all lighted ready to fire a broadside into her till luckily she shewed her colours and brought to. This same *Jerry O'Brian* is a noted provincial privateer and lately had the assurance to look into Halifax, but found the port well guarded with Men-O-War, otherwise it would have laid the town under contribution.'

More conflict between the Americans and the men of Whitehaven was to come, for two years after Daniel Brocklebank and the *Castor* had almost met their end, the famous

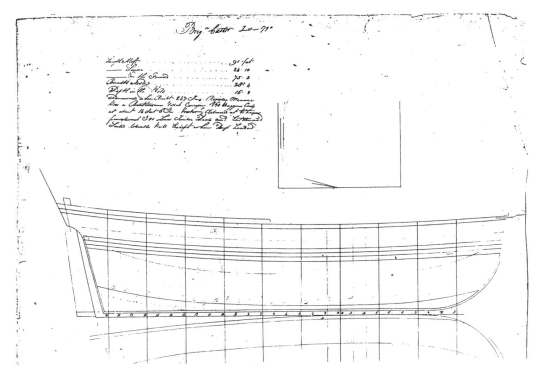

Lines of the brig Castor, *1790.*

American naval officer, John Paul Jones arrived off Whitehaven in his celebrated privateer *Ranger*, with the intention of destroying the place! Paul Jones's vessel had been well equipped for this task at the port of Nantes and mounted 18 six-pounder guns. Jones landed with a party of 30 armed men, dashed to the crowded harbour and quickly set fire to three of the 200 ships then in the harbour, which action might well have destroyed the greater part of the Whitehaven fleet, but fortunately did not.

Early in 1779 Daniel Brocklebank left New York in the *Castor* bound for Whitehaven. It was to be an eventful voyage for our Cumberland mariner for shortly after leaving the American port he chased and sank a small enemy merchantman. He continued across the Atlantic, and when almost in sight of the Irish coast he met up with the notorious American privateer, *General Sullivan*, which at the time had under its control a British ship which it had taken only a few days earlier. Daniel Brocklebank joined forces with another British ship then in the vicinity, the *Lively* of Bristol, and together they chased off the American vessel and recaptured her prize. The *Lively* and the *Castor* then escorted the vessel into Cork where her grateful owners paid the usual salvage money.

At this time privateering was general, and many armed private vessels were commissioned by governments to attack and capture vessels of enemy states. The whole history of the Merchant Service in the 18th and early 19th century is one long saga of such attacks and counter-attacks. Vessels were often taken and retaken within the space of 24 hours, and many a shipping fortune was founded on the acquisition of an enemy prize. No doubt the above interesting experience prompted young Daniel Brocklebank to apply to King George III for his official licence to become an accredited privateer. In August 1779, 'Letters of Marque' were granted to Daniel Brocklebank, authorising him to 'seize and destroy the ships, depots and goods belonging to the King of Spain'. Armed with this useful document, and with no less than 26 guns aboard the *Castor*, Daniel Brocklebank entered into a new phase of his career. In addition to the 26 guns he also had a highly qualified crew of no less than 45 armed men aboard.

The life of a privateer was however by its very nature a somewhat insecure one, so perhaps being mindful of this fact Brocklebank decided not to put all his eggs into one basket; he shrewdly implemented a policy of diversification by placing orders with Whitehaven shipbuilders for additional vessels. The first such vessel to be constructed was the *Pollux*, which was promptly renamed the *Precedent*, built by Spedding and Company. On the loss of the *Castor*, wrecked at Jamaica in 1781, he took command of this new ship, but then handed over command of the vessel to Captain Wise, and whilst under this master's command she was lost off the coast of Ireland in 1791.

In 1782 Messrs Spedding's built to the order of Daniel Brocklebank the 18-gun brig *Castor*(2), which again was commanded for a while by him, but sold after seven years. In 1786 Messrs Spedding and Company completed their final order for Brocklebank, this being for the brig *Cyrus*, which remained in Company service for 11 years before being sold. Two more vessels were then built at Whitehaven for Daniel Brocklebank, these being the brigs *Zebulon* and *Dolphin*, built in 1787 and 1788 by Henry Stockdale and Company, a noted local shipbuilder. In the same year that this last vessel was built, Brocklebank launched from his own recently acquired yard the first of 29 vessels to be built there before his death. From this point in time the construction of ships, rather than the trading of them was to provide his main source of income.

Although it was clearly Daniel Brocklebank's policy to build ships for sale, rather than to trade them on his own account, he retained shares in vessels that he built, and also held shares in other ships, one of the latter being the *Musgrave*. The *Musgrave* was an interesting vessel, a brig of 136 tons burthen, built on the coast of Cumberland in 1771. The years 1796–97 found this vessel sailing under the command of Capt Samuel Wise of Workington. Alas, the accounts which have survived show that the eighth voyage of the *Musgrave* dated the 15th April 1797, showed a net loss of £2.3.4¼, which figure it would seem merely added to the accumulated financial problems then being experienced by the respective owners.

To resolve the problems the Brocklebanks took steps to sell the brig. The owners arranged a meeting, which took place on the 22nd April 1797 at Workington, which resulted in the following statement being added to the final page of the *Musgrave* accounts:

'We the undersigned part owners of the brig *Musgrave*, having this day examined the foregoing accounts find a balance due to us from Capt. Wise of £262.15.11 and likewise a cargo of coals unpaid for amounting to £49.4.0 making £311.19.11 and it is hereby agreed by us, the present

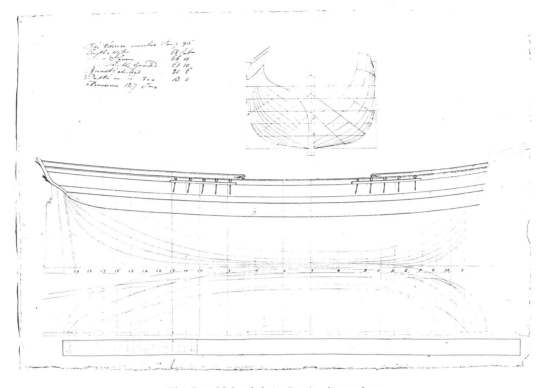

The Brocklebank brig Carrier *lines plan.*

owners that Mr Askew of Harrington be empowered to sell the said vessel to pay and settle all just accts., and divide the residue amongst the owners. . . .'

Soon after Daniel Brocklebank sold his shares in the *Musgrave* he was to suffer the loss of his son, Capt Daniel Brocklebank Jnr., then commander of the *Alfred*, and only 25 years old. The *Alfred* had voyaged to Montego Bay, Jamaica, only to find the harbour filled with slave ships; conditions being what one might expect on these ships, yellow fever was prevalent, and in the hot humid air of Montego Bay it rapidly spread to vessels not engaged in the notorious trade. Daniel Brocklebank contracted the disease, and died after a short illness. He was buried in the churchyard of St. James, Spanish Town on the 21st July 1798.

Thankfully however the days of slavery were now numbered, for only two months before Daniel Brocklebank had died at Montego Bay, himself, in a very real sense a victim of the system, the British Government drew up and passed a lengthy Act for the improvement of the conditions of slaves, usually styled the 'Amelioration Act', which in itself was a major step on the road to the system's complete abolition some years later.

24

CHAPTER 3

With the Jeffersons 1780–1824

The island of Antigua, where Capt Henry Jefferson married Miss Anne Tweedie in 1780, has a long and fascinating history, but it is sufficient to state here that the island was first discovered by Europeans when Christopher Columbus landed a party there in 1493, but contented himself with merely giving the island the beautiful name of Santa-Maria-de-la-Antigua, after a church by that name in Seville. The formal long-term settlement of the island by the British dated from 1632, when Sir Thomas Warner despatched a party of settlers from the parent colony of St. Christopher's, but regrettably the importation of slaves from Africa soon followed this development, providing the labour to work the plantations. Life for these unfortunate slaves would begin at sunrise, and continue until dusk with severe punishment being meted out to any who relaxed from their labour.

The life-style enjoyed by the white inhabitants of 18th century Antigua stood in stark contrast to that experienced by their black field workers. Most of them ate, and in particular drank to excess! After a typical night's drinking it is doubtful if many of the plantation owners were capable of arousing themselves – let alone working in the fields at sunrise.

In most of the great plantation houses the ordinary drink of the men was punch or grog, but madeira wine and porter were introduced at the tables of those considered to live well, and at the houses of the island's principal merchants and planters claret was served, the best being imported from London. Some also came from Ireland, but the greater part of this luxury was smuggled in from the French and Dutch at Guadaloupe and St. Eustatius. The history of this particular enterprise dated from as far back as 1710, when the administrator of the day, one Daniel Parke was promptly murdered for attempting to stop it! The coastline of Antigua was particularly well adapted to this clandestine traffic, its many secluded bays, coves, and hidden harbours providing just the environment so much appreciated by smugglers of all nations – then and now.

As well as the fine wines, the tables of the rich would be laden with a profusion of good foods, and as an additional diversion a theatre was established at St. John's, the first performance being given in 1788.

Such then was life on the island of Antigua at the end of the 18th century, when Henry Jefferson married Anne Tweedie. It is not clear from remaining records just how long Henry and Anne Jefferson remained on the island before they returned to Whitehaven, but I would hazard a guess that it was in the 1790s. The firm's accounts for the year 1814 have survived, which clearly indicate that many years of sustained work must have been put into their Whitehaven wine business, building it into a very substantial enterprise. Amongst other things these documents also give us an interesting insight into the drinking habits of old Whitehaven.

Without a doubt the Earl of Lonsdale was the Jeffersons' best customer – at one time running up an account of £369.16.9 – which amount was promptly paid – one imagines much to the relief of the Jeffersons. In contrast to this the late Lord Muncaster's account showed the amount of only £10.10.0 as being outstanding. Most of the local clergy seemed to have relatively modest accounts with the firm, whilst Thomas & John Brocklebank seemed to be amongst the firm's best customers. The regular customers also included Miles Ponsonby, shareholder in Abraham Wise's ship, *Maranham*, Thomas Manley, Capt Piele, owner of the *Caras*, the churchwardens of St. Nicholas, and Admiral Lutwidge. To cater for their needs the Jeffersons carried a varied stock valued at no less than £8,427.16.7.

In 1817 Messrs William Wilson and Company of Whitehaven built and launched the 161-ton brigantine *Thetis*, which vessel they traded between Workington and America until about December 1823, under the command of Capt John Taylor. At the above time she was chartered by Jeffersons to undertake voyages to Antigua for the firm – Capt Taylor remaining with his ship. The *Thetis* was eventually bought by Jeffersons in 1825. Prior to this, in 1817, Thomas & John Brocklebank built to the order of Robert & Henry Jefferson the brig *Doris* – which vessel they traded to Brazil, Charleston, and St. Domingo, until she was lost on Heneaga in 1825. At the time of her loss the *Doris* was on passage from St. Domingo to Falmouth; fortunately Capt John White, his crew, and some of the cargo were saved.

The acquisition of the *Thetis* and the *Doris* in the second and third decades of the last century seems to have marked a new phase in the development of the firm, although few early Jefferson records have survived, apart from the West Indies Diary of young Henry Jefferson, in which he writes an account of his voyage to Antigua in the brig *Thetis*, and his business and social life whilst on the island. From this document it is clear that at this point in time the firm of Robert & Henry Jefferson were much involved in the business life of the colony – as shippers and bankers – but not yet as plantation owners, for no mention is made of their own plantation. However, at the time of emancipation ten years later in 1834, Government compensation figures make it clear that Robert & Henry Jefferson were very substantial plantation owners at that time. From these facts one may reasonably deduce that the Jefferson family acquired the Yeaman Plantation on Antigua at some point in time just prior to emancipation. Short extracts taken from Henry Jefferson's Diary give us an interesting insight into both 19th century shipboard life, and the life of a 19th century colonial businessman, and these are reproduced as Appendix D.

26

CHAPTER 4

With Thomas & John Brocklebank – 1801

The year after Daniel Brocklebank Jnr. died at Montego Bay, John Brocklebank, who had acted as master of the *Scipio*, settled in Liverpool, and in the year 1799 founded the firm of Brocklebank and Hebson. They were merchants in the South American trade, having a small number of vessels. John, however, like Daniel Brocklebank before him also tried his hand at privateering. This John Brocklebank eventually took up residence at Wavertree, then a village near Liverpool, and to distinguish him from other members of the family bearing the same name became known as 'Wavertree John'.

Despite the demoralising loss of his son, Daniel Brocklebank remained active as a shipbuilder, for he completed three vessels at his yard in 1798. The 12 gun ship *Montgomery* was launched the following year, and the *Active*, *Ariel*, and *Cumberland* were completed in the year 1800, the latter vessel being built for John Hartley, a well known Whitehaven merchant. Alas though, some five months after the launch of Hartley's fine new vessel, Daniel Brocklebank, founder of the Brocklebank Line, died, the following short notice of his death appearing in the 'Cumberland Pacquet' on the 10th March.

> 'On Saturday, in Roper Street, in this town there passed away in the fifty-ninth year of his age, and highly respected by all who knew him, Mr Daniel Brocklebank, shipbuilder and ropemaker. Mr Brocklebank in the course of a very active life made twenty-five voyages across the Atlantic, and after quitting the sea and settling as a shipbuilder, to which business he was originally brought up, he built at this port twenty-five ships.'

Following Daniel Brocklebank's death the firm passed into the hands of his two remaining sons, Thomas, then aged 27, and his younger brother John, then aged 22, the business at this point becoming known as Thos. & John Brocklebank. During the last days of May 1801 the Brocklebank brothers launched their first vessel following their father's death; this was the Brigantine *Matty*, built for Capt Hutchinson. The *Dryad* launched in November of the same year brought to a close the year's production at Bransty under the direction of the founder's sons.

Thomas & John Brocklebank launched two ships at Whitehaven in 1803, these being the

264 ton ship *King George*, and, at the end of September the patriotically named vessel *Volunteer*, the local reporter describing the latter launch in the following terms: 'Friday morning a new ship (one of the largest ever built in these parts) was launched here by Messrs T & J Brocklebank. The weather had more the resemblance of spring than of the declining season of the year, and the great number of people assembled on the occasion were gratified with one of the finest launches that could possibly be seen.'

The year 1804 was another active and interesting one for Thomas & John Brocklebank. The snow *Queen Charlotte* and the brigantine *Beaver* were constructed that year, and the Brocklebank Brothers were now trading four ships on their own account, these being the *Active*, *Dryad*, *Experiment* and the *King George*. On the 3rd April Thomas & John attempted to sell two vessels by placing the following advertisement in the 'Cumberland Pacquet': 'For sale or private contract a new vessel on the stocks 215 tons register measure and copper bolted, may be launched in two months. The brigantine *Active* 114 tons per register, two years old, apply Thomas & John Brocklebank, Whitehaven – 5th March 1804.' A further attempt to sell the above vessels was made via the 'Cumberland Pacquet' on the 29th May, but no doubt because of the fragile and risky political situation, no buyers appeared ready to purchase. The *Experiment* was offered for sale on the 29th May, but no sale was made, and it is understood that soon after this date she was captured and ransomed!

On the 2nd November a public auction was held at the house of Mrs Ann Buckham, in King Street, Whitehaven, to sell the recently captured French schooner privateer *Caroline*. The vessel it would seem was admirably fitted out for her trade as a privateer, carrying 12 six pounder guns, muskets, pistols, cutlasses, and boarding pikes. Intending purchasers were invited, via the local press, to obtain further details, prior to the sale, from Mr Spital (Grocer) in Roper Street. Really serious bidders were informed that full inventories relating to the ships stores and armaments could be inspected at the houses of Mrs Barnes at Harrington, Mrs Robinson's at Workington, and Mrs Nelson's at Maryport. The vessel was advertised as copper bottomed, and suitable for the straits or West Indies Trade. The purchasers were Thomas & John Brocklebank, who actually employed her as a privateer, Capt Gregg being appointed master.

Whilst the Brocklebank privateer *Caroline* cruised for her proud new owners, the Brocklebank brig *Queen Charlotte* was herself captured whilst outward bound by the French privateer *L'Emperor*, which powerful vessel carried 14 guns and 120 men. Luck was with the *Queen Charlotte* however, for only two days later H.M. Frigate *Carysfort* (28 guns) recaptured the Brocklebank brig and escorted her into Barbados. She was later allowed to proceed on her voyage to Grenada under escort of H.M. schooner *St. Lucia*. Much was happening in the West Indies in 1805, the French were busily engaged in plundering various islands, whilst at Basseterre they decided to demand £18,000, and £8,000 currency for *not* plundering the town and murdering the inhabitants.

Thomas & John Brocklebank's venture into privateering proved to be short-lived, for on 9th July 1805 Mr Spital, grocer, was once more called upon to act for the Brocklebanks and the other smaller shareholders in the privateer *Caroline*, by arranging its sale – when she was again advertised as 'the remarkably fast sailing coppered privateer'.

The only ship to be launched by Thomas & John Brocklebank in 1805 was the 301-ton,

The Brocklebank brig Swallow. *First command of Capt Abraham Wise.*
(Photograph from Liverpool Public Libraries.)

six gun ship *Hercules*, which was placed under the command of Capt Caffey who traded her to Jamaica for the firm. The year drew to a dramatic close with Admiral Lord Nelson destroying the fleets of France and Spain off Cape Trafalgar, but as we are aware, being killed himself aboard his flagship *Victory*.

The next ship to be launched by Brocklebanks was the *Swallow* (2), a small brig of 114 tons register. She was placed under the command of Capt Waite, who took the ship to the Baltic for the firm shortly after her launch. In 1807 the firm launched the eight gun snow *Brown*, built to the order of Richard and William Whiteside, which was followed in 1808 by the launching of the *Dryad* (2). In 1809 Brocklebanks launched my great-great grandfather's second command, the Fisher-Brocklebank brig *Maranham*, which ship Abraham Vaux Wise was to command from September 1810–February 1814.

The combined Brocklebank–Wilson Fisher fleet – 1810.			
Brown	220 tons	Capt Robert Fell	(Wilson Fisher)
Swallow	114 tons	Capt J. Bell	(Wilson Fisher)
Maranham	154 tons	Capt Abraham Vaux Wise	(Wilson Fisher)
Balfour	310 tons	Capt W. Fraser	(Brocklebank)
Hercules	301 tons	Capt H. Jackson	(Brocklebank)

The Brocklebank Line and the East India Company.

In the year 1813 Thomas & John Brocklebank, together with other ship owners, continued to take an active interest in public demands for the ending of the East India Company's trade monopoly to the East Indies – they had much to gain by breaking this monopoly. The East India Company was an English commercial company that was chartered by Queen Elizabeth in 1600. The Company obtained from the Government a lucrative monopoly in trade between England and the East Indies, which monopoly had much to do in inhibiting the actual size of ships in the British Merchant fleet. By the close of the 18th century the East India Company had in effect become ruler of a large part of the Indian sub-continent.

Such was the wealth and power of the East India Company that its commanders could make fortunes large enough to retire on, after making only two or three voyages to the east, but before the close of the year 1813 this historic monopoly was at long last broken. Brocklebanks were amongst the first to enter the port of Calcutta, as free trading merchants and ship owners, thus establishing their links with Calcutta which were to last for more than one and a half centuries. The ship that they were later to build specifically for this lucrative trade was their famous Indiaman, *Princess Charlotte*, but the launch of this great ship was not to take place till almost three years later.

Life at sea for Brocklebank commanders in 1813 continued to be hazardous – the firm's brig *Westmorland* on a voyage from Archangel to Liverpool, with a cargo of wheat was captured by a Danish privateer and sent to Bergen. The presence of American and French privateers in the Atlantic was now forcing all British merchant vessels to proceed across the western ocean in convoy – under the escort of a man-o-war. The spring of 1813 found my ancestor, Capt Abraham Wise, commander of the *Maranham* laying off Jamaica, awaiting with others the arrival of H.M. escort ship *Vengeur*. The *Vengeur* duly arrived in April, and the convoy set off on the long and hazardous passage across the Atlantic. As luck would have it the ships in this particular convoy were not attacked by privateers – but nevertheless it did experience more than its fair share of troubles:

The first ship in the fleet to run into difficulties was the *Ann Maria & Catherine* commanded by a Capt Hillyard – and bound for London. She sprang a leak on the 5th May, struggled to remain with the fleet, but, unable to do so parted on the 23rd, making her way alone to Bermuda. The *Princess Mary* under the command of Capt Storey, and also bound for London, sprang a leak on the 28th May; the vessel kept up with the convoy for the next few days, but like the *Ann Maria & Catherine* was also obliged to leave the fleet. She parted

30

on the 2nd June, making her way to Halifax, Nova Scotia. Captain Abraham Wise of Whitehaven kept the *Maranham* with the fleet, leaving the convoy, and H.M.S. *Vengeur* only when across the Atlantic, on the 15th June, when he parted and made for Whitehaven. The *Eliza*, Capt Holmes, also sprang a very severe leak, which caused her to founder, but fortunately the crew were saved, whilst the *Mercantor* seemed to lose her way, eventually running aground on Port Royal Keys.

On the 5th February 1814 John Fisher and Miles Ponsonby, two of the shareholders in the *Maranham* sold their shares leaving Wilson Fisher and the Brocklebank brothers as the sole remaining owners. Under this new ownership command passed to Capt John Holliday. Capt Abraham Vaux Wise, of Brigham, now had important business of his own to attend to at the nearby port of Harrington; it was the building of his own 235 ton vessel – which he was to name the *Eleanor* – after his wife, Eleanor Wise, daughter of John Braithwaite. For the next few years Abraham traded his ship between London and Barbados, but alas this particular maritime venture was not a success, for the various partners could not agree on trading policy. On the 27th October 1817 Abraham Wise sold the *Eleanor* to Messrs Sanderson and Walker of Lancaster, which gentlemen put Capt Hatherthwaite in command of the brig. For the next ten years, until his death in 1827, the life of Abraham Wise becomes something of a mystery. From the parish records he remains listed as a mariner, but only Lloyd's Registers provide us with a possible clue as to his last command; for here the name of Capt Wise is listed against a Scottish built brig, named after the God of War – *Mars*!

The Brocklebank fleet continued to grow at an incredible pace; the partners were now trading no less than ten vessels, and these small brigs were being traded to a truly amazing number of ports, which included St. Petersburg, Cronstad, Revel, Archangel, Alexandria, Alicante, Barcelona, Trieste, Leghorn, Oporto, Cadiz, Gibraltar, Montreal, Maranham, Antigua, and Barbados. At the firm's Bransty building yard their craftsmen continued to turn out excellent vessels. The *Westmorland* (1) having been captured the previous year – the year of her construction – Thomas and John replaced her with the *Westmorland* (2) early in 1814. On the 19th February William Morrison was appointed master and Brocklebank wrote to their insurance brokers, Messrs Pulsfords asking them to insure the ship for £4,000.

Robert Pulsford was contacted again on the 2nd April, the Brocklebanks writing to him in the following terms:

'Pulsfords – you will no doubt have learnt that the *London* overset at Honduras. This is a very unpleasant circumstance, Captain Frazer writes of date the 16th January that they had on the evening succeeded in getting her upright without any damage whatever excepting the cutting away of the Top Masts, and that he would be ready to take in again in three days. Make up insurance on the ship to £7,500, and £2,000 of freight valued at £3,500; on *Balfour* at or from Tobago or port of loading in the West Indies to London valued at £7,000, and £1,000 on freight valued at £2,500.'

The Brocklebank's plans, made in 1813, to enter the East India trade, came to fruition with the completion of the *Princess Charlotte* in 1815 –

'On Wednesday morning a new vessel called *Princess Charlotte* was launched from the building yard of Messrs Thomas & John Brocklebank, she was 514 tons register measure (which we are

31

The Princess Charlotte *built at Whitehaven in 1815.*

informed is 7 tons more than any ship hitherto built at this port), and is believed to be a vessel of uncommon strength and beauty. The weather was delightful, and a great concourse of people computed at not less than 6,000 witnessed her gallant descent from the stocks a little before 10 O'clock. It is what is termed a dry launch; and after smoothly running (or rather gliding) about 80 yards with scarcely any apparent diminuation of speed, she stopped. The tide was then flowing; in little more than half-an-hour she was afloat, and soon after 1 O'clock she was towed safely into the harbour.'

The *Princess Charlotte* was registered at the port on the 11th January the following year (1816), and Capt M'Kean was placed in command – this master being one of the firm's most experienced commanders. A few weeks after her registration Brocklebank's first great 'Indiaman' sailed majestically past the Whitehaven harbour walls – bound for the distant Indies.

32

Some months later in the summer of 1816, the *Princess Charlotte* made her way across the Indian Ocean – being carried towards the Indies by the gentle south-east trades. On about the 2nd August she sailed past Krakatoa, passed through the Straits of Sunda, and on the 5th she was lying at anchor off Batavia. Between 1811 and 1818 Java was controlled by the British – Batavia being the island's main port. The poverty of the place was appalling, the cruel oppression of the Dutch colonialists having reduced the inhabitants of this beautiful island to the level of disease ridden paupers. By 1815, Europeans had moved out of the town, taking up residence on the higher and healthier ground to the south of the port.

The first thing that young Capt John M'Kean discovered on his arrival at Batavia was that, whilst the East India Company may have lost its monopoly of Eastern trade, this historic institution was still very much a power to be reckoned with. Being an astute man, and wishing to put himself in a favourable position with the Company, M'Kean offered the *Princess Charlotte* to the East India Company as a troop transport – such vessels at that time being in great demand (and short supply) by the British authorities. The young Brocklebank commander's offer was accepted, the *Princess* being sent off to Calcutta with a party of troops. On the way the vessel called at various ports, which included Samarang and Sourabaya, and at each port the shrewd young master took notes on the cargoes that were available – prices, and other points of commercial interest.

On completion of her troop carrying duties the *Princess Charlotte* made her way back to Batavia, arriving at the port in February 1817. It was at this time that H.M.S. *Alceste* was wrecked in the Straits of Sunda. Some 260 survivors reached the shore, amongst whom was no less a person than Lord Amherst – Governor of India!

Many of the survivors were picked up by the ship *Ternate*, but Lord Amherst and forty other survivors reached Batavia in the *Alceste*'s boats. M'Kean was sent out to pick up the remaining survivors, not knowing at the time that all the survivors had in fact been picked up by the *Ternate*. Captain M'Kean took his ship back to Batavia, and in April sailed for Calcutta once more – still under charter to the East India Company, which institution released her from their service in September. She loaded a fabulous cargo, and about the 15th September made her way down the Hooghly River, and at last headed for home.

News of the Indiaman's movement were slow in reaching Whitehaven and Liverpool, but on the 10th March 1818 the 'Cumberland Pacquet' at last carried a small notice which indicated that the ship had indeed left Calcutta in September last. Eleven days later the same paper brought news that the *Princess Charlotte* was off the Cape of Good Hope. How Thomas and John Brocklebank's hopes must have risen upon receipt of this news, for the ship was long overdue. On the 24th March 1818 the *Princess Charlotte* sailed proudly up the Mersey – her epic voyage over at last. Captain M'Kean must have been a very happy man, pleased that his voyage had proved such a success – for the holds of his great ship contained a cargo of tremendous value. In her holds the vessel carried 2,500 bales of cotton, 552 bags of sugar, 200 bags of saltpetre, 4,000 bags of rice, 452 bags of ginger, and one pipe of madeira, the total value of this one cargo being no less than £28,000 – which resulted in an estimated profit for the firm of £10,651 – a vast sum by the monetary standards of the day. The profits from this, the firm's first voyage to the east, at last gave Thomas & John Brocklebank the freedom they needed to hasten other developments, but of prime consideration now was the completion of the firm's next Indiaman – the *Perseverance*, now already under construction.

The following year, 1819, Thomas & John Brocklebank embarked on another interesting, but alas, short-lived venture – the operation of a passenger service from Whitehaven to America. The brig *Constellation*, under the command of Capt Thomas Fell was put into this service, it being decided that the brig should carry cargo and passengers to St. John's, New Brunswick, instead of the more usual destination of New York. This move was in fact designed to overcome the problem created by the 1816 maritime acts which made it illegal for any vessel to carry more than one passenger per five tons vessel weight. Thomas Brocklebank, shrewdly noting that the act did not apply to the colonies consequently decided to run his service to the colony of New Brunswick!

Adverts were duly placed in the Cumberland press extolling the virtues of the 'fast-sailing coppered brig *Constellation*', which was stated to be a commodious and roomy vessel, fitted up with convenient berths, which passengers would find most desirable. Alas, this new service did not prove a success, its failure in fact owing much to the fact that the *Constellation* sank a few weeks after her departure whilst off the coast near the port of Halifax! The 145 passengers aboard the 187-ton brig at the time of her wreck lost all their belongings, but fortunately, not their lives; for a passing schooner picked them all up and took them into Halifax where they all appealed to the 'kindness and liberality of the community to take care of them'. Further efforts were made to get this service re-started after this minor set-back, but demand for it now, perhaps not surprisingly, did not justify its continuance.

The year 1819 marked another more lasting event in the history of the firm of Thomas & John Brocklebank; Thomas obtained a seat in the office of the firm's Liverpool agent – Messrs Thomas and Isaac Littledale. This was but the first move towards the establishment of the firm's own office in the rapidly developing port of Liverpool – their own office in fact being opened at Exchange Buildings the following year. From now on Thomas Brocklebank was to direct the firm's operations at Liverpool, whilst his brother John was to look after the interests at Whitehaven. There can be little doubt that this move was prompted by the recent inauguration of the firm's East India service. In September the *Princess Charlotte*'s sister ship, the *Perseverence* was launched at Whitehaven – it was again quite an occasion, as the following article taken from the pages of the 'Cumberland Pacquet', the 28th September will indicate:

'Tuesday last, a beautiful new ship was launched by Messrs Brocklebank. She is named the *Perseverence*, register measurement 513 tons; will carry a thousand tons. She is 131 feet 6 inches upon deck, and is intended for the East India Trade. The vessel upon the stocks has been viewed with admiration by numbers of nautical men from various parts, and unanimously pronounced one of the most complete specimens of naval architecture that has yet been produced at any port in the United Kingdom. The day was beautifully fine. She left the stocks at ten minutes past eleven in the forenoon, and glided into the water in a style the most majestic that can be conceived, affording a most gratifying view to an immense crowd of spectators, who not only crowded the quays, but also lined the hills on each side of the harbour, making as it were a complete frame to one of the most interesting pictures ever beheld. The material of which she is built, and the excellent workmanship are described by competent judges as being in no degree inferior to that symetry in her interior, which strikes the eye of every observer.'

34

Whilst the children of Abraham and Eleanor Wise played near their home on St. Bee's headland, overlooking Whitehaven, far below them in their yard at Bransty, Thomas & John Brocklebank continued to produce many of the ships that they and other Cumbrian youngsters would one day be sailing on. Their brig *Manchester* was launched in 1824 – a vessel which was destined to remain in Company service for almost half a century. The *Affleck* was launched the following year, but sold upon completion to Capt Fell of Whitehaven, who traded her between London and the West Indies. These launches were followed in rapid succession by the completion of the *Grecian*, *Superior*, *Gazelle*, *Courier*, the *Meteor* and in 1827 the Jefferson brigantine *Lady Shaw Stewart*, which famous Whitehaven ship was registered at the port on the 30th June 1827. Her first master, whilst in the Jefferson Company service, was Capt John Taylor, but the young boy, Joseph Wise of Sandwith – at this time six years old, was destined to command this vessel only fifteen years later, in 1842.

On the 27th November 1827 the 'Cumberland Pacquet' reported the launch of another vessel, upon which Joseph's elder brother Abraham Vaux, would soon be serving as mate to Capt Daniel Brocklebank Jnr., she was the *Oberon*: 'On Friday 23rd inst., was launched from the ship building yard of Messrs Thomas & John Brocklebank a handsome new coppered schooner of about 150 tons register, called the *OBERON*, she is intended for the American trade.' The launch of the *Oberon* was followed by the launch of a paddle wheel steamer, one of only two steam vessels built by the firm; her length was 127 feet and her single steam engine generated 120 horse-power, whose no doubt noisy efforts were supplemented by fore and aft sails on her two masts. To carry away into the atmosphere the masses of pitch black smoke that her engine developed she was fitted with a tall thin funnel of exceptional height. This revolutionary craft was named *Countess of Lonsdale*.

Soon after the launch of this craft Thomas & John Brocklebank's highly skilled craftsmen employed at their building yard formed a trade union. Such a development was not entirely unexpected, as for some time the men and the boys working in the yard had been showing 'strong symptoms of a refractory spirit'! The members of the newly founded union soon developed a most interesting method of persuading non-members to join their ranks, which was duly reported in the local press – 'It appears that on Tuesday the apprentices seized two men who did not belong to the union and mounted them upon poles successively paraded them through the streets. They were met at the foot of Duke Street by Mr Brocklebank who endeavoured to prevail on them to liberate the men but in vain. A scuffle ensued. Mr Brocklebank was either knocked or thrown down and did not rise again without soiled apparel and a bloody face.' John Brocklebank, upset at developments, made his way to the yard, sacked his men, and closed the place down. Good relations however were quickly restored for he soon agreed to meet the men's representatives, after which he agreed to open the yard again on the following Monday morning.

The firm continued to expand, until once more the Brocklebank family was to suffer a sad loss. On a day late in February 1831 John Brocklebank mounted his horse, and began to ride towards Whitehaven; alas, as fate would have it a small child suddenly ran in front of him. He reined sharply in order to avoid the child and was thrown from his horse. The shock of this fall must have caused some internal injury, for following his fall he felt very

35

unwell. On Sunday the 13th March he died at his home, and on the following Tuesday the 'Cumberland Pacquet' published his obituary:

'On Sunday afternoon last in the parish of Irton, where he had been residing for a short time, John Brocklebank Esq. of the firm of T & J Brocklebank, ship builders. Mr Brocklebank had laboured under some indisposition for some weeks past. As it was alarmingly sudden, but finding himself worse than usual, he returned to his room where he expired within half-an-hour.'

Thomas Brocklebank was to survive his brother by fourteen years, during which time the firm was to develop and enlarge its interests enormously.

CHAPTER 5

Eighteen Hundred and Thirty Two

In January 1832, Messrs William Wilson & Co. of Whitehaven, shipbuilders, launched their latest vessel, another *Perseverence*, a 237-ton barque built to the order of James Gunson. Soon after her launch, a crew was signed, and then on Saturday the 14th January, she set sail for Pernambuco; on the following Tuesday the 'Cumberland Pacquet' recorded her departure in the following words – 'The *Perseverence*, Gibson, new barque, which sailed hence for Pernambuco on Saturday last, was spoken by the *Hebe*, White, off Black Coomb on the following day.' Aboard the *Perseverence*, on this maiden voyage, was a young apprentice by the name of George Wise, now just 14 years of age. One wonders what this young lad's thoughts were as the barque sailed slowly past Ravenglass, and the brooding mass of Black Coomb mountain, just to the south of this small Cumbrian port. George Wise was destined to spend the next five years of his young life aboard this deep-sea barque, voyaging to South America, New South Wales, and China.

Just over one month later Messrs Thomas & John Brocklebank launched the 99-ton schooner *Bransty* (3) from their yard at Bransty, Whitehaven. This small, but well-proportioned vessel was to be traded to the Gulf of Mexico, and used by the firm for coastal voyages. Command was given to Capt R. Wilson, and amongst his crew on the schooner's maiden voyage was an apprentice by the name of Abraham Vaux Wise – George Wise's elder brother. Abraham Wise was now 19 years and 8 months old – surprisingly old in fact to start life as a ship's apprentice. I have no doubt that this delay in sending young Abraham to sea was occasioned by the death of his father in 1827, when one assumes he had to play the role of 'father' to his younger brothers and sisters, prior to more permanent arrangements being made. At what time their brother John embarked on a seafaring career it is difficult to say, but from information that does exist it is clear that he did, but alas died whilst very young. It would be more than two years before Abraham and George's younger brother Joseph began his long life at sea, and over eight years before Francis Wise joined his brother Abraham – bound as an apprentice to Thomas & John Brocklebank.

Some three short months after young George Wise left Whitehaven, his future employers, Thos. & Jno. Brocklebank, completed yet another vessel, which was to be added to the growing fleet now being managed by the surviving Brocklebank brother, the local Whitehaven reporter recording the occasion in these terms – 'A Handsome new barque of the burthen of three hundred and thirty eight tons per register, was launched from the yard of Messrs Brocklebank's at this port on Saturday last, called the *Patriot King*, and intended for the South American trade.' Twenty years from this date George Wise would be in command of this famous vessel, but until he joined his brothers at Brocklebank's in 1845, his career at sea was an interesting and varied one.

After serving his time with Messrs Gunsons he shipped as 2nd mate aboard the Workington snow *Cammerton*, making one voyage to the West Indies with Capt J. Hewitt. In the main this small craft was traded between the ports of Liverpool and London, to the West Indies, South America, and, on occasion North America. Only rarely did the *Cammerton* return to her home port of Workington. After this voyage George shipped as 1st mate on a coasting vessel – the Maryport built brig *Sarah*, this being before shipping as 2nd mate on the Chepstow registered snow *Emma*, upon which vessel he shipped for California by way of Cape Horn, just about two years after Richard Henry Dana had completed his well recorded voyage over this same route.

The *Emma* was an interesting vessel, having been built at the port of Chepstow in 1828 by Messrs Buckle & Davis. The Buckle family of Chepstow were the greatest of all the builders of ships at that port, John, and George, his son, and various partners – James, Davis, and others – producing some very fine ships. The *Emma* was snow rigged, and had one deck, with a high poop, and on her bows she carried a woman's figure-head. At the time of her launch the ship's main owner was Richard Morris, a well known Chepstow merchant, but amongst the subscribers at this time was a Monmouth banker by the name of James Silvanus Fortunatus Brown Bromage! When George Wise joined the ship Richard Morris held 28 of the 64 shares, and John Davis, partner in the firm that built the ship, held 12.

The *Emma* carried a crew of 16 – Captain, 1st and 2nd mate, a cook, a steward, a carpenter, and two young apprentices, the remainder of the crew being seamen. When George Wise served aboard this vessel the master was Capt John Gething, a native of Chepstow, then aged 33, the first mate being a Mr Maddack, a young Liverpudlian, who had last served on the ship *Rival*. The *Emma* was open for charter, to take freight anywhere in the world, which on reflection might well have been the factor which prompted young George Wise to serve aboard her. After just experiencing a rather hum-drum spell aboard a local coasting vessel, a voyage aboard the *Emma* – to the fabulous coast of California – would have been an appealing proposition to any young and ambitious 19th century mariner.

Before joining Brocklebanks in 1843, young George Wise was to serve on two other vessels, these being the *Matilda* and the *Catherine*. The *Matilda* was again a snow, built at Bideford in 1831, but owned by Messrs Worrall & Co. of Liverpool – her port of registry. Whilst on this ship George Wise served as 1st mate to Capt Hodgson, taking the ship to Genoa. After this voyage he served as 1st mate aboard the 300-ton Nova Scotia ship *Catherine* – voyaging down the coast of North America. In December 1843 he joined his elder brother Abraham – now master of the *Kestrel* – and his younger brother Francis, now an apprentice on the *Dryad* – at Brocklebanks, his first appointment in the Company's service being that of 2nd mate aboard the *Princess Royal*.

Abraham Wise remained with the *Bransty* until August 1834, but before he had completed his apprenticeship he was transferred to another company ship – the 130-ton *Tampico*. In April 1836 he finished his term of apprenticeship, then shipped as an ordinary seaman aboard the *Tigris* – making a long voyage to Calcutta and China, after which voyage in this capacity he was – (rather suprisingly) – then made 1st mate to Capt Daniel Brocklebank aboard the *Oberon* – rapid promotion indeed – even by the standards of the 19th century. No doubt the fact that he was the second generation of the Wise family to enter the Company service had something to do with this situation, but at the same time it is doubtful if sentiment alone could have influenced his unusual rise in status – he must have shown much promise as a mariner. The Daniel Brocklebank that Abraham was now serving with was the son of Capt Ralph Brocklebank – the grandson of John Brocklebank – the founder's brother.

Voyage of the *Oberon* Liverpool to Bordeaux & back 28th Feb. 1839				
Name	*Age*	*Place of Birth*	*Quality*	*Last Ship*
Danl Brocklebank	29	London	Master	*Oberon*
Abm Wise (23833)	26	Whitehaven	Mate	*Oberon*
John Musson	32	Liverpool	2 Mate	*Oberon*
Henry Holmes (15680)	25	Welford	Seaman	*Colonist*
John Brown	34	Belfast	Seaman	*Albanian*
Hugh Kelly	25	Newry	Cook/stwd	*Crown*
Saml Kirkpatrick	20	Dal—	Seaman	*Crown*
Richard Audland	15	Liverpool	Apprentice	*Oberon*
Geo Fletcher	15	Liverpool	Apprentice	*Oberon*
			Signed. Danl Brocklebank.	

Whilst the Brocklebank Brothers developed their fleet, and the two elder Wise Brothers learned the art of seamanship, Robert and Henry Jefferson continued to trade their ships to Antigua, which island was shortly to undergo fundamental social changes. By the celebrated Act of the Imperial Legislature, passed in 1833, compulsory labour was summarily abolished throughout the British Empire. The effects of this act were mitigated by the fact that it was not immediately enforceable until some years after this date. West Indian Planters were also given the option – if they so chose – to implement a system known as 'apprenticeship' – as a sort of interim system, between the formal abolition of slavery by the above Act, and the slaves complete freedom. To their eternal credit the Planters of Antigua – men who had profited by the system for generations – decided that enough was enough, laid aside all claims to 'apprenticeship', and gave their negroes immediate freedom.

It might be imagined – by those that have not examined the facts – that only plantation owners in the West Indies owned slaves prior to emancipation. This was not the case. On the island of Antigua the published figures make it quite clear that almost every white inhabitant of the island owned at least one or two; clearly these would be used as house servants. Most of the medium-sized plantations seemed to have made do with about 100 negroes, whilst the larger plantations required the services of many more black workers. The estate of Sir E. Codrington, Bart, which was to be found at the centre of the island, required the services of 190 workers, Sir H. W. Martin, Bart, managed with 319, whilst the vast estates run by Robert & Henry Jefferson required the services of no less than 455. However, despite the size of the Jefferson plantations prior to emancipation, there are indications that they were sympathetic to emancipation – indeed, given the size of their holdings at this point in time it is difficult to see how the islanders could have adopted the policies they did in 1833, had the Jeffersons held other views.

In 1834 the Jeffersons were operating their shipping enterprise with three vessels, these being the brig *Thetis*, voyaging to Antigua at this period under the command of Capts Benjamin Wheelwright and William Harper, the *Lady Shaw Stewart*, and the latest addition to their fleet – the brigantine *Derwent*, named after the Cumberland river of that name. This last vessel was built by Jonathan Fell & Co. of Workington; she was a vessel of 221 tons burthen, measuring 87 ft 6 ins.

Command of the *Derwent* was given to Capt Wilson Harper, who by all accounts was a very capable mariner, which fact one might infer from the following notice which appeared in the 'Cumberland Pacquet' on 8th July 1834: 'The *Derwent*, Harper, from Antigua at this port yesterday, with a cargo of rum and sugar for Messrs R & H Jefferson – see advertisement – The *Derwent* made her passage in the unusually short period of twenty-five days, having reached Dunleary on the 25th day after leaving Antigua, where she remained until the tides had improved to admit her entering this port.' It was however aboard the Jeffersons' older vessel, the *Lady Shaw Stewart*, that young Joseph Wise was to serve his time. On the 21st December 1834 the 13-year-old son of Capt Abraham Vaux Wise climbed aboard the *Lady Shaw Stewart*, made himself known to the vessel's master – Capt John Taylor – and thus began a life behind the mast which was to span the better part of half a century.

The *Lady Shaw Stewart* was a typical West Cumberland square-sterned brigantine – small, but exceptionally strong; for the development and design of these vessels took several factors into consideration. Firstly, as mentioned, vessels built for the heavy coal trade had to be strong, for clear and obvious reasons. In addition to this, however, all the West Cumberland harbours dried out at low tide and the ships were thus obliged to take the ground. One can imagine the strain this put on these small wooden craft, particularly if they were laden with upwards of 200 tons of coal when the tide ebbed and left them high and dry. The hulls under these conditions took a particularly heavy pounding, to the extent that a great many of them were built with a 'double-bottom'. That is to say, the entire underwater section of the ship had a second layer of heavy timber – the two being sandwiched together by a thick mixture of oakum and tar. So when the need arose for firms such as Jeffersons and Brocklebanks to send these craft across the Atlantic, they were sturdy enough to tackle such voyages – and even longer ones.

The *Lady* (as she was sometimes affectionately referred to in the Cumbrian press of the day), measured just 85 ft 5 ins in length, and had a maximum beam of 22 ft 1 in – her holds were 14 ft 11 ins deep. Being a brigantine she had two masts, and on her bows she carried a figure-head. The stern however was the most interesting feature of these small craft, for they were square, built in a manner redolent of Capt Bligh's famous *Bounty* – the master's cabin being situated here, with the square windows of this cabin running across the full width of the vessel, from which the master would look out over the wake of his vessel. Beneath these windows would be hung the ship's long boat which was kept aboard not just as a lifeboat, but as a working vessel whilst the craft lay at anchor, near some port or bay where quayside accommodation was not available.

From the early crew lists that I have examined it is clear that the *Lady Shaw Stewart* usually carried a crew of 12 to 13, a typical crew comprising the Master and his 1st and 2nd mates, a carpenter, and a cook/steward, the remainder being seamen or apprentices, four or more of the latter sometimes being carried. The *Lady Shaw Stewart* did not usually carry a bosun or sailmaker, but on occasion she did list amongst her crew a cooper. It would clearly be this latter individual's responsibility to look after the many valuable casks of Jeffersons' famous rum that the *Lady* would bring back to Whitehaven from Antigua. The masters of these vessels would usually be paid about £8.0.0 per month, the first mate and carpenter £4.4.0, the cooper, if carried, £3.0.0, the 2nd mate £2.15.0, and the seamen £2.10.0, reasonable rates for the time when we consider that some land-based workers then often only received 7/-–8/- wages per week! Such were the conditions aboard the *Lady Shaw Stewart* in 1834 when Joseph Wise joined her.

During the year 1835 the *Thetis* and the *Lady Shaw Stewart* continued to ply between the West Indies and Whitehaven for their owners, but an entry in the maritime column of the 'Cumberland Pacquet' dated 17th May 1836, indicates that their vessel the *Derwent* was despatched to China. 'The *Derwent*, Hewitt, of this port, from Liverpool at Canton on the 31st December.' Here I think it is clear that the Jeffersons were attempting to establish connections in the East Indies and China, emulating the Brocklebanks, and others, following the ending of the East India Company monopoly. For them however the venture does not seem to have been a successful one, for I can find no trace of their having repeated the exercise.

During his early months aboard the *Lady Shaw Stewart*, Joseph Wise first served under Capt John Taylor, prior to serving under Capt Hewitt, before this master left to take the *Derwent* to Canton. In 1836 however Capt William Steele was appointed master, who remained with the ship for several years, and whilst serving with this master Joseph Wise gained much useful experience, for the ship then made many voyages between Whitehaven, Liverpool, or London, and Antigua – and many other ports in the West Indies.

In February 1837 the 'Cumberland Pacquet' published the sad news that Joseph's elder brother John had died, the notice in the obituary column reading as follows: 'On his passage out from Liverpool to Bombay, Mr John Wise (died) aged 21 years, grandson of Mr John Braithwaite, late assistant overseer of the township of Whitehaven.' Throughout the same year Joseph remained with Capt Steele aboard the *Lady Shaw Stewart* – in June the papers reported that the vessel had left Whitehaven on the 1st June in order to take in a cargo at Liverpool, she later sailed for Antigua on the 16th June, and was off Kinsale on the 24th, when she spoke another vessel reporting that she had experienced thick and foggy weather, and had only seen one light after sailing. On Tuesday the 4th July the 'Cumberland Pacquet' had disastrous news to report – it was their later, and fuller account, of the loss of the *Thetis*.

'We last week announced the disastrous loss of the *Thetis*, of this port, belonging to Messrs Jeffersons off Cape Finisterre. A letter has since been received from Capt Harper, from which it appears that the loss of the vessel was purely accidental and owing to a cause which no human foresight could have guarded against. On the 16th May, when in latitude 39, 52 and longitude 14, 36, the vessel struck, just as the moon had set, against what in all probability, was a sunken wreck, and stove in her bow parts. The consequences were most disastrous, in a few minutes the vessel went down, before the whole of the crew and passengers could get into the boat. Mrs Deane and her child, and John Black were drowned with the sinking wreck, and the Captain gained the boat by swimming.

For eight days the Captain, eight of the crew and Mr Lennard, a passenger suffered the most dreadful privations from hunger and thirst, when they were providentially picked up by a Spanish brig, the master of which treated them with the greatest kindness and humanity. One man, the cook, died in the boat. The other sufferers were taken by the Spaniards to Malaga, from whence they will be sent home by the British Consul.'

Disaster struck the Jefferson fleet again this year, when sickness ravaged the crew of the *Lady Shaw Stewart* and Joseph Wise was lucky to escape unscathed. Reports reaching Cumberland in November 1837 written by Capt Steele indicated that when the vessel was at Demerara a terrible fever struck down many of the ship's crew. Captain Steele himself became infected, but recovered, but Joseph's fellow apprentice, a youth named Scott died, as did a passenger, Mr John King of Scotch Street, Whitehaven, and Mr Ninnes and Mr Redfern – 1st and 2nd mates of the vessel.

Captain Steele added that the fever had spread to an alarming extent, and that the crews of very few vessels then at Demerara had entirely escaped the infection. At the date of his letter home however the fever had subsided, the place then becoming as healthy as normal. One is left wondering at this point as to how the vessel managed to return to Whitehaven following the loss of the 1st and 2nd mates – did they manage to sign other officers whilst in this port – or did Joseph Wise, or another apprentice, assume the role of mate during this emergency? I cannot say, but what is clear is that the *Lady Shaw Stewart* was soon back in normal Company service.

Upon the loss of the *Thetis* in May 1837 Robert & Henry Jefferson promptly placed an order for the vessel's replacement, the builder they chose being Lumley Kennedy of Whitehaven – which gentleman had formerly been employed as yard manager by Thomas & John Brocklebank, prior to setting up in business on his own account. The ship they ordered from Lumley Kennedy was the larger brigantine, *British Queen* – a vessel of 218 tons burthen, that Joseph Wise was to command for almost 13 years. The *British Queen* ran down Kennedy's slipway in May 1838.

On Tuesday the 17th November 1840 the 'Cumberland Pacquet' reported the launch of another Jefferson vessel – 'On Thursday last, a copper fastened sloop, called the *Midge*, burthen per register 38 tons old measurement (28 new) was launched from the building yard of Messrs Lumley Kennedy and Company, at this port. The *Midge* was built for Messrs Jefferson and is intended for service in the West Indies. She will sail hence for Cadiz in a few days, with a cargo of coals under the command of Mr James, mate of the *Lady Shaw Stewart*, where she will take a cargo of wine and proceed from thence to the West Indies.'

42

From surviving material we find that the *Midge* returned directly to Whitehaven after obtaining her cargo at Cadiz, and on the 27th January 1841 my ancestor Joseph Wise stepped ashore 'feeling sick'! The following day Mr James took the sloop to Lancaster with a part cargo, returning to Whitehaven on the 10th February. Here Joseph rejoined the *Midge* and then took the tiny craft across the Atlantic to Antigua, again acting as mate to Mr James. The *Midge* was sold to George Athil of Antigua in December 1843. Thomas James, and Joseph Wise returned to the *Lady Shaw Stewart* early in 1842, the former as master, the latter as mate. But as the following notices placed in the 'Cumberland Pacquet' on the 5th and 12th July 1842 confirm this was Joseph's last voyage as mate.

July 5th 'The *Lady Shaw Stewart*, James, from Antigua, at this port on the 30th ult. after a passage of 40 days. All well, with a cargo of sugar etc for Messrs R. & H. Jefferson. Capt J reports the following vessels as being at Antigua when he left:– The *Antigua Packet*, M'Knight, for London; the *Belgrave*, Donaldson, would sail for this port about ten days after the *Lady* left; the *James*, Hunt, for Belfast, in four or five days; and the *Zephyr*, Lieut. Wilson in charge, in three days for Liverpool, the crew of which vessel had been murdered on the coast of Africa. The *Lady Shaw Stewart* has landed her inward cargo, taken onboard an outward one, and expects to sail tomorrow for Antigua.'

July 12th 'The *Lady Shaw Stewart*, Wise, sailed hence for Antigua on the 6th instant.' Seven years, and seven months after beginning his career as a Jefferson apprentice, Joseph Wise was now beginning his career as a Jefferson master – many adventures lay ahead of him, as we shall see.

In 1833 Thomas & John Brocklebank launched one of their most famous vessels, the 364-ton ship *Jumna*; command was given to Capt Pinder, who took her from Whitehaven to Liverpool and loaded a cargo for Calcutta. He arrived back from Calcutta on the 24th February 1834, having completed the voyage in the record time of eight months and two days. Less than three months later she was ready to sail again; Capt Pinder made his way to the Prince's Dock on the 14th May 1834, and *Jumna* was towed out into the Mersey. This, according to the Liverpool newspapers, made maritime history, for *Jumna* was the first ship to sail direct from the Mersey to China.

Trade with China at this time was difficult, for the opium traffic, then at its zenith, was causing much concern to China's rulers, all of which led to the notorious Opium Wars, then in progress. Despite these obstacles Pinder was not long in returning. Early in 1835 he was back, Gore's 'Liverpool Advertiser' noting the event in these words – 'This is we believe the quickest voyage to China and back ever known. It is the more remarkable when it is stated that the *Jumna* lay two months at Canton owing to the dispute with Lord Napier and the Chinese.

The *Jumna* is the first ship that has made the voyage between this port and Canton direct. Captain Pinder is noted for making quick voyages to the East having performed two voyages to Calcutta, the first in the *Patriot King* in eight months and three days, the other in the *Jumna* in eight months and two days.'

Captain Pinder was to make one more voyage to the Far East for the firm, before he became Brocklebank's first Marine Superintendent in the Summer of 1836. At the time of this appointment he could look back on 22 years' service at sea – 15 of them as master. He remained as Superintendent at the Liverpool Office until his death on the 2nd September 1851.

Throughout the 1830s Brocklebanks' building yard remained as busy as ever; in March 1834 the beautiful little brig *Rimac* was launched, named after the South American river Rio Rimac, and later to be commanded by Francis Wise. In November of the same year the 'Cumberland Pacquet' commented on the launch of Brocklebank's latest vessel – the *Ituna* –

> 'On Tuesday afternoon last, a very handsome brig of 221 tons per register, was launched from the building yard of Messrs Brocklebanks at this port. She was built for Mr Anthony Bell, Grocer, Lowther Street, and upon leaving the stocks was named *Ituna*, which is the ancient designation of the river Eden in this county.'

The range of vessels built by Brocklebanks at this period was extremely varied. In 1836 they launched the Indiaman *Tigris*, a vessel which was to be traded between Liverpool and the East Indies by the firm for almost three decades before being lost. In contrast to this they launched the 61-ton sloop *Mite* from the firm's Bransty yard in July 1837 – a vessel intended for the trade between Whitehaven and Ravenglass! She remained in company service for three years before being sold to new owners. The *Mite* remained afloat until she was burnt in 1865.

In 1838 the firm launched one of their most famous vessels, the *Patriot Queen* – 'A splendid new ship of 547 tons, new register measurement, was launched from the building yard of Messrs Brocklebank, at this port, called the *Patriot Queen*, and intended for the East India trade. This magnificent vessel made a beautiful launch; she is coppered and copper fastened, and is the largest, with the exception of the *Princess Charlotte* and the *Perseverence*, ever built at this port. The *Patriot Queen* will be commanded by Capt Hoodless.' In 1839 the smaller Indiaman *Aden* was launched, whose first commander was Capt Henry Ponsonby, late of the *Princess Charlotte*. Later in the same year the third vessel to be named *Swallow* by the firm was launched, but she was an ill-fated craft. On the 15th June 1840, she sailed from Guayaquil, but alas, Capt Nelson and his crew were never seen again, her fate remaining a mystery.

Ships being traded to India by Thomas & John Brocklebank – 1840				
Balfour	310	Brig	Foster	Bombay
Princess Charlotte	514	Ship	King	Bombay
Crown	297	Barque	Kerr	Bombay
Herculean	317	Barque	Grindale	Bombay
London	351	Ship	Benn	Calcutta
Hindoo	266	Barque	Mawson	Calcutta
Patriot King	338	Barque	Roddock	Calcutta
Lord Althorp	233	Brig	Jackson	Calcutta
Jumna	364	Ship	McGill	Calcutta
Earl Grey	242	Brig	Bell	Calcutta
Tigris	422	Ship	Robinson	Calcutta
Patriot Queen	547	Ship	Hoodless	Calcutta
Santon (2)	345	Barque	Huxtable	Calcutta
Aden	339	Barque	Ponsonby	Singapore/Canton

The Fleet of Robert and Henry Jefferson – 1840				
Lady Shaw Stewart	181	Brig	Steele	Antigua
British Queen	218	Brig	Kennedy	Antigua
Derwent	221	Brig	–	–
Midge	28	Sloop	James	Cadiz–Antigua

CHAPTER 6

At Brocklebanks and Jeffersons – 1841–50

The main event at Brocklebanks in the year 1841 was, without doubt, the launching of their famous Indiaman, the *Princess Royal*. The vessel was designed specifically for the East India trade, and upon her launch at Bransty on Monday the 8th March she was placed under the command of Capt Daniel Robinson.

The only other vessel to be launched at Whitehaven by the firm in 1841 was the barque *Valparaiso*, which, as her name might suggest, was mainly traded to that port, for the first few years under the command of Capt Dixon. The 1841 launches brought the number of vessels being traded by the firm up to 37.

Meanwhile at Jeffersons, young Joseph Wise remained in command of the *Lady Shaw Stewart*, his older colleague, Capt Thomas Kennedy, remaining with the firm's brig *British Queen*. The ships ran their regular service across the Atlantic to Antigua, returning to Whitehaven and Liverpool heavily laden with rum, sugar, and molasses. On the 25th October 1842, Capt Wise, completing probably his third voyage to the island in the capacity of master, reported 'that all was well', and that he had 'spoke' the schooner *Albion* (Capt Riley) of Whitehaven, when off Tuskar on the 22nd. With slavery now a thing of the past Joseph was now clearly voyaging to a more hospitable place. For 19th century mariners however, the problems of actually getting a sailing vessel safely into St. John's harbour, Antigua, and back across the Atlantic remained formidable ones.

At certain seasons of the year the prevailing winds in the West Indies made an approach to the island particularly hazardous. Added to this is the fact that the coastline of Antigua is nothing short of a mariner's nightmare, a jagged mass of shoals, small islands and rocky headlands, all awash with tricky tides and currents. For any vessel to be driven ashore on such a coast, disaster was certain. Jefferson masters, in particular, must have been well versed in these dangers, for in all the years that their craft voyaged to the island I can find no record of one having come to grief there; all of which I think must speak highly of their collective skills as mariners.

In addition to the aforementioned dangers, Capts Kennedy and Wise also had to contend with the very real dangers posed by pirates – still highly active in the Atlantic at

46

this time – Capt Kennedy having a particularly interesting close encounter with such characters in August 1842. On his arrival back in Whitehaven in September, he published the following fascinating account of his adventures in the Whitehaven papers –

'On the 5th August, at 4 p.m. in lat 38 30 long 51 14 W the *British Queen* saw a vessel steering to the north west, carrying a heavy press of canvas, wind E by N light breezes. The *British Queen* was by this time by the wind, going N by E about 2½ knots per hour. At six Capt Kennedy made her out to be a schooner, carrying a maintopsail, and observed her to haul her wind after them, but as she had passed a large ship to windward, it was deemed prudent not to wait for her, Capt Kennedy did not like her appearance; and from her rig could not but regard her as a suspicious looking craft.

From six to eight p.m. the stranger hauled right up by degrees in the wake of the *British Queen*, and at 8 p.m. she was about four miles off. After this it became very moderate, and at midnight it was a complete calm. During the whole night afterwards it was so extremely dark that the strange vessel was never seen, though a good look-out was kept, as all on board the *Queen* doubted her intentions being good. At day-light (4 H 30 m.a.m.) on Saturday, both vessels lay becalmed, the stranger with the greater part of her sails clued up, bearing from the *British Queen* about 3 miles distant. At 5 a light breeze sprang up from about N. by E. in favour of the *British Queen*, and before the suspected vessel got it the *Queen* had gained considerably ahead of her. She made all sail and stood after the *British Queen* by the wind yet was unable to maintain her ground.

At 8 a.m. she hove her maintopsail to the mast for about ten minutes, and hauled a flag at the maintopmast head; owing to the great distance however it could not be made out, but the impression on board the *British Queen* was that it was a Spanish flag. After this she ran away to the S.E. carrying all sail for about an hour, and then hauled up after the *British Queen* again as if determined to come up with her. The *British Queen*, however still gained on her, and about half past ten she stood away again to the S.E. and soon after that stood about S. At noon she was fully eight miles astern, and at 2 p.m. she was not visible from the deck of the *British Queen*, at which hour the wind got variable and very light. At four she was in sight again, when the *British Queen* tacked to the north, and almost immediately afterwards the stranger tacked also. The wind backed again, and the *British Queen* stood to the eastward, steering all night about N.E. and in the morning the suspicious looking vessel was not in sight.

Captain Kennedy is confident from the conduct of those on board the strange sail that she was either a piratical vessel or had a mutinous crew on board. She had the appearance of a Spanish vessel, her head was painted black; had long lower masts, and very square yards, short bow-sprits and jib-booms. She had no Fore Royalmast, and all her sails were new, except the mainmast. She had a boat over her stern, and when last seen was standing to the north at dusk on Saturday night.'

Even more adventures lay ahead for Capt Kennedy, for on the 8th February 1843 one of the worst earthquakes ever recorded struck Antigua and other islands in the Leeward group. On land the effects were devastating – even at sea the effects were dramatic. Captain Kennedy left Whitehaven for Antigua on the 28th December 1842, after having been put back twice by 'foul winds', and when disaster struck on the 8th February he was close to the island. Ships' reports, including Capt Kennedy's, regarding the event read as follows: The *Thames*, the Royal Mail Steam-Packet Company's ship, Capt Haste, was passing Antigua at the time of the shock. Captain Haste says, 'The *Thames* was brought up as if on a reef of rocks, to his own dismay, and the dismay of all on board, and continued for a short period to jump and kick as if beating on rocks.' 'The brig *British Queen*, Capt Kennedy, from Whitehaven, 17 3' north long 58 45', ship going six knots, felt a severe shock of earthquake, which stopped her way when 160 miles due east of the island, on the 8th, which lasted about four minutes. A French brig coming to St. Thomas's, of Tortola felt the shock so severely, he (the captain) thought that the vessel had struck on a rock.'

On Antigua the extent of the damage caused by this earthquake was immense. About one-third of the shops and houses of St. John's were destroyed; the remainder were left so shattered and torn that they were rendered untenable. Some of the houses were in fact completely twisted around by the force of the event. Of the island's 172 sugar mills, 35 were entirely levelled with the ground, 82 were split and damaged very severely, and of the remainder almost all suffered some damage.

As luck would have it Joseph Wise, with his Antigua bound brig the *Lady Shaw Stewart*, was only three days out from Whitehaven when this terrible disaster struck the island.

The Brocklebank brig, *Dryad* (4), built by the firm in 1837 was a remarkable vessel, for although she was of only 251 tons burthen she was traded around the globe by the firm. She remained in company service for 25 years, and was actually afloat until November 1894 when she was wrecked. The brig's first master was Capt Askew, followed by Capts Rickerty and Hansen. On the 14th September 1840, 14-year-old Francis Wise, the last of the five Wise brothers to go to sea, began his five year term of apprenticeship aboard this ship. Whilst aboard this vessel he was to voyage to Singapore, Valparaiso, Arica, Iquique, Buenos Aires, and back to Singapore – covering well over a hundred thousand miles before completing his term.

The *Dryad* carried a crew of 14, the composition being almost identical to that carried by Jefferson's *Lady Shaw Stewart*, that is Master, 1st and 2nd mates, carpenter, a steward, a cook, four seamen, and four apprentices. The only difference here being that she carried a cook *and* a steward, and, not surprisingly, no cooper. As was often the case with Brocklebank ships a high percentage of all crews – particularly the officers – were Cumberland men. They were also usually very young; for the voyage of 1843 the crew list shows that Capt Rickerty was then 30 years old; his mate, Davey Curwen, 23; Thomas Fearon, 2nd mate, 20; and the carpenter 23; all of them from Whitehaven.

It was whilst young Francis Wise was serving aboard the *Dryad* that his elder brother George at last entered the services of the Brocklebank Line, becoming 2nd mate to Capt Daniel Robinson aboard the firm's famous new Indiaman, *Princess Royal*. Daniel Robinson, born in 1803, was a direct maternal descendant of the Reverend Daniel Brocklebank, his grandmother Margaret, being Capt Daniel Brocklebank's sister. Daniel Robinson's brother Joseph never went to sea, but nevertheless played a crucial role in the development of the Brocklebank Line – that of building yard manager at Bransty.

It was on this voyage of the *Princess Royal* in 1840 that a young man by the name of Richard Robinson, from Workington, made his first voyage as an apprentice – a young man who was destined to become master of the almost legendary tea clipper *Fiery Cross* of 1860. Captain Daniel Robinson remained in command of the *Princess Royal* until April 1844, before handing over command of the ship to Capt William Hoodless – for at that time Daniel Robinson was to assume command of the even larger Indiaman, the *Robert Pulsford*, about the launch of which the Whitehaven press had much to say –

48

'On Thursday morning last, a splendid new ship was launched from the building yard of Messrs Brocklebank's at this port called the *Robert Pulsford*, in compliment to R. Pulsford esq., one of the most eminent insurance brokers of his day, and an old and particular friend of the Brocklebanks. This really beautiful vessel is the largest ever built at the port of Whitehaven; she is entirely copper fastened, coppered to her bends, and as regards model and substantial workmanship she cannot be excelled.

She sports a full length figurehead of the gentleman whose name she bears, and which is said to be an admirable likeness, not merely as regards features, but the whole contour of the body. Be this however as it may, it is an admirable specimen of the art of carving, to which the talented artist (Mr Robinson of Liverpool) appears to have imparted vitality itself. Her stern was also carved by the same clever workman and it is in reality a beautiful and rich specimen of carving on wood. The *Robert Pulsford* is intended for the East India trade, under the command of Captain Robinson, late of the *Princess Royal*. We may observe in conclusion that the launch was what may be termed a dry one: the ways were of great length, along which she glided with perfect steadiness even to their extremity, at which point she was most lustily cheered by a whole army of carpenters who had bestowed upon her many a day of anxious labour.

Shortly after launching the much admired *Robert Pulsford* Messrs Brocklebank built and launched the schooner *Roland Hill* which vessel was sold upon completion. The next vessels to be built were the *Courier* (2) and the barque *Sir Henry Pottinger*, in both of which vessels Francis Wise would soon be serving – the former as master – the latter as mate to Capt McWean. Meanwhile the firm's brig *Patna* – later to be bought by Jeffersons – continued to develop Brocklebanks' fast growing links with the Middle Kingdom – and Hong Kong – the colony just established by Admiral Sir Henry Pottinger. The value of one entry passed at the Customs House for the *Patna*, when bound for Hong Kong in 1844, amounted to £45,025, in respect of 3,012,147 yards of cotton cloth. It was in this year also that Ralph Brocklebank, cousin and partner of the first Sir Thomas Brocklebank first became involved in establishing a reputable Sailors' Home at Liverpool.

Ralph Brocklebank was the descendant of the Reverend Ralph Brocklebank, the son of 'Corbridge' John Brocklebank, of Hazleholme, Cleator Moor, Cumberland. Ralph was born at Cleator Moor in 1803, and spent his boyhood at this village near Whitehaven. In 1826 he came to Liverpool and started his life's work with the firm.

In October 1844, Capt Wilson Fisher, father of Thomas Fisher, died at his home at Keekle Bank, near Whitehaven at the age of 67. Within a few hours of the New Year, 1845, Daniel Bird, son of the founder's sister, Margaret, died at his home in Whitehaven. Daniel Bird had been the able manager of the firm's Whitehaven yard for many years, and it was following his death that he was succeeded at the yard by his sister's son, Joseph Robinson, brother of Capt Daniel Robinson, the newly appointed master of the Indiaman *Robert Pulsford*.

Ten months later, Thomas Brocklebank passed away at his home, Greenlands. Throughout his long life he had been noted as a man of retiring disposition, and as a merchant he had few equals. Most importantly however, he was considered to be one of the best shipbuilders of his day – his ships being noted for their strength and sea-worthiness. At the time of his death he had directed the operations of the firm for 45 years. He was a member of the Liverpool Dock Trust, and a director of the Bank of Liverpool from 1833 until his death. Upon the death of Thomas Brocklebank the cousins Thomas Fisher and

Ralph Brocklebank found themselves in sole charge of the family enterprise, the former being the sole surviving male descendant of the firm's founder, Capt Daniel Brocklebank. Under the terms of his uncle's Will, Thomas Fisher was obliged to change his name to Brocklebank, and so it was that in 1845 the only son of Capt Wilson Fisher became Thomas Brocklebank, senior partner with Ralph Brocklebank in the old established firm of Thos. & Jno. Brocklebank of Liverpool and Whitehaven – a partnership which was to last for over 40 years.

Meanwhile at Jeffersons, Capts Kennedy and Wise continued to ply between White-haven and Antigua – Kennedy in command of the *British Queen*, Joseph Wise remaining in command of the *Lady Shaw Stewart*. The movements of the vessels being noted at regular intervals in the 'marine intelligence' columns of the 'Pacquet'. –

13th February 1844, 'The *British Queen*, Kennedy, sailed hence for Antigua on the 6th instant – put into Douglas on the 8th having had very rough weather, and sailed again on the 9th.'

May 14th – 'The *Lady Shaw Stewart*, Wise from Antigua at this port on the 9th instant, after a passage of 47 days, all well; experienced strong easterly winds, and was detained upwards of a week in the channel. Captain Wise reports leaving the following vessels at Antigua: the *Kyanite*, Lister, would sail for this port in three weeks; the *British Queen*, Kennedy, had nearly finished discharging her outward cargo, and would load for England. The *Lydia*, for Liverpool, and the *Jamaica* for London, would both sail in about three weeks. On the 24th April, in lat 47 57 N long 11 23 W spoke the barque *Ellengrove* from Dominica for London. On the 30th off Cape Clear, spoke the *Eucles*, from Calcutta. On the 6th instant, when off Tuskar, spoke the *Marmion*, from Liverpool for Halifax – the *Lady Shaw Stewart* will be ready for sea again tomorrow morning.'

10th September 1844 – 'The *Lady Shaw Stewart*, Wise, from Antigua at this port yesterday evening with a cargo of sugar and mollasses for Messrs R & H Jefferson. 50 days passage: all well. Capt. W has kindly handed us the following report:– On the 29th July spoke her Majesty's frigate *Beak*, from Jamaica for Barbadoes. On the 5th August, spoke the barque *Harriet*, of and for Swansea from St. Jago de Cuba. On the 6th instant off Cork, spoke the schooner *Jubilee*, from Liverpool for Gaspee, which vessel desired to be reported.' December 3rd 'The *Lady Shaw Stewart*, Wise, will be ready to sail hence for Antigua on Thursday.' 'The *British Queen*, Kennedy, from Antigua arrived off this port on the 29th ult., after a passage of 38 days, all well; received orders and proceeded for Liverpool: experienced most severe weather for three weeks and lost foreyard.'

17th December 1844 – 'The *Lady Shaw Stewart* sailed hence for Antigua on the 10th instant.' 14th February 1845 – 'Extract of a letter from Capt. Greggs of the *Scipio*, dated at sea on Saturday last at noon – I yesterday parted company with the *British Queen*, Kennedy, from Liverpool for Antigua, off the Calf-of-Man, wind N.N.W.: We were both carrying double reefed topsails, with a heavy sea. The wind during the night veered to the northward, so that I have no doubt the *British Queen* will get down the channel.'

On the 25th February 1845 the 'Pacquet' carried a most dramatic account of disaster aboard the Jefferson brigantine *Lady Shaw Stewart*, relating to the above mentioned voyage of the ship which commenced on the 10th of December –

'The *Lady Shaw Stewart*, Wise, hence at Antigua on the 20th January, after a passage of 41 days. Sailed from this port on the 10th December, and on the night of the 12th when off Tuskar, with

50

the wind at the S.E., and blowing strong, the crew when attempting to reef the mainsail, the mainyard broke in two, when three of the crew were precipitated into the sea and unfortunately met with a watery grave. Every exertion was used by Capt Wise to rescue the poor mariners, but the night being extremely dark, and the sea very high, his efforts proved to no avail.

The carpenter who was also on the yard at the time it gave way, fell inside the railings and was saved: another seaman succeeded in getting hold of the fore brake, and made his way to the deck by the foretopmast backstay. Soon after the yard gave way, the foretopmast came down: On the following day got another yard and topmast up, which in about three hours afterwards came down again off Holyhead light.

In this disabled state an attempt was made to run the ship back to this port, and after contending for some time with the waves, the wind veered round to the eastward, when Capt Wise deemed it advisable to proceed on his voyage. The vessel being in this crippled state may in some degree account for the length of the passage, particularly as they encountered favourable winds. The names of the sufferers are: Charles Tyson (son of the late Mr John Tyson, plasterer) John Little and Samuel Taylor, all seamen belonging to this town, the last named whom has left a widow and four helpless children to deplore their untimely loss.'

Joseph Wise remained as commander of the *Lady Shaw Stewart* until the 28th February 1846, at which time the ship was sold to Buckingham and Company, who placed their master, Capt Roper in command. Joseph Wise was then given command of Capt Kennedy's old ship the *British Queen*, which he was to remain with for many years. Some nine months after Robert and Henry Jefferson sold the *Lady* to Buckingham & Co. reports reached Whitehaven concerning their old ship, for it would seem that on the 28th October Capt Roper left the Liverpool docks and anchored in the Mersey, prior to sailing for the port of Payta. The steamer *Sea King* making her way down river, bound for the open seas ran straight into the *Lady* causing her some considerable damage, all of which obliged her new master to put back into port for extensive repairs. However, back at Whitehaven I have no doubt Joseph Wise, and many others, were pleased to learn that the fine old brig had survived the incident.

Following the launch of the barque *Sir Henry Pottinger* in 1845, no other ship was launched by Brocklebanks until 1847, when the firm launched two ships, one of them being the strangely named craft *Crisis*, the other being the *Thomas Brocklebank*. The former vessel was placed under the command of Capt Gibson, the latter under the command of Capt H. Ponsonby, both ships making their maiden voyage to Calcutta. The 629-ton *Thomas Brocklebank* was destined to remain on the run to Calcutta until sold by the firm many years later, whilst the smaller ship *Crisis* was to make most of her voyages to China – Hong Kong, and Foo Chow Foo in particular.

At Jeffersons Capt Joseph Wise was now making record passages across the Atlantic with his new command the *British Queen*, as this short item published in the 'Cumberland Pacquet' in January 1847 illustrates – 'The *British Queen*, Wise, from Antigua and Belfast at this port on the 2nd instant – 43 days passage to the former port. On the 19th December, in lat 51.11 N long 9.54 W spoke the barque *Ajax* for Valparaiso. The *Queen* under the able seamanship of Capt Wise has performed three West Indies voyages within the twelve months, a feat which reflects great credit on her commander for his perseverence and activity.'

In the same year that Jeffersons' vessel nearly met her end in the Mersey, luck nearly ran out for Thomas & John Brocklebank's splendid old *Westmorland*. Built in 1814 she was still in active service in 1846, most of her voyages to date having been made to either North or South America. In January 1846 however, the *Westmorland* had a very narrow escape from total disaster, as the following report taken from the Whitehaven press clearly indicates:

'January 6th – The *Westmorland*, Fulton, from Liverpool for Bahia, was driven on shore during a heavy squall on the north side of the entrance of Ravenglass Harbour on the 30th ult., with loss of mainmast and bowsprit, having been run into by a large American ship, the *Epamiminondas*, on the morning of the above date, between the Calf-of-Man and point Lynas. The *Westmorland* has since been got into deep water, and by discharging her cargo it is expected that in the course of a few tides she will be got into the harbour.' 'January 20th, The *Westmorland*, Fulton, which vessel was on shore near Ravenglass was taken up the slip at this port on the 14th instant, to undergo examination.' 'January 27th – The *Bransty*, Russell, was towed to Ravenglass on the 24th instant, and will take in the cargo landed from the *Westmorland* and thence proceed to this port again.' 'February 3rd – The *Westmorland*, Fulton, was launched from the patent slip at this port on the 30th ult., after being thoroughly overhauled; got a new mainmast, bowsprit, and re-coppered.'

When Joseph Wise obtained command of the *British Queen* his younger brother Francis Wise, now aged 20, was serving as 2nd mate on the *Bonanza* to Clement Mossop of Whitehaven – this skipper now being an 'old man' of 28 years of age! Francis Wise was not to join the *Sir Henry Pottinger*, as 1st mate to Capt William McWean until April 1849, which was perhaps fortunate for him.

The *Sir Henry Pottinger* left the Mersey, bound for Calcutta, on the 16th July 1847. The voyage was to be a disastrous one, for the Indian Ocean is noted for dreadful cyclones, and as fate would have it, one occurred on the 14th January 1848 when Capt McWean was taking the *Sir Henry Pottinger* through these dangerous seas. The terrific winds screamed through the rigging, until such sail as remained on her was torn to shreds. The vessel was hurled from side to side by the unremitting fury of the winds until eventually, with a crack like thunder the mainmast split in two, and came crashing to the deck. Soon the remaining masts gave way, and the bowsprit also snapped in two. On deck the scene was one of chaos and disaster – broken masts – rigging – and shreds of sail, all awash with the huge seas whipped up by the cyclone.

Captain William McWean, his officers and crew, struggled heroically to save their ship, all working feverishly to cut away the tangle of broken debris that was now threatening to drag the ship down. Night descended, but still they worked on, until their task was completed, and the Brocklebank Indiaman was saved. One member of the crew did not survive this terrible ordeal, he was the youngest apprentice aboard the ship – George Smith, age 14, from Kent – who was drowned, we must presume swept away whilst working with his fellow seamen to save his ship. (On the following voyage it is interesting to note that the *Sir Henry Pottinger* carried two carpenters.) Captain McWean came from Whitehaven, and at the time of this incident was 34 years old.

In December 1847 George Wise was appointed commander of Brocklebank's barque *Esk*, which at this time was 19 years old, having been built at Whitehaven in 1828. The vessel was a small barque of 217 tons, mainly traded by the firm to Pernambuco and Bahia, and at the time of George Wise's appointment as master she had seen eight previous commanders. One can imagine that George Wise was more than pleased to obtain this post, his first as master, for his younger brother Joseph, and his elder brother Abraham had now been masters of their own ships for some time.

Crew of the *Sir Henry Pottinger* on her voyage to Calcutta from Liverpool, May 1st 1849.

Name					wage		
William McWean	age	36	Whitehaven	Master		–	
Francis Wise		23	Cumberland	Mate	£4	10	0
John McBride		24	Argyle	2nd Mate	£3	10	0
George Scott		23	Dean	3rd Mate	£2	15	0
Joseph Quinton		24	Whitehaven	Carpenter	£4	10	0
James Knowles		32	Liverpool	Steward	£2	15	0
John Wright		27	Liverpool	Cook	£2	10	0
Michael Fielding		30	Cornwall	Seaman	£2	5	0
George Kingham		26	Middlesex	Seaman	£2	5	0
William Hundle		20	Whitehaven	Seaman	£2	5	0
William W. Boncher		16	Carmarthen	Seaman	£2	5	0
John Peebles		29	Dundee	Carpenter	£5	0	0
Harry Thompson		16	Ravenglass	Apprentice			
Thomas Thackray		17	Bootle	Apprentice			
Henry Grindall		18	Crosshouse	Apprentice			
Phillip Graham		18	Parton	Apprentice			
Robert Johnston		19	Eclesfield	Apprentice			

CHAPTER 7

Whitehaven 1850

On the 1st June 1850 Capt Joseph Wise arrived back in Whitehaven with his ship the *British Queen* – heavily laden as usual with rum, sugar, and molasses for Robert & Henry Jefferson. He then made a particularly 'fast passage' to St. Nicholas Parish Church, at which place he married Hannah Glover on the 2nd June. Hannah was the daughter of Capt John Glover, master and owner of the well known Whitehaven brig, the *Massereene*.

The Glovers, like so many other Whitehaven maritime families, had links with the Brocklebank Line and the Fisher family. John Glover's first command was the brig *Kitty*, built by William Palmer at Whitehaven in 1765 for Capt Fisher – and about which remarkable vessel we will hear more later. Hannah's late brother was Capt James Glover, born in 1815, who died at Whampoa China in 1848, whilst in command of the Boadle brothers' barque *Rajah Bassa*. The Boadle family of Whitehaven were well-known ship-owners and mariners – one time partners of the Brocklebank family.

Thomas & John Brocklebank held shares in the Boadle ships, *Helvellyn* and *Avoca*, which vessels were commanded by the Boadle brothers. With these ships they attempted to start a shipping Line between Liverpool and New South Wales, Australia. On the outward passage they would call at Melbourne, Hobart, and other ports, but on the return passage they would trade the ships via India, China, and Malaya, the ports where they in fact later traded their ship *Rajah Bassa* – last command of young Capt James Glover. It would seem however that Thomas Brocklebank was not very impressed with the venture, for none of the firm's own ships were ever traded to Australia.

How had the town of Whitehaven developed since the early decades of the last century – a great deal it would seem, despite the general decline in the maritime trade. The compilers of Mannix and Whellan's Cumberland Directory, published in 1847, have much to tell us of interest about the town at this time – speaking first about the harbour and its development they make these observations –

'The New West Pier was commenced in 1824, and finished in 1839, at a cost of above £100,000. It is a noble building of great strength, extending northward from the west pier, to the length of about 300 yards, and on the magnificent round head at the end, which cost £30,000, stands the light house, with a revolving light and three reflectors. There is another half tide house on one of the inner piers, and another on St. Bee's head, a lofty promontary about three miles S.S.W. The new north pier is also a splendid structure, finished in 1841, at a great expense, and has a light

A presentation mug given to Capt John Glover of the Masserene, *and now in the Whitehaven Museum.*

house or harbour guide. Indeed, no town, perhaps in the kingdom can boast of two such splendid piers as Whitehaven.

A great improvement has recently been made on the south side of the harbour, by removing the old unsightly hurries, widening that part of the quay, and erecting a substantial iron roadway, supported by iron pillars, with close iron hurries for delivering coals into the vessels, thus opening a good access to the baths, and to the unequalled promenade on the west pier, and its

55

spacious parapet, where a walk of nearly a quarter of a mile direct out to sea from the old quay is afforded. The first iron hurry was placed here in 1837. Though spring tides rise about eighteen feet, and the neap tides eleven feet, thus enabling vessels of 500 to 600 tons burthen to enter, the old or inner harbour is dry at low water, but is accessible without any danger, about two hours after high water; and since the erection of the outer pier, is remarkably secure.

On the north wall, the coals are lowered to the ships' hatchways by a novel hydraulic arrangement, the invention, we understand, of the late Mr Mattheson, engineer to Messrs Tulk & Ley. The coals are dropped from the waggon, into a box supported by an unseen rod, which, on turning a tap, is permitted to descend, by forcing water from a cylinder below, into an ornamental tank placed on columns over the waggon; when the coals are let fall into the hold, the water, again descending, raises the empty box. This is intended chiefly for small vessels, and is a manifest improvement on some of the clumsy mechanism at Newcastle and other coal ports. On the south of the harbour various mechanical devices are in operation for returning the empty waggons by the descent of the laden ones; and an air cylinder is applied as an effectual break on the steep inclined plane. Railways were in use here, and at most coal ports, in conveying coal

Coal hurries, Whitehaven Harbour in 1907.

56

from the mines to ships, long before public railways for passengers and general traffic were formed; but the distances are too short for the advantageous introduction of locomotive power. The first iron railway in the Kingdom was laid from a pit near the town to the harbour.

Of late years the demand for coals to Ireland has exceeded the existing means of supply, vessels having frequently to wait from four to six weeks for a turn to load; but various works now in progress warrant the prospect of a great and permanent increase at no distant period. Near to the noble pier on the west, the attention of every stranger is attracted to a series of towers and castellated erections, of a style of architecture, magnificent of design and execution rarely to be seen, presenting the appearance seaward, of extensive fortifications and furnished inside with enormous steam power, appropriated however to afford a better security to the trade and prosperity of Whitehaven, than could be given by the most powerful aray of warlike fortifications. These engines are connected with two shafts of great depth, cased from top to bottom with the strongest cemented stone work, impervious to water. A large quantity of coal is daily raised here, whilst the great work is progressing, which, when completed, will probably be the deepest, the most productive, and the most remarkable coal mine in the world; opening out such a supply of the best coal from underneath the sea, and the adjacent headland, as may not for centuries be exhausted.'

Owing to the close friendship which existed between the Earl of Lonsdale, George Stephenson, and Henry Jefferson, the Cumberland railway lines were rapidly developed; to the extent that the Maryport to Workington line, operational in 1846, was pushed southwards, reaching Whitehaven on the 18th March, 1847. Henry Jefferson was one of the first to promote the Whitehaven Junction Railway, and one of the first directors when the line was projected in 1844, having amongst his colleagues in the directorate at this time, his brother Robert, who was chairman of the company, Viscount Lowther, Mr Heywood, the Rev Henry Lowther, Mr John Peille, and other leading local citizens.

WHITEHAVEN COLLIERIES.

WANTED a Number of PITMEN, as HEW-ERS, who will meet with constant Employment and liberal Wages.—Comfortable DWELLING HOUSES, with SMALL COAL. for their Fires, for the above Description of Workmen, are allowed Gratis.

By the Introduction of Sir HUMPHREY DAVY's admirable SAFETY LAMP, the Danger of Collieries, infected with Fire Damp, is greatly diminished; as every Man may carry his Security in his Hand.

Any Class of Men, who are able and desirous to labour, may soon be taught the Duty.

Colliery Office, 12 July, 1819. (26)

FEMALE EDUCATION.

Advertisement for miners in the 'Cumberland Pacquet' 1819.

With commendable foresight the Earl of Lonsdale had laid the first stone of the town's famous Lonsdale Hotel on the 26th September 1846; it covered an area of 6,000 square feet, contained a spacious ball room, a coffee room and eighty bedrooms – and was conveniently situated at Bransty, contiguous to the proposed Whitehaven Junction Railway Station! This enormous establishment was considered at the time to be a great ornament to the town and harbour; all it required was a steady stream of visitors – which duly arrived with the opening of the line in 1847. The rail tunnel from Bransty to Corkicle was started in 1850 and completed in 1852. Prior to 1852 there was a break in the line, the Whitehaven and Furness line terminating at Preston Street Station, the Whitehaven Junction Railway terminating at Bransty Station.

The combined efforts of George Stephenson, Robert & Henry Jefferson, and the Earl of Lonsdale, to bring the railway lines into Cumberland were welcomed by many, but opposed by others. Prominent amongst those who opposed their efforts was none other than Cumberland's most celebrated citizen – the poet William Wordsworth! On learning about the introduction of one projected Cumberland Line he penned the following lines – making it *abundantly* clear what he thought about such ventures!

Proud were ye, Mountains, when, in times of old,
Your patriot sons, to stem invasion war,
Intrenched your brows; ye gloried in each scar:
Now for your shame, a power, the Thirst of Gold,
That rules o'er Britain like a baneful star,
Wills that your peace, your beauty, shall be sold,
And clear way made for her triumphal car
Through the beloved retreats your arms enfold!
Hear ye that whistle? – As her long-linked train
Swept onwards, did the vision cross your view?
Yes, ye were startled; – and, in balance true,
Weighing the mischief with the promised gain,
Mountains, and Vales, and Floods, I call on you
To share the passion of a just disdain.

By 1850 the principal approach road to Whitehaven, which ran in from the north side of the town, ran between banks, one side having been laid out as gardens, the other overgrown with great oak trees. In the town itself all the streets, lanes and roads were now well paved and lighted, and the pavements flagged with hard highland stone. Oil lamps for street lighting had first been adopted at Whitehaven in 1781, but from the time that the gas works were established in 1831, the town had been well lit from the town's two gasometers. By 1847 the town and harbour were illuminated by 261 gas lamps, and almost all the private shops and houses in the town were supplied with well-purified gas – at the extremely low price of 4s per 1,000 cubic feet.

The town boasted an excellent Subscription Library, which occupied a handsome building in Catherine Street, and the local Theatre was in Roper Street, but owing to the fact that the taste for dramatic literature had been on the decline in the town for some years, few productions worth seeing were ever presented there. For those who obtained their pleasures from drinking their needs were particularly well provided for, for in 1847

58

there were no less than 88 hotels and inns, and three beer houses, situated within the town boundaries. There was also a 'Temperence News Room' at No. 2 Tangier Street, which was established in 1847 – but alas, in the year in which it was opened membership had risen to only 40.

The town's savings bank occupied a large and handsome building in Lowther Street, Henry Jefferson was the President of this establishment, William Miller the treasurer, and Isaac Hayton, secretary. They opened for business every Saturday evening, from six to eight. Apart from the Savings bank, the town also had two other banks, these being the 'Bank of Whitehaven', and the 'Whitehaven Joint Stock Bank', Henry Jefferson also being a director of this latter bank. In 1847 the town had two newspapers, these being the 'Cumberland Pacquet', which was published every Tuesday by Mr Robert Gibson, at No. 26, King Street, which was the oldest newspaper in the county, having been established in 1774, by Mr Ware. The 'Whitehaven Herald', which was commenced in 1830, was, in

Wellington Pit, Whitehaven, c 1900.

1847, published by Mr George Irwin, at 13 Lowther Street. Mr Gibson advocated Tory principles, whilst Mr Irwin favoured the Whig policy.

In 1850 ship building was carried on to a considerable extent at Whitehaven, Thos. & John Brocklebank's yard being situated at Bransty, and managed by Mr J. H. Robinson, the firm's Rope Works also being at the same place, but managed by Mr J. Jones. Lumley Kennedy's yard was at the North Harbour, and Mr Hugh Williamson, also a noted builder of ships, lived at 9 Sandhills Lane; Robert Hardy, another ship builder lived at 82 Scotch Street. In 1847 no less than 119 master mariners were listed as householders living within the town boundaries of Whitehaven, which figure would of course not include Whitehaven sailing masters who were not householders, nor those who lived outside of the town boundary; all of which gives some indication of Whitehaven's dependence on its maritime trade at this point in time. In all the average number of men navigating Whitehaven vessels in the 1840s was estimated to be 2,252. The total number of vessels belonging to Cumberland in 1840 was 502, with an aggregate tonnage of 73,372.

With the decline of Whitehaven, and the rise of Liverpool, during the second part of the 19th century, a large percentage of these Cumberland mariners moved south to the booming new port, the links between the two places being particularly strong during the transitional period. In the 1840s and 1850s the Whitehaven Steam Navigation Company's vessels sailed regularly between Whitehaven and Liverpool, performing three voyages weekly during the summer period, and two in winter.

The Whitehaven coal trade

Whilst Joseph Wise, and his brothers, continued to sail across the great oceans for Robert and Henry Jefferson, and the Brocklebank Line, Joseph's father-in-law, Capt John Glover, continued to sail as master and owner of the collier brig *Massereene*, with the Whitehaven coal fleet. Many of the masters in this considerable fleet were owners of their own ships – making them a highly independent group of mariners. In the main this fleet confined itself to voyaging to ports in the St. George's, and Bristol Channels – Ireland in particular being the destination of much of Whitehaven's best coal.

Being harbour-bound at Whitehaven seemed to have been something of an occupational hazard for John Glover and his colleagues, as the following extract taken from the 'Whitehaven Herald' of Sat. August 10th will illustrate:

'On Saturday last about twenty vessels left this port for Dublin and other ports. A strong wind from the S.W. sprung up a few hours after their departure, which gradually increased to a moderate gale when most, if not all of them put back again on Sunday and Monday. A large fleet of laden vessels are at present windbound in our harbour. This morning (Friday) however, the weather became quite moderate, and large numbers are putting to sea.'

Apart from keeping the fleet in port, too much wind could also bring the collier brigs into port more quickly than desired:

'The brig *Massereene*, Glover, from this port, coal laden, when going up Dublin River on the evening of the 10th inst. ran against the quay wall, drove her anchor through her bows, and sunk, but has since been raised and is now alongside the quay discharging.'

60

'Corves' or baskets used in the William pit c 1870.

Alas, John Glover's days as an independent mariner with the collier fleet were now numbered – for soon he was destined to make his last voyage in this life. In March 1853 he signed a fresh crew and took his beautifully named ship down the channel to the bustling port of Liverpool. But whilst at this port he died there under the following sad circumstances – duly reported in the Whitehaven press: '... as Captain Glover, of the brig *Massereene* of Whitehaven, lying in the Wellington dock, was going on board, he fell between the vessel and the quay; and though promptly taken out of the water by Mr John Doley, his mate, and police officer 88, he died immediately.' The date of his untimely death being July 29th.

Upon the death of his father-in-law Joseph Wise became the reluctant owner of the brig *Massereene*, which he promptly advertised for sale in the Whitehaven press. A few weeks later his first son was born, whom he named John Glover Wise after the lad's grandfather. To allow Joseph Wise to put his affairs in order Robert & Henry Jefferson engaged Capt

William Hunter, as relief master for the *British Queen*, but poor old John Doley, late mate of the *Massereene* experienced some difficulty finding a new berth, for like many old mariners, the surviving crew lists show he was illiterate, and could not sign his name! However, the crew lists for the voyage of the *British Queen*, dated the 25th January 1854, show that his old skipper's son-in-law, Joseph Wise, had engaged him as cook on the brigantine – bound for the distant island of Antigua!

CHAPTER 8

At Brocklebanks 1849–55

As a general rule most of the vessels now being produced at Brocklebank's Bransty building yard tended to be ships, rather than small barques, or brigs; instead of producing one or two small craft each year the firm was now concentrating on producing perhaps one larger vessel per annum. The *Harold*, launched in 1849 was a ship of 666 tons burthen, but the *Petchelee* launched the following year was an exception to the emerging policy for she was a barque of only 393 tons burthen; she was nevertheless a very fine ship, whose fine lines and appearance, at the time of her launch, clearly impressed the local reporter – even though he failed to obtain the vessel's name:

> 'This morning (Friday) a really noble looking new ship was launched from the building yard at this port, of T & J Brocklebank, Merchants, Liverpool. In her construction every application of skill has been combined that could contribute to her strength and speed; and she will deservedly take her place amongst the fleet of far famed Indiamen owned by that eminent firm. We understand her registered tonnage is 393, but could not learn what she was christened.' ('Whitehaven Herald', 13th July 1850.)

In 1851 the Indiaman *Arachne* was launched, a ship of 654 tons burthen. She carried a crew of 27, and on her maiden voyage to Calcutta she was commanded by Capt Adamson. In 1852 an even larger vessel – the 852 ton *Martaban* – was launched by the firm; Capt Adamson handed over command of the 12-month-old *Arachne* to Capt Roddock, and had the honour of being given command of the *Martaban*. The launch of this latter vessel was quite an event in the history of Whitehaven, as the following report, first printed in the 'Carlisle Journal' and later reprinted in the 'Liverpool Mercury' on October the 26th will indicate:

> 'Ship Launch at Whitehaven. – On Friday last, the noblest vessel ever built at this port was launched from the yard of Messrs Brocklebank. The extreme fineness of the day enabled the inhabitants of the town to gratify the desire to witness the launch which the dimensions, beauty, and general character of the splendid ship had excited. Accordingly, long before twelve o'clock, the hour appointed, they were seen hastening from all quarters towards those points which commanded a favourable view of the locality; and by noon, not less than five thousand persons, including a great number of elegantly attired ladies, had assembled on the North Pier and the adjacent stand points, the whole presenting a very gay and animated appearance. Shortly after twelve, all the preparations being complete, and the tide being at its height, the word was given,

63

the crutch was knocked away, the time-honoured ceremony of breaking a bottle of wine on her bows as the name she now bears, *Martaban*, was gone through, and the mighty mass glided gracefully into the element on which, we trust, she is destined to achieve a signal success, amid the heart-stirring cheers of the assembled multitude. The dimensions of the *Martaban* are 827 tons o.m., and 852 n.m. She is not only the largest ship ever built at Whitehaven, but the longest in proportion of length to beam; her length for measurement being 171 feet 2 inches, and her extreme breadth 32 feet. She is a flush ship, and has a full length female figure-head, in Asiatic costume, beautifully executed by Mr Brooker, of Maryport. Her through fastenings are all of wrought copper, and her other bolts of mixed metal. All the materials and the workmanship are of the highest character, and the vessel is intended to class A 1 at Lloyd's for 14 years. She is intended for the East India trade, and will be commanded by Captain Alexander Adamson, late of the *Arachne*.

Captain Adamson's 1st mate on the maiden voyage of the *Arachne* in 1852 had been young Francis Wise, late 1st mate of the *Aden*, and *Sir Henry Pottinger*, but at the time when Capt Adamson was given the command of the great Indiaman *Martaban*, young Francis Wise, now aged 27, was given command of the firm's smallest ship, the brig *Courier*.

The brig *Courier* (2) was a tiny vessel by our standards, 135 tons burthen, and just over 80 feet in length, from which figures one might suppose the firm had built her for the coastal trade, but this however was not the case. Almost unbelievably the *Courier* was a West Coast South America trader, serving in this hazardous trade for 11 years. The coasts that the crews of the *Courier* were most familiar with were not those of North Wales, Ireland, or Scotland, but those of Cape Horn, and Tierra del Fuego. This brig was the smallest vessel ever traded round Cape Horn by Brocklebanks – and perhaps one of the smallest ever to be placed in this trade, by any owner. She was however a remarkable vessel, and well able to stand the hammering the Cape Horn seas gave her, for after rounding Cape Horn for 11 years for the firm, she was to remain in service for other owners for a further 39 years.

Voyage of the *Courier* – Liverpool to Lima – October 7th 1853, July 25th 1854					
Francis Wise	master				
Michael Fletcher King	mate	£4	4 0		monthly wage.
Thomas Thompson Reed	2nd mate	£3	10 0		
William Nuttall	Carpenter	£5	0 0		
Mark Graham	Apprentice				
John Brown	Steward/Cook	£3	0 0		
Mathew Short	Seaman	£2	10 0		
J. Allan	Seaman	£2	10 0		
John Orren	Seaman	£2	10 0		
George Williams	A.B.	£40	0 0 +		
George Mayfirst	A.B.	£40	0 0 +		

With the exception of the last two crew members, all the above were signed on for the voyage at Liverpool on the 5th October 1853, the last two, however were signed on, on the 10th March 1854, whilst the *Courier* was at Callao. Apart from the fact that they both received the wage of £40 per month, against the then going rate of £2.10, the crew list also

64

indicates that further to this they received an advance of £80 each on joining the ship! Why did Francis Wise pay these two men these large sums of money to join his brig at Callao? Clearly it must have been for some service given to the firm, and paid in the form of wages for a single voyage. Perhaps they had both remained in Callao for some time on Company business? It is hard to say, so must remain as something of a mystery. Young Francis Wise remained in command of the *Courier* until the 15th November 1855, when he was given command of the larger Cape Horn brig *Rimac*.

On the 1st January 1852 George Wise left the *Esk* and became commander of the firm's Indiaman *Patriot King*, which vessel carried a crew of 17 men. George Wise's 1st mate for this voyage was Mr A. Williamson, who was described by the firm as '. . . a steady attentive officer, and a good scholar, and also a good navigator.' Abraham Wise, as always, remained in command of his WCSA trader, the *Kestrel*, but most of his voyages around Cape Horn in this brig seem to have been uneventful. Disasters aboard ship were however noted, and in this context the following recorded incident which occurred on the *Crisis* is worth mentioning.

On the 12th March 1854 the 426-ton Brocklebank ship *Crisis* left the Mersey, bound for Bombay, under the command of Capt J. Bell from Whitehaven and on board were two young apprentices, Herbert and Storrs, both of them Liverpool lads. There was to be a tragic start to this, the second voyage of the *Crisis* under Capt Bell's command.

Crew list of the Kestrel *for a South American voyage, 1843.*

'After the steam tug left the ship the tow rope was coiled abaft the main mast and lashed to all appearances secure, however shortly afterwards a gale of wind came on and whilst wearing the ship off Holyhead she gave a heavy lurch, causing the rope to burst its lashings and sally to leeward crushing two of the apprentices, Storrs, and Herbert, against the lee bulwarks. Poor Storrs only lived twenty minutes after the accident. Captain Bell immediately put back in the hope of saving Herbert's life, and arrived in the river on the 14th inst., when he was at once removed to his own home where he expired at noon the following day. Eight of the crew refused to proceed again in the ship and were sent to jail for 31 days, with hard labour. Shipped another crew and sailed again on the 17th. Christopher Hill and Thomas Combes from the *Harold* filling the places of Herbert and Storrs.'

Despite this tragic start to the voyage of the *Crisis* in 1854. the ship arrived safely at Bombay later in the year, and from there made her way to Whampoa, Hong Kong, and Amoy, returning to Liverpool in 1855. Captain Bell made two more voyages in the *Crisis*, these being to Hong Kong and Foo Chow Foo in 1855, and to Hong Kong and Foo Chow in 1856, before handing over command of the ship to Capt Black in 1857.

Following the launch of the *Martaban* in 1852, no ships came from Brocklebank's yard until 1854, when they launched their famous Indiaman the *Aracan*, a ship of 864 tons which carried a crew of 25. Without a doubt the *Aracan* was one of the finest clipper ships ever built on the coast of Cumberland; she became noted for making fast passages to India and China, and is reputed, on one occasion, to have raced and beaten the tea clipper *Fiery Cross*.

Apart from building and launching the *Aracan* in 1854, the firm departed from its normal practice by also buying a ship from another builder in this year, this being Capt John Ponsonby's ship, *Mindanao*, named after the beautiful island of that name in the Philippines. The 'Cumberland Pacquet' of the 16th May had this to say about the launch of this famous ship: 'On Friday last a very handsome new clipper ship was launched from the building yard of Mr Richard Williamson, at Harrington, the new craft received the name *Mindanao*, is 482 tons, o.m. 477 tons n.m., copper fastened throughout, and is classed A1 at Lloyds 13 years. The vessel has been built for Capt John Ponsonby, of this town, and no expense has been spared, or skill in architecture wanting to make her an ornament to the county, and fully a match for any of the noble clippers whose swiftness is the admiration and boast of the age.' Despite the above notice John Ponsonby was in fact the ship's commander, although he may have held shares in the vessel. From the time of her launch she was always listed as a Brocklebank ship. Captain Ponsonby remained in command of this ship for 11 years, but despite her name he never took her round the Cape of Good Hope to the Philippines, or the East Indies, but traded her almost exclusively for Brocklebanks to Callao and Valparaiso on the West coast of South America.

On the 28th June 1854, Capt Abraham Vaux Wise took the Brocklebank brig *Kestrel* down the Mersey once more, laden with a general cargo, and bound for Lima, by way of Cape Horn. His mate on this fateful voyage was Peter Bowman, a young man of 26 from Workington Cumberland. On the *Kestrel*'s passage from Islay, Abraham Wise contracted yellow fever, and died from this tropical malady on Wednesday 17th January 1855, being buried at sea on Friday the 19th. He left a wife and three young daughters, Mary Eleanor, Sarah Hannah, and Eliza, who, I think, lived at Cockermouth at this time. So ended the life of the one time 1st mate to Capt Daniel Brocklebank.

Whitehaven Harbour in 1856 with the brigs Bee *and* Favourite.

William Ray – Marine Superintendent – his early days at sea with Francis Wise

Of all the mariners who sailed with the Brocklebank Line, none is more famous than William Ray, who was born at Hensingham, a village to the south of Whitehaven on 31st August 1839. On the 12th October 1854, he began a career with the Brocklebank Line that was to span almost six decades, rising from apprentice to master, and then becoming the firm's first Marine Superintendent. Fortunately for us he left a brief written account of his life at sea, in which he paid particular attention to his early days afloat, as an apprentice serving under Capt Francis Wise aboard the Cape Horn brig *Rimac*. But his interesting story begins in the following manner:

'When I was fourteen years of age I was at St. Bee's School, in Cumberland. That was in 1853. At the midsummer examination one of the examiners was the Dean of Hereford, Dr Cox, and it appears that he was rather impressed with my general knowledge in the course of the examination, so much so that he interviewed the head master. The then head master of St. Bee's School was the late reverend Miles Atkinson, D.D., who, I afterwards learned, was a rector in the Earl of Harewood's parish attached to the Mansion.

Dr Cox interviewed this gentleman, and said he found there was a boy in the Commercial School called Ray, who displayed rather out-of-the-way knowledge of general subjects, but that he was somewhat deficient in mathematics. It was his wish, if the discipline of the school allowed it, that this boy should be taken out of the class so that he might study mathematics for the next twelve months. If the boy made the progress that was expected of him, he (Dr Cox) would get him into the Civil Service. So far so good. But it happened that Dr Cox did not return at the end of the twelve months, for the reason that he was dead, and at the next midsummer examination some other gentleman came in his stead.

The plan having fallen through in this way, the question now arose – What was I to do? I decided to go to sea. At that time it seemed a strange thing to the country people that a boy like myself should express a desire to go to sea – I explained to them, however, that as a boy I had been brought up on the shores of the Solway Firth, and had seen the shipbuilding and shipmanning going ahead on that West Cumberland coast – principally by the firm of Thos. and Jno. Brocklebank, who were the most prominent shipbuilders and shipowners in that neighbourhood, and built some of the finest ships that ever floated on the ocean. Not only were they the best built ships: they were the fastest ships, as I myself proved afterwards when I was master of several of them.

So I came to Liverpool, and was bound apprentice to the firm of Thos. and Jno. Brocklebank for five years. This was in 1854. At that time, the firm had ships sailing all over the world. They had ships going to Calcutta, to China, to the East and West Coasts of South America, and to many other places. Of course this was in the days when steam had hardly been thought of, and all the ships were wooden ships.

For my first voyage I was drafted as an apprentice in a little vessel called the *Rimac*, of 212 tons register, carrying a cargo of about 340 tons weight, and trading around Cape Horn. My first voyage in the *Rimac* was under the command of a master who was the most tyrannical and selfish individual you could possibly imagine, and although the instructions from the owners was that the people on board should always have a sufficiency of good food without waste, he, in his position of master of the ship, took no notice of this instruction, and seemed to take a delight in apportioning as little as possible, and the consequence was a most unhappy voyage.

68

Brocklebank brig Rimac.
(Photograph by Merseyside County Museums.)

Some years ago he went to his own place, and we will therefore say no more about him, more especially as he was succeeded by one of the finest shipmasters and the most gentlemanly and courteous man that I have come across in my career. This gentleman revolutionised the state of things on board the little craft, and it seemed to be his greatest pleasure to make everybody as comfortable as he knew how or circumstances would allow. I made three voyages around Cape Horn with this Captain. We had, of course to meet the same weather in this little ship as I had on my first voyage, in navigating that stormy corner of the world, which brought exposure to the elements, when we were often cold, wet, and miserable, and which really meant the survival of the fittest. These three voyages were nevertheless very happy voyages in spite of the rigours of the climate and the hardships we experienced, for the captain and officers did everything in their power to soften our position and make things easier for us.'

The *Rimac* returned to Liverpool on the 19th September 1855, thus completing the voyage William Ray refers to above; the vessel remained in port until the 16th November, when she set sail once again for Lima, via Cape Horn. The new master of the *Rimac*, of whom young William Ray thought so highly, was in fact Captain Francis Wise, late of the *Courier*, and newly promoted to this larger brig. Both young men were to sail together for

69

the next three years, Francis Wise, as we shall see taking good care of his lively young apprentice, William Ray from Cumberland, who continues his story about those years on the brig *Rimac* with Capt Francis Wise:

'I recall one interesting episode – during my third voyage, I believe. We were at the Chinca Islands, islands remarkable for the tremendous quantities of guano exported. The chief officer of the ship sent myself, the eldest apprentice, and another apprentice, by name George, to bring the captain who had gone ashore on business, back to the ship for dinner, the midday meal. George went up to the store at Chinca Islands, which was kept by a man named William Grace, who was some years afterwards Mayor of New York. Under his Mayorality the Tammany Ring was upset.

At that time there was a captain of the port at the Chinca Islands – a Peruvian Official – and there was a man-of-war in the harbour as a sort of guardship, and for the maintenance of order. As I was waiting for the captain, a boat belonging to the Peruvian man-of-war came alongside of our boat. In the course of a minute or two the captain of the port, and the captain of the man-of-war walked down the jetty and took up their positions in the stern of this boat. They were in full regimentals, and were evidently going on board the man-of-war for their midday lunch. When they shoved off from the jetty, the man in the bow of the boat had a boat-hook, and instead of putting this boat-hook in the jetty and shoving the boat off by this means, he had the cheek to stick his boat-hook in the bottom of our boat. I was sitting in the stern waiting for the captain, and this was too much for me. I happened to have in my hand a hard wooden tiller, made of teak, which the captain used instead of yoke lines to steer the boat. I brought this down on the boat-hook handle and smashed it.

The rest of the boat crew of the man-of-war had their oars at the perpendicular ready to drop in the water at the signal of the coxswain. One of them, seeing me break the bow oarman's handle, dropped his oar onto me instead of the water, but fortunately only hit me on the shoulder, dazing me for half a minute or so. When I recovered he was standing there grinning, as if he had performed a very notable feat. The boat was too far away for me to get at him, but I had the tiller in my hand, and I let drive with it and got him across the eyes and over he went into the water. Before I could realise what was happening the coxswain gave orders to the rest of the boat's crew – about eight of them – to manhandle me. In the boat (a very unstable platform) it was difficult to make any resistance, so the result was I was dragged on the jetty like a bag of potatoes.

Once on the jetty, where there was more space to move about, we had quite a little scrap, half a dozen of these fellows and myself, and before it was finished I dare say they learned something of the St. Bee's playing fields. Whilst the fighting was at its height, two gendarmes marched in with fixed bayonets. I had to bow to force majeur, and was marched up the jetty between these two gendarmes. Of course I didn't know what they intended to do with me – I didn't much care – but at the inner end of the jetty the ground rose considerably before we got up to the level of the top of the island, and the way up was simply a rough unpaved road.

As we were going up this road there was quite a crowd of Peruvian Ragtag and Bobtail, jeering at the English boy and telling him what was in store for him. Prominent among this jeering crowd was an oldish man, and as I gathered the purport of his remarks, I stopped suddenly between the two gendarmes and made a bolt for him. The old chap in his hurry to get away fell and rolled down to the bottom of the hill, and the ragtag and bobtail ran too, so I was clear of them. We resumed our march to the jail, and I was finally landed there. This jail was simply a structure of four walls, built on the bare ground, and had no roof, but was furnished with two lines of stocks. I was ushered into the jail and put in the stocks.

Alongside of us there was a Frenchman. He was Bo'sun of a French ship then in the harbour, and

70

had tried to desert from her. He had been caught and sent to jail. He spoke a little English, and a Frenchman is always a pleasant companion in my experience. We became very friendly, and I said 'Do they give you anything to eat in this place?' (It was then 2 o'clock in the afternoon and I was beginning to feel hungry), 'They don't give you anything to eat, and if your shipmates don't bring you anything from the ship you'll go hungry.' I remarked, 'How about sleeping on this bare ground, with our legs in the stocks? – don't they give you a pillow or anything?' The Frenchman laughed and said, 'They'll take us around the island for exercise about 4 o'clock, and you must then look out for as big a stone as possible for a pillow.'

I must tell you the chief officer came on shore that afternoon and brought us a good supply of food, and at 4 o'clock we were taken around the island for exercise. I followed my friends advice, and selected a suitable stone for a pillow. That night I felt like Jacob at Bethel, the only difference being that I did not see the angels ascending and descending as he did. But strange to say later on – about 8 o'clock – that night, a number of ladies belonging to the island turned up and were allowed to see the poor prisoners in the stocks. These ladies brought a big supply of fruit of all kinds and lemonade. I think they were really more deserving the name of angels than were those that ministered to Jacob, who confined themselves to going up and down the ladder.

Next morning a deputation interviewed the captain of the port on my behalf, and the result was that I was taken out of the stocks and released, the Captain of the port kindly explaining that it was because of the insult offered to himself and the captain of the man-of-war that I was put under arrest, not because of the injury I had done ...

My release was effected on the solicitation of a gentleman called Forbes, a Scotsman, who was building a jetty for the Government on the middle island at the time; also by William Grace, the owner of the store already mentioned, and our captain. The acquaintance I then made with Mr Grace was a lifelong acquaintanceship, and several years afterwards, when I was a chief officer of the same ship, and found myself in a very difficult position, Mr Grace was of great assistance to me. I served the usual five year apprenticeship, and finished my time in 1859....'

The Brocklebank Ships and Masters 1855

Departures of the Brocklebank Fleet recorded at Rumford Street Liverpool.

Ship	Master	(Master's place of birth)	Sailed for	Date	Number of men
Dryad	J. Chambers	Liverpool	Lima	Jan 9th	13
Patna	G. Rogers	Plymouth	Hong Kong	Jan 10th	
Thomas Brocklebank	J. Rorison	Gatehouse	Calcutta	Jan 17th	27
Horsburgh			Valparaiso	Jan 21st	15
Sir Hry Pottinger	R. Barnes	Cumberland	Lima	Feb 8th	16
Harold	J. Mann	Liverpool	Calcutta	Feb 20th	27
Aden	H. Fletcher	Whitehaven	Shanghai	Feb 25th	15
Bonanza	A. Penrice	Workington	Callao	Mar 4th	10
Westmorland	A. Halliday	Gatehouse	Pernambuco	Mar 11th	11
Petchelee	T. Overend	Lancaster	Callao	Mar 30th	17
Callao	G. Fletcher	Liverpool	Callao	Apr 4th	11
Lord Althorp	W. Ronald		Lima	Apr 22nd	13
Aracan	A. Adamson	Edinburgh	Shanghai	May 4th	35
Princess Royal	M. Mawson	Whitehaven	Calcutta	May 9th	27
Kestrel	P. Bowman	Workington	Callao	June 2nd	13
Tigris	George Wise	Whitehaven	Calcutta	June 5th	23
Crisis	J. Bell	Whitehaven	Hong Kong	June 6th	20
Patriot King	Osborne	Liverpool	Lima	June 22nd	17
Patriot Queen	J. Bell	Liverpool	Calcutta	June 28th	25
Camana	P. Smith	Liverpool	Callao	Aug 30th	11
Florence Nightingale	C. Mossop	Whitehaven	Calcutta	Aug 17th	40

Ship	Master	(Master's place of birth)	Sailed for	Date	Number of men
Jumna	J. Sharp	Scotland	Bombay	Sept 5th	18
Earl Grey	E. Curwen	Beckermont	Valparaiso	Sept 14th	
Comorin	S. Roddock	Scotland	Calcutta	Oct 8th	35
Courier	J. Candlish	Kirkudbright	Callao	Oct 17th	9
Westmorland	W. Pole	Scotland	Pernambuco	Oct 19th	13
Martaban	M. King	Whitehaven	Calcutta	Oct 30th	35
Arachne	M. Mawson	Whitehaven	Calcutta	Nov 16th	27
Rimac	Francis Wise	Whitehaven	Lima	Nov 16th	12
Patna	G. Rogers	Plymouth	Hong Kong	Dec 8th	17
Robert Pulsford	Tho. Smith	Sanwith	Calcutta	Dec 11th	
Thomas Brocklebank	J. Rorison	Gatehouse	Calcutta	Dec	27

CHAPTER 9

Life at Sea and Ashore for 19th Century Mariners

It might be appropriate, at this point in our story, to examine in greater detail the manner in which 19th century masters, mates, seamen, and apprentices lived. The ships that they manned were themselves things of great beauty, admired by all, but in stark contrast, the seaman's life was one of danger and great hardship – even whilst serving under a kindly Brocklebank master such as Francis Wise! Ashore these men were at the mercy of the 'Crimps' – a sort of international dockside mafia, that exploited men, masters, and even ship owners – without the slightest hint of class discrimination; the ordinary seaman however was their prime target.

Let us imagine we are back in Liverpool on a cold December evening in 1855. The Brocklebank ship *Aracan* has just berthed in the Prince's Dock, and young Jack Tar has been paid off; he makes his way out on to the Dock Road, where all is a scene of frantic activity. Cart horses struggle to pull their huge loads to the great warehouses, whilst hansom cabs dash past them, carrying the wealthy city merchants, shipowners, and masters, to their comfortable homes in the better parts of the city – but Jack is alone on the wet cobbled streets of this vast city, he has no home to go to; his only consolation being the ten months pay he carries in his wallet. Where should he spend the night? How should he spend his hard earned pay?

Like a vulture homing in on an injured beast, the Liverpool 'Crimp' spots his prey. Soon 'Jack' is not alone any more for the crimp has found his latest victim. First he takes the poor unsuspecting lad to his lodgings, and then takes him on a guided tour of the Liverpool gambling houses, brothels, shops, and ale houses. Eventually the young seaman is presented with an enormous bill – inflated by the crimp's 'commission' on all services rendered. Unable to pay, the only hope he has of meeting this is to sign on again for another ten month voyage – perhaps only hours after completing his last voyage – just in order to meet the bill.

Being enterprising men, the crimps did not rely solely on the above source of income; having exploited the seamen they now turned their attention to the masters and owners who required a crew. By brute force, threats and murder the crimps placed themselves between the seamen wanting a berth on a ship, and an owner or master wanting a crew for his vessel. Both sides of the shipping industry being obliged to pay the crimps a handsome 'commission' before the former còuld obtain a ship, and the latter a crew. As might be expected though, even here the poor seaman suffered most. An unscrupulous, unpopular master might find it difficult to obtain a crew for his ship, and under these circumstances he would often approach the crimps with a view to obtaining one by force. In this manner men were often 'shanghaied' – that is drugged, or knocked unconscious in some low dive by the crimps and ferried out in this state to the waiting ship. In this manner many a poor man, often not even a seaman in the first place, woke up in the forecastle of some unknown ship making its way down the Mersey. Clearly this state of affairs could not be allowed to continue.

In many ports, including Liverpool, that were plagued by these 'land sharks', efforts were made to establish reputable Sailors' Homes, which would provide reasonable accommodation for the sailors, and a venue free from the attention of crimps, where crews could be signed without the payment of commission. A crimp's 'commission' for finding a sailor a new berth was £1 – a huge sum in those days; by contrast a Sailors' Home would make the same arrangements for one-and-sixpence. I am pleased to note in this respect that the crew lists of my ancestors would indicate that they almost always signed their crews at the Sailors' Home in Liverpool. This was in fact common practice for all Brocklebank masters – for Ralph Brocklebank had helped to establish this particular home. At this home a proper scale of wages and fees was established, and the crimps found their evil occupation gone. This is not to suggest that the wage paid to any seamen of the time was particularly adequate – it was not; but the establishment of a recognised scale was at least a step in the right direction.

Most 19th century sailing ships, certainly those belonging to Jeffersons or the Brockle-bank Line, carried several young men known as apprentices, whose aim and ambition was to become officers. With Brocklebanks and Jeffersons, as we have seen, the term of apprenticeship usually lasted four–five years. In the main these boys came from middle-class families; often they were the sons of other mariners.

If the aspiring officer came from a non-seafaring family he was entering a life that was far more rigorous than either son or parents could possibly imagine. With mariners such as the Vaux Wise brothers, or James Glover, they would harbour no such illusions. If an apprentice on say a larger Brocklebank Indiaman or clipper did become an officer he immediately obtained a much higher standard in his working and living conditions; for there was a stark contrast between living conditions of the crew crammed in the forecastle, and the quarters of the 'afterguard' under the poop deck.

Traditionally the master's accommodation was at the stern, where in earlier vessels, such as Jeffersons' *Lady Shaw Stewart*, large windows looked out over the wake. However, the gradual development in hull design saw this square stern replaced by the round and elliptical varieties, which dictated a different pattern of accommodation. In the larger sailing vessels, there was a roomy saloon, off which the master had his sleeping cabin and often a day cabin and office as well. The off-duty mates would eat with the master in the saloon, which was often as well furnished as a home ashore – complete with marble-topped sideboard, piano, and even potted plants.

74

But while this was the case on the larger vessels, life for men like my great-great-grandfathers, John Glover and Abraham Vaux Wise, on small brigs such as *Swallow* and *Massereene*, would be little better than for the men who served under them. The 'cabins' of the captain and mate of a coasting brig or schooner were basically cupboard berths tucked into the angles of the stern, while master, mate and crew all ate together in a tiny saloon, access to which was obtained by a steep ladder – a far cry from the elaborate companionways of the later Brocklebank ships.

The hardest and most dangerous job on any sailing ship was that of 'going aloft' but the oldest seaman, and the youngest apprentice all had to undertake this arduous task. There was no escape. In emergency situations even the services of the cook, the steward, and the carpenter could be called upon in order to get the sails furled. The lower yards of a merchantman projected well over the ship's sides, on a large vessel this could mean working at a height of 60 ft above the sea or decks; the t'gallant yard could be up to 140 ft above the deck. Let us imagine for one moment that we are with Abraham Wise on the poop of the *Kestrel*, fighting her way round Cape Horn in the depth of winter. Abraham's mate, young Peter Bowman, would be standing near him on the poop deck, perhaps near the weather rigging. Only the poop and fo'c'sle of the *Kestrel* would be showing above the furious white cauldron of water. To all intents and purposes she would be submerged beneath the massive seas that continually swept over her.

Perhaps the full fury of this 'Cape-Horner' has caught even the experienced Mariner Abraham by surprise – sails still have to be taken in, a few words to his mate, and the voice of Peter Bowman would roar out, and be carried away on the wind. 'Now up and stow them lads.' Fearfully the crew would then scramble aloft on the ratlines between the shrouds – until they were level with the right yard. They would then have to make their way out along the yard, sliding down the foot-ropes towards the lee yardarm, which, with 'Cape-Horn' seas could be almost dipping into the hissing water below.

Now the seamen of the *Kestrel* would be faced with the seemingly impossible task of obeying Peter Bowman's command to stow the sails. The much quoted saying, 'one hand for the ship and one for yourself' never really worked, for there were few jobs that could be done one-handed, particularly stowing sails. The men would now have to lay on their stomachs across the yard, drenched to the skin, and half blinded by wind, sleet and spray; the constant danger of being hurled into the icy black water below them for ever in their minds.

In these freezing southern latitudes off the Horn the men would find the sails of the *Kestrel* as hard as iron. Abraham's men would now begin clawing at the folds of the huge area of canvas, attempting to bring it close enough to the yard for gaskets to be passed around it. Nails could be torn from frostbitten fingers as the men struggled to subdue just one of the brig's sails. If after all of this they were fortunate enough to reach the deck of the *Kestrel* in one piece it is doubtful if they would get so much as a hot drink to revive them – for under such conditions it is more than likely that the cook, and all his utensils, would be afloat in the galley.

As we have seen with Joseph's crew on the *Lady Shaw Stewart*, men did inevitably fall from the yards, and it has to be said, these falls were usually fatal. If they fell onto the hard deck broken legs or ribs could be mended, but with more complicated injuries the men stood almost no chance of survival. Life aloft was extremely dangerous, but life on deck was far from safe. A following sea could sweep the helmsman – and the Skipper – away, and huge seas often swept over the ships, particularly small ones like the *Kestrel*. Men could be plucked from their positions by these seas as if they were a piece of flotsam, and hurled against a pin rail or capstan – their ribs being smashed like matchwood.

In the small and isolated world of a Jefferson or Brocklebank brigantine the master's word was law; he was chief navigator, business manager, judge, paymaster, Doctor and Surgeon. When sickness struck, or accidents occurred he was the only available medical authority for hundreds of miles. Captains were supposed to be able to diagnose and treat all manner of diseases and be able to set (or amputate) broken limbs, caused in the main by falls from the rigging. Amputations were however usually a 'joint operation', captain and carpenter working together on the unfortunate victim.

Seaman's Medical Guide, 1863 – the treatment for the bite of a dog is an obvious omission put right here.

76

By the 1860s it was very properly felt that ships' masters might perform the medical aspects of their duties better if given some rudimentary guidance. As a consequence of these humanitarian considerations several guides were produced, one of these being the 'Seaman's Medical Guide', another being the 'Ship's Captain's Medical Guide' – These Guides were specifically designed for ship-board conditions, all symptoms being graphically described, with the appropriate treatment being listed alongside:

'RESTORING SUSPENDED ANIMATION, Lose no time; but do things quietly and orderly. Avoid all rough usage, crowding and hurrying. Never hold up the body by the feet; nor shake nor roll it, nor rub with salt or spirits. Do not inject tobacco-smoke, or infusion of tobacco, nor attempt to take away blood.' (The Seaman's Medical Guide)

'APPARENT DEATH FROM STRANGLING OR HANGING. From the return of the venous blood being stopped by the action of the rope, &c., round the neck, the face is rendered black, the eyeballs start from their sockets, and the nostrils are wider than in natural death. After the rope, &c., has been removed, the taking of blood from the arm, or even the jugular vein, is advisable, as well as all the other means directed under DROWN-ING, except artificially warming the body, which will in most cases be unnecessary. The bellows will be the most important agent.' (The Seaman's Medical Guide)

'The Ship's Captain's Medical Guide' has an interesting section dealing with the replacement of a dislocated shoulder joint. The master is given clear and detailed instructions on how to apply his heel to the patient's armpit; I am however pleased to note here that the Captain *was* advised to take off his boot before starting! Ships usually carried a medicine chest which contained patent medicines, mercury, quinine, laudanum, and 'purging pills', also various numbered mixtures. The old story goes that if a master found himself in an 'out of stock' situation with say a number ten mixture, recommended for a particular malady, he would make good the deficiency by using say a 'four' and a 'six', but I must confess that I have my doubts about the truth of this particular yarn.

The same guide had some very interesting thoughts on the treatment of V.D. Sufferers who showed suspect symptoms after connection with a 'foul woman' were advised to soak the afflicted parts in near boiling water, or sit on cold metal! I think this particular 'cure' may well have deterred the patient from further sexual adventures with 'foul women', but did it rid the patient of his complaint? I rather doubt it. The 'Seaman's Medical Guide' placed a great deal of faith in the curative powers of barley water, gruel, and cream of tartar – even as a remedy for serious gunshot wounds?

> 'Gunshot wounds fortunately seldom occur in merchant-ships. They are difficult to manage, and liable to mortify. Should a ball have passed into the belly or chest, there is little hope of recovery: the sufferer will often bleed to death (internally) in a few hours. The most perfect quiet is desirable; keep the head low, and supply cooling drinks, such as Barley-water and Gruel, with the addition of Lemon-juice, or Cream-of-Tartar....!'

So much for the medical aspects of shipboard life in the 19th century, but closely related to this was the question of food.

Before the days of refrigeration all provisions taken aboard a merchant ship for a long voyage had to be preserved in some way, for this reason salt pork and beef featured very greatly in mariners' diets. The beef usually tended to go as hard as leather, whilst the salt pork often turned almost black, streaked with lines of bright green! Horse meat was often sold to ship's masters or owners as pork or beef, but given the usual state of the end product hardly anyone noticed – or cared. In theory good meat, if properly salted and packed should keep in excellent condition for years. In practice the casks were often damaged whilst being loaded, and the heat of the tropics, working on the contents of such a cask would complete the damage to the contents. When the cook eventually opened such a cask it would give off a stomach-turning stench, nevertheless it was rarely 'wasted', just cooked for a little longer.

Ship's biscuits were made from lumps of baked dough, the dough was beaten flat, put into moulds, and baked as many as three times; needless to say they became as hard as iron, and had to be soaked in water before they could be eaten. If salt water should spoil the biscuits they were simply re-baked in the galley stove, which made them even harder. It is small wonder that these biscuits proved more attractive to the ship's weavils than the ship's crew, the former often being found by the latter in great numbers inside the biscuits.

Not all ship's masters or owners kept their crews hungry; the more responsible ones added dried fruit, marmalade, raisins etc. to their men's diet, and as we have seen from the log of the Jefferson brig *Thetis*, whilst laying at Montego Bay, large quantities of fresh meat were often bought for the crews whilst the vessels were in port. I suspect conditions varied greatly regarding mariners' food, being very much affected by the different attitudes of Captains and owners.

The galley on most ships was extremely small, but it was in these cramped quarters that the ship's cook was expected to produce palatable meals from the dubious material provided. The cook was plainly a man of some importance, for the men he served had little to live for whilst at sea other than eating or sleeping. As on shore there were good cooks and bad cooks, but all too often this worthy well deserved the opprobrious title of 'Old Slush' given to him by the long-suffering captain and crew; on many occasions after the ship had left port it was discovered that he had few, if any, credentials for his job. It was often remarked that the failings of this particular character caused more discontent at sea than did all the Bully Forbes, Capt Blighs, and man-driving officers put together.

With the exceptions of the cook, carpenter, bosun, and sail maker, if carried, all crew members were allotted to a watch. It was the mate's responsibility to arrange these watches, and this he did by mustering all hands on deck soon after sailing. The crew obtained such items as tobacco, soap, clothing etc. from the captain's 'slop chest', the management of which was one of the master's privileges. The captain being in a position to set his own price, this provided him with a useful secondary source of income. Given several fines, and a few purchases from the master's slop chest, a seaman could often end up with next to no cash, after a long and arduous voyage.

On joining his ship a seaman would first report to the mate, whose responsibility it was to see that he was allotted a berth in the Forecastle, which was originally in the bow of the ship, and below decks. These cramped and unhealthy quarters had little ventilation and light, and were often flooded during bad weather. Water leaking from above was a constant problem, and more experienced seamen would often make brave attempts to overcome the problem by rigging oilskins over themselves.

Superstition was rife amongst 19th century mariners. When the ships were approaching the Cape of Good Hope – known as the 'Cape of Storms' – the 'Old Salts' would take the young seamen on one side and fill their heads with stories about sea monsters, and phantom ships, favourite amongst the latter type of yarn being the legend of Capt Vanderdecken, the Flying Dutchman – the ghostly mariner condemned by the Almighty to sail off the Cape for ever – with only one man as crew. It is said that his ghostly ship will pursue other vessels, and, on overtaking them, Vanderdecken can be seen on the poop deck – holding out a letter – roaring out across the wild seas that he would like it posted. But no sane mariner would be lured into this trap – for to approach the ghost ship, and take his dreaded letter would spell disaster for those concerned. One can well imagine the effect that this yarn would have on the impressionable mind of a young 19th century mariner – particularly if it was well told!

Discipline, and other aspects of life at sea were governed by the Merchant Shipping Acts. These acts made it obligatory for Crew lists and agreements to be drawn up and signed by each member of the crew before sailing. Crew lists varied in shape and size, but they were usually very large sheets, upon which were printed general details and conditions of service, and in many cases the disciplinary code; a space always being left here so that a master could add, at his own discretion, a further clause, or clauses. I have noticed in this respect that many of my ancestors thought it prudent to add a clause here specifically directed against the use of knives and drink: – 'No grog or sheath knives allowed!'

A space was always left on the crew list so that the master could insert the actual details of the voyage, but these did tend to be rather vague, or exceptionally inclusive; typically they would give a master voyaging to the Far East the freedom to call at any port in India, China, and the South Pacific before returning to any port (or ports) in the United Kingdom (or Europe) – the duration of the voyage was however usually limited to two years. On this last point though, masters were often inclined to obtain from their crews a further signature, greatly extending the terms and conditions of the original agreement. In theory this was always done by 'mutual consent', but one is left wondering how a dissenting minority that refused to sign, whilst 10,000 miles from home, would have fared. Offences were punishable on a scale numbered one to twenty-two, the following being some of the more noteworthy:

Offence	Fine
Bringing, or having on board spirituous liquors	3 days pay
Carrying a sheath knife	1 days pay
Smoking below	1 days pay
(For the Cook) – Not having any meal of the crew ready at the appointed time	1 days pay
Interrupting Divine Service by indecorous behaviour	1 days pay
Not being cleaned, shaved, and washed on a Sunday	1 days pay
Washing clothes on a Sunday	1 days pay
Secreting contraband goods on board with intent to smuggle	1 months pay

79

Drunkenness was covered by rule 9 which cut the allowance of provisions, i.e. for the first offence 'Two days half allowances of provisions'.

Although things may well have been more informal on the smaller brigs, life aboard all ships was a great place for etiquette and ceremony. The poop was considered sacred ground, seamen not being allowed to go there without orders. The men lived in the fo'c'sle, and the officers lived aft – hence the expression 'afterguard'. In the fo'c'sle a strict code of etiquette existed, it being considered a great insult to his fellow ship-mates if a man should lock his sea-chest. The captain always addressed the mate as 'Mr' which officer always took command of operations in the fore part of the ship – the anchor, the head-sails, the towing hawser etc. The captain and his junior officers' place was aft. If an officer had learned the art of navigation as an apprentice he was said to have come aboard 'through the cabin window', if he had worked his way up through the ranks he was said to have come aboard 'through the hawse-hole'; the hawse-hole being in the bows.

Under normal circumstances the captain was as aloof on the ship as any King among his subjects. Custom and practice demanded that he did not converse with anyone but the mate, orders being conveyed to the crew via this officer. This life of grand and gloomy isolation, imposed on the masters by years of tradition, caused some captains to develop silent and eccentric personalities, some turned to drink because of the loneliness of their lives, but the majority learned to live with this particular occupational hazard, remaining in full command of themselves, and their ships.

Notwithstanding the aforementioned occupational hazard, the Brocklebank sailing masters were acknowledged to be amongst the finest in the world. Whether bringing their great ships through the straights of Sunda, rounding the Cape of Storms, or approaching port, their navigational and maritime skills could not be bettered. At Liverpool, when conditions were favourable, commanders such as William Hoodless, Rorison, Caleb Brown, George Wise, or Clement Mossop, would take much pleasure in demonstrating their skill to those ashore. They would see to it that their great Indiamen were brought into the Princes Dock whilst still under sail, and without the assistance of a tug! The huge sails would then be taken in with split second timing by the crews already stationed on the yards – perhaps a 100 feet or more above the decks.

We can well imagine the excitement at this point in time, the end of a 32,000 mile voyage. Friends and relatives of the crew would be thronging the dock side eager to catch a glance of the loved one they had not seen for almost a year. The mooring ropes would be thrown to the men on the quayside, the gangway lowered and those aboard would hasten ashore, home at last. No doubt if the vessel carried a particularly valuable cargo, Thomas Brocklebank himself would be there, anxious to go aboard to confer with his commander; his tall figure, great shock of white hair, and top hat set at its characteristic jaunty angle, making him immediately recognisable amongst the crowd.

The scene when these great ships left port was, if anything, even more impressive; crowds would usually gather to witness the event, for the crew would climb into the rigging, raise their caps and give three hearty cheers as the vessel moved silently away. Then, as the crew prepared to set all plain sail, a sailor's voice would roar out 'Hurrah for Reuben Rantzau'; the men would then roar back – 'Rantzau ... boys ... Rantzau', then the chantying would begin in earnest:

Solo 'Rantzau was.....no...sailor,'
Chorus 'Rantzau......boys...Rantzau'
Solo 'Rantzau......was a....Tailor'
Chorus 'Rantzau......boys....Rantzau'
Solo 'Rantzau....joined the beauty.....and did not do his duty....'
Chorus 'Rantzau.....boys.....Rantzau..........

It must indeed have been a stirring scene to witness, the chantying, the last shouted farewells, the tears and the cheers, as the sails were set, and the clipper ship moved out into the Mersey – bound for the Cape – the Indian Ocean – or on to the Straights of Sunda, the South China Seas and the distant port of Foo Chow Foo on the Min River.

Many of the finest sea-chanties ever written were based on, or at least adapted to relate to Liverpool – the town itself, or the many famous shipping lines that once sailed from the port. And how they captured the spirit of old Liverpool town – and the great days of sail. Sea-chanties were to sailors, what marching songs once were to soldiers, they gave zest, swing, and energy to men, as they hauled on a halliard, or tramped around a capstan. There were various kinds of chanty, each adapted for a particular task. There was the capstan chanty, the chanty sung when hauling on the halliards, and the chanty used when working the tacks and sheets which set the sails. The rhythm of each was exactly suited to the work it was chanted to, to the tramping of feet around a capstan, or the united heaving on a line. One of those adapted to suit the port of Liverpool went as follows:

BLOW THE MAN DOWN

Solo O blow the man down, bullies, blow the man down.

Chorus Way-ay, blow the man down,
O . . . blow the man down in Liverpool town. . . .
Give a man time to blow to blow the man down.

Solo As I was a walking down Paradise Street,
A saucy young bobby I happened to meet . . .

Chorus

Solo Says he . . . you're a Black Baller, by the cut of your hair,
I know you're a Black Baller by the clothes that you wear.

Chorus

Solo You've sailed in a packet that flies the Black Ball,
You've robbed some poor Dutchman . . . of boots clothes and all.

Chorus

Solo O Bobby, O Bobby, you do me great wrong,
I'm a Brocklebank sailor man, just home from Hong Kong.

Chorus

CHAPTER 10

At Brocklebanks and Jeffersons 1856–61

In the main the Indiamen of the Brocklebank fleet were built for reliability, and strength, rather than just speed. They were never intended to compete with the best clippers, built specifically for the China tea trade, which required, above all else, fast vessels; the best tea clippers could on occasion make the passage home from China to the U.K. in under 100 days. Nevertheless, the Brocklebank vessels, under good commanders, could also make exceptional passages; the *Crisis* and the *Aden* are on record as having returned from Hong Kong to Liverpool in 95 and 97 days respectively.

There can be no doubt at all however, that the Brocklebank clipper *Aracan* was the finest and fastest ship ever built by the firm at Whitehaven; only perhaps the *Everest*, built later in 1863, and used on the China run, could be considered in the same class. As already mentioned, *Aracan* is reported on one occasion to have raced and beaten the *Fiery Cross*, perhaps one of the finest tea clippers ever built. On the 20th April 1856 George Wise, leaving the *Tigris*, assumed command of the *Aracan*, sailing for Calcutta on that date. On this passage she broke all records for a Brocklebank Indiaman, arriving at Calcutta only 86 days later, and on her passage home she made the run in 91 days, arriving at Liverpool on 5th December 1856.

Early in 1857 George Wise married, and set up home at 79 Duke Street Whitehaven, near the address of his brother Joseph, who at that time lived at 10 George Street. The *Aracan* was due to sail again on the 27th of January, so we must assume that shortly after his marriage, he left his young wife, Hannah, and returned to Liverpool. Sadly Hannah Wise was never to see her husband again – for the next voyage of the *Aracan* was to be a tragic one. On the 27th January 1857 the *Aracan* duly set sail for Calcutta, carrying a large crew of 35 men all told. As on the last voyage, his first mate was Mr Charles Howe, from Halifax Nova Scotia, about which officer, the firm made the following comments regarding the voyage of 1856: 'Last two voyages mate the *Aracan*, a very steady attentive man, might do well as the master of a ship.' In 1857, at the start of the above voyage, he was praised again, for against his name in the same 'Officers and apprentices Book' are written these words: '4th voyage mate the *Aracan*, conduct good – Capt Wise reports would make a better master than mate.'

Brocklebank ship Tigris.
(Photograph from Merseyside County Museums.)

One hundred and three days later the *Aracan* arrived safely at Calcutta, and after discharging and re-loading she set sail once more for Liverpool in June. Wednesday the 1st July found the *Aracan* in lat. 13.55 N, 89.18 E and crossing the Bay of Bengal in a heavy gale when James Frost, seaman, fell to his death, the account of the incident, taken from the official log book of the *Aracan* reads as follows:

'James Frost, seaman, when in the act of bending the jib was either washed or fell accidently overboard. Hove the life buoy overboard and put ship round and used every exertion to save him, but without effect, it blowing a heavy sea at the time, with sea running fearfully high, so that no boat would live without endangering other lives; ship under double reefed topsail at the time, consequently the man met a watery grave.'

Following the normal custom and practice at sea, the mate, Mr Charles Howe, then gathered the unfortunate man's effects together, and offered them for sale to the crew, but could get no purchasers; and so ended the life of one poor unfortunate 19th century mariner – more tragedy was, however, to follow on this voyage.

83

At 4.30 a.m. on the 8th September 1857 the *Aracan* was almost at the end of her voyage home, for she was off the coast of Anglesey, the South Stack Light bearing E.N.E. 12 miles distance, at which time and place Capt George Wise, master of the vessel, was drowned, for he also went over the side of the ship. . . . . . . which was going at the rate of six knots at the time and on an ebb tide. The ship was immediately brought to the wind and boat put out with 2nd and third mates and three hands in her, after the boat left the side the ship was put on the port tack, after the lapse of one hour the boat returned having seen no appearance of him, the boat was then taken in and ship put on proper course.'

Following the death of her commander in September 1857, the *Aracan* was brought safely back to Liverpool by the mate, of whom George Wise thought so highly, Mr Charles Howe of Halifax. Command of the ship was then given to Capt T. Selkirk from Gatehouse, late master of the *Princess Royal*. The *Aracan* sailed for Calcutta on 6th November under the command of her new master, whilst Mr Howe became Captain Howe, master of Capt Selkirk's old ship the *Princess Royal*, which set sail for the same port some three weeks later on the 1st December.

William Ellery goes to sea

On the 17th December 1856, the 25-year-old Brocklebank barque *Hindoo* left the Mersey, bound for Pernambuco. On board was a 17-year-old apprentice by the name of William Ellery, who was destined to become one of the Line's most noted commanders. Like his fellow apprentice, William Ray, still at this point aboard the *Rimac* with Francis Wise, Ellery was also to leave a written account of his life, from which I quote. Unlike William Ray, he did not serve with one of the Wise brothers, but served in two ships once commanded by George Wise, the *Tigris* and the *Patriot King*, and the *Arachne*, later to be commanded by Francis Wise; and about his life aboard these ships he has much to tell. About his background, and early days, he writes as follows:

'I come of an old Cornish family. My immediate ancestors were farmers in the village of St. Columb Minor, not far from Penzance. The great Napoleon is reported to have said that if you scratch a Russian you find the Tartar. I know not if this is true or not, but I do know that Cornishmen easily take to the sea; and in my own case, when things went irretrievably wrong with the farm and the year 1848 found the family transplanted to Liverpool, my thoughts as a very little boy often turned seaward, no doubt influenced by the shipping of the port, and the beautiful sight so often presented of vessels entering and leaving in full sail, those being the days when steam was only just coming in.

Something was also due to heredity, that mysterious chain which so powerfully links us to the past. In the days of Queen Elizabeth certain of my forebears were seafaring men, and during the same century another branch settled in America. When therefore, the time came that I must choose a profession, that of the sea took possession of me, and in due course I was apprenticed, at the age of seventeen, for four years with the reputable firm of Messrs T and J Brocklebank, which I believe to be the oldest shipping firm in the world. . . . It was in the year 1856 that I began to serve my four years apprenticeship in the barque *Hindoo*, 256 tons register, bound to Pernambuco, Brazil; and I finished my term at the end of this voyage in the barque *Lanercost*, which traded between Liverpool and the West Coast of South America. There were three other apprentices on each vessel, the crew all told numbered sixteen, a very fair arrangement,

84

providing ample labour for working, yet there was plenty to do for all hands, and we beginners were taught our duties as sailors thoroughly well.

When going around Cape Horn in the winter time my fingers have been often so frost-bitten that they were black and blue, and the circulation had to be restored by rubbing them energetically with snow. There was plenty of rough weather, our little vessels were knocked severely about, the decks were often awash with green seas, rigging and decks were covered with snow and ice, yet everyone was expected to be alert and in his place when wanted. The work was undoubtedly hard, very hard, but it made sailors of us. I shall never forget one experience in the *Lanercost*. It was in July 1858, the depth of winter in those latitudes. We were bound to Callao with a general cargo, and on nearing the Horn encountered very severe weather, with snow and ice, the thermometer showing 14 degrees of frost. The jibboom was carried away, and brought down the fore topmast.

I was sent aloft to help clear away the wreck, and before obeying the order I took off my oilskin coat and trousers. When I came down from aloft I was almost literally frozen stiff, but crawled to the lee side of the spars to recover my oilskins. To my intense chagrin they were not there. Afterwards they were found in shreds in the pighouse, the animals having drawn them through the iron bars, and gnawed them to pieces. My circulation was restored by persistent rubbing with snow, and after a hard night's work I went on the half-deck, got some old canvas and made a jumper, painted it to make it waterproof, the paint freezing as applied, and I again faced the weather. However trying the work, it was always cheerfully done.

The vessels were always extremely well found, but the food was better imagined than described, except by the old salts saying that we "lived on the smell of an oilrag." Hard biscuits – and it was fearfully hard in those days – and a weak decoction of cocoa nibs, served for breakfast. One-and-a-half pounds of beef – mahogany-coloured and almost as hard – and one-and-a-quarter pounds of fat pork were served on alternate days, with a pint of pea soup one day and the next "duff," each man being allowed half-a-pound of flour with which to make this delicacy, which was baked flat and stiff, and eaten with molasses. A curious mixture called "dog's body" was made as follows: Half of your pea soup, broken up biscuit, a dab of molasses, and a piece of fat pork saved from dinner. These ingredients were put in the oven by the grace of the cook (alias the doctor). While it was in the oven Jack was always thinking of the savoury treat in store for the meal called tea, with his biscuit and liquid.

We were strangers to milk and butter, but the tea was sweetened with sugar. For supper we had to depend on savings from the earlier meals. On Saturday our dinners consisted of boiled rice, which the sailors dignified by the name of "strike-me-blind." On Sundays the fare was sometimes varied by what the cook called "currant duff," but the difficulty of the eaters was to find the currants. Three quarts of water were served out daily to each of us to answer all purposes, drinking, cooking, and washing, that is until the supply was exhausted. Our ablutions were generally performed with salt water, and salt water soap – a thing hardly ever heard of now-a-days. The result was never satisfactory, the salt causing boils, the salt water not cleaning the skin, and it was a genuine pleasure when rain fell so abundantly as to enable us to collect it from the decks and wash in it.

Lime juice was served out once a week in a bottle previous to 1864, after which date, owing to the prevalence of scurvy, lime juice had to be served out daily. I have seen men's teeth drop out and their legs badly swollen from scurvy. No vegetables were carried in those days. I knew an old sailor who suffered from the disease, and whose remedy on landing in Liverpool was to go to Parliament fields (then unbuilt upon), dig a big hole in the earth, and remain there for a few hours with a bottle of rum and his pipe. He persisted in declaring that the treatment did him a lot of good!

As I have said the work was hard and plenty of it, but the men did not shirk their share, though there were rare cases of malingering. Sundays brought no relief to the daily routine, as the Sailors Catechism testifies: "Six days shalt thou labour and do all thou art able, and the seventh day holy-stone the deck and scrape the cable." There was no religious services on board, and if any boy or man kept alive a sense of his spiritual duties he had to do it in private. At the port of debarcation the discharge and loading of the cargo on the West Coast was done by the ship's company.

On arrival in the Mersey, after the ten or eleven months voyage to Callao and back, crimps regularly boarded the vessel, and as poor Jack was then flush of money, and really no wiser than "a bearded infant", he was fleeced right and left by boarding-house keepers, pierhead jumpers, and their various allies. I have known cases in which sailors were cleared out in less than a week, and had to take a ship again. Such abuses led to much stricter regulations connected with the advance note, and a very great improvement in the life of Jack ashore.'

Outward bound with the sailing fleet of Thomas & Jno. Brocklebank – 1857

Date	Ship	Commander	Destination	Crew
January 4th	*Princess Royal*	T. Selkirk	Calcutta	26
January 27th	*Aracan*	George Wise	Calcutta	35
February 23rd	*Harold*	J. Rorison	Calcutta	27
February 27th	*Callao*	W. Pole	Lima	11
March 22nd	*Dryad*	J. Chambers	Valparaiso	13
March 24th	*Tigris*	G. Fletcher	Calcutta	21
April 10th	*Aden*	J. Howson	Hong Kong	16
April 14th	*Lanercost*	T. Tully	Callao	15
May 1st	*Hindoo*	W. Kelly	Pernambuco	15
May 5th	*Earl Grey*	W. Bell	Bahia	13
May 12th	*Flo. Nightingale*	C. Mossop	Calcutta	40
May 15th	*Sir Hry. Pottinger*	R. Barnes	Valparaiso	16
May 21st	*Kestrel*	P. Bowman	Callao	13
June 13th	*Comorin*	S. Roddock	Calcutta	35
June 20th	*Lord Althorp*	W. Ronald	Pernambuco	14
June 27th	*Petchelee*	P. Smith	Callao	17
July 9th	*Crisis*	J. Black	Hong Kong	19
July 23rd	*Robert Pulsford*	T. Smith	Calcutta	26
July 18th	*Patriot King*	W. Lowden	Valparaiso	17
August 8th	*Camana*	J. Jordain	Callao	11
August 29th	*Herculean*	J. Bell	Hong Kong	26
September 6th	*Arachne*	J. Sharp	Calcutta	27
September 20th	*Valparaiso*	E. Curwen	Lima	15
October 3rd	*Hindoo*	M. King	Pernambuco	15
October 4th	*Martaban*	J. Joughlin	Calcutta	34
November 6th	*Aracan*	T. Selkirk	Calcutta	35
November 18th	*Thos. Brocklebank*	W. Kelly	Calcutta	27
November 18th	*Rimac*	F. Wise	Callao	14
November 20th	*Lord Althorp*	W. Ronald	Valparaiso	13
December 1st	*Princess Royal*	C. D. Howe	Calcutta	25
December 11th	*Globe*	A. Penrice	Callao	13
December 12th	*Earl Grey*	W. Bell	Bahia	13

The building of the clipper-barque 'Antigua'

On Tuesday the 1st June 1858 Messrs Robert & Henry Jefferson attempted to sell the brig *British Queen*, which was at the time still under the command of Capt Joseph Wise, the following advertisement being placed in the columns of the 'Cumberland Pacquet':

ON SALE

The brig *British Queen*, 218 tons, o.m. AE 1 in red, now discharging her cargo from Antigua, at Liverpool. This vessel was built at Whitehaven by Messrs L. Kennedy and Co., in 1838, classed A1 for 12 years, with the addition of being copper-fastened instead of treenailed from the first futtock heads to the gunwales. Is abundantly found in stores, and could be sent to sea at trifling expense. Apply in Liverpool to Messrs Jefferson and Taylor, Apsley Buildings; or in White-haven to:

ROBERT & HENRY JEFFERSON

28th May 1858

It would seem however that no suitable offer was received for the *Queen*, for she remained in the service of the Jefferson Company, Capt Joseph Ledger taking over command of the brig later in the year. The *British Queen* was eventually lost off Newfound-land on the 6th May 1861, whilst under the command of Capt William Hinde. Seven days after attempting to sell the *British Queen*, Messrs Jeffersons registered their new vessel, the Whitby-built clipper barque *Antigua* at Whitehaven.

Despite the excellence of Cumberland built ships it should not surprise us that Robert & Henry Jefferson should have obtained this vessel from a Whitby yard, for the port of Whitby was also responsible for producing some of the most soundly built ships ever launched. Shipbuilding had been carried on at Whitby since time immemorial, the skill of the town's shipbuilders being acknowledged, and responsible for bringing much business to the town. The strength and durability of Whitby built ships may be inferred from the great age some of them attained, the *Sea Adventure* built in 1724 being a noted instance. This vessel braved the storms for some 86 years, and was only lost on the Lincolnshire coast in 1810, when she was carried up by a violent storm and deposited high and dry in a farmer's field some distance from the sea. The *Happy Return*, a small Whitby coaster wrecked in the early 1800s, was reputed to be over 100 years old when she finally met her end.

As was the case with Whitehaven on the West coast, many of the port's smaller vessels were employed in the coasting and coal trade; whilst at Whitehaven much of this trade was with Ireland, at Whitby a very large proportion of the trade was with London. The number of small Whitby vessels employed in this trade was quite staggering. Richard Wetherill, the author of 'The ancient port of Whitby', states that he had once counted 400 in sight at one time from the Whitby cliffs. The life of these North Sea mariners was extremely hazardous, the area being noted for sudden gales, strong and difficult currents, and many sandbanks. It was however just such conditions that produced some of the world's greatest mariners, Capt Cook, of course, being the most famous.

The Whitby shipbuilder that Robert & Henry Jefferson had selected to build the *Antigua* was Barrick. The first mention of the Barrick family as shipbuilders at Whitby would seem to be about 1786, but they may also have built ships before this date. The York and North Midland Railway Company bought part of the yard, but shipbuilding continued in the remaining portion, with one slip, using a dry dock for repair work, and it was this small yard that produced the Jefferson clipper barque *Antigua*, whose sailing from the port on Thursday the 10th June 1858 was a notable and impressive event – well recorded in the pages of the 'Whitby Gazette' on Saturday the 12th:

'New ship. – We are glad to see that the glory of our good old town, as a shipbuilding port is not quite gone for ever; and those who are wont to tell of the sunny days when that branch of trade was high in its zenith, would be glad to be reminded of those prosperous times, when on Thursday last, they were privileged to witness the sailing of the *Antigua*, a superior ten years classed ship, and of a most beautiful model. Since the launch of the vessel from the building yard of Messrs H & G Barrick, the time has been fully occupied with fitting out and equipping her, in a complete manner, as a regular West India trader, under the superintendence of Capt. Forsyth, on behalf of her owners, Messrs Robert & Henry Jefferson, merchants & shipowners, Whitehaven. The departure of the vessel was rendered more than usually interesting in consequence of her sailing direct for the West Indies, and having on board seven passengers, with part of a cargo of manufactured goods from Manchester, Glasgow, and Paisley. Captain Wise, who has been appointed master (and is very proud of his "yacht"), is an able seaman, and has already made forty-four trips to Antigua in only two vessels.'

The *Antigua* was a three masted barque, of slender design, but with a square stern. She had a length of just over 107 ft, with a beam of 25 ft 3 ins; at her bows she had a female figure-head. The majority of the shares in the *Antigua* were held by Henry Jefferson Jnr., of Springfield, Whitehaven – 28 of the 64. Henry Jefferson Snr, and Robert Jefferson, both of Rothersythe, Whitehaven, held 14 shares each, the remaining eight being held by Joseph Wise, then also of Whitehaven. Joseph Wise was to remain in command of this vessel from the time of her launch in 1858, until the 10th September 1863, at which time he handed over command of the barque to Capt Joseph Morgan. The launch of the *Antigua* brought the number of ships in the Jefferson fleet to three, for it would seem the *Derwent* sold previously, had now been bought back by the firm in 1851. Mr Henry Barrick of Whitby retired from business some eight years after building the *Antigua*, but sadly then suffered a complete loss of sight, and was thus unable to see the beautiful vessels that his yard had once produced.

William Ray completes his apprenticeship at Brocklebanks

On the 11th October 1859 William Ray completed his time as an apprentice, and, as was customary at this point in a young officer's career, he made his way home in order to take a well earned holiday, after which it became necessary for him to decide what he was going to do. After some consideration he returned to Liverpool, and made his way back to the offices of Thomas & John Brocklebank in Rumford Street; it being his intention, if the firm's marine superintendent had nothing to offer him, to ship before the mast to Australia. The great Australian gold rush was still on, and young William Ray had clearly caught 'Gold Fever', for once at Australia his considered intention was to run away and make his way to the goldfields, and a potential fortune. However, at Rumford Street the firm's Marine Superintendant said he could go aboard the *Harold* as third mate, which prospect it is clear did not particularly appeal to young William Ray, who continues his story:

'In those days servitude as third mate did not count for the next certificate, so that third mate of the *Harold*, although as much as I ought to have expected, was not very attractive to me. I went on board the ship, however, and thought it over. Next day the Marine Superintendant sent for me and said, "Your old ship the *Rimac* is going into graving dock. The second officer has joined the *Tigris*, the chief officer is on leave, and I want you to take the ship into Canning Graving Dock." This was in the Prince's Dock in Liverpool. I took the ship into graving dock, and the necessary work being done there, I was confirmed in the position of second officer. This was the very utmost I expected, seeing that the twelve months' servitude as second officer would enable me to pass the next degree as chief officer. We went to the West Coast of South America. We had a very pleasant voyage together. I, at all events, got along with the captain very well, though the chief officer and the captain did not seem to agree so well. We loaded a cargo of guano at the Chincha Islands again, and came home to Queenstown for orders.

We got our orders on arrival at Queenstown to go to a place called Tayport, on the opposite side of the Firth of Tay to Dundee. The voyage lasted over twelve months, and I took the opportunity of passing for chief officer while there.' (This was at Leith, he sat the exam on the 29th of December 1860, and received his Certificate on 5th Jan. 1861.) 'After the cargo was discharged the chief officer left, and the master of the ship was instructed to go to Leith for a cargo of cannel coal for the Gas Company of Lima. Instructions had been given to the captain to put me on the articles if I passed as chief officer. Accordingly we went to Leith and ultimately sailed for Callao. Unfortunately the captain elected to go round the north of Scotland, which I thought at the time was not a very advisable thing to do, and so it proved. After passing through the Firth at the north of Scotland, and getting to the west round Cape Wrath, we had a most strenuous time, for it was in the middle of winter. Gales of wind, one after the other, sprang from the south west and continued so long that it was 70 days before we crossed the equator – a passage which should have been made, even from Leith round the north of Scotland in say 40 days. This made a very long passage to Callao.'

Eventually the *Rimac* found her way to Callao, at which place young William Ray soon discovered that the master of his ship was rather fond of hard liquor – to the extent that he went ashore the moment the ship docked, and was not seen again for three weeks – most of his time being spent in the local taverns. William Ray, left in charge of the ship spent these weeks seeing to the discharge of the cargo – and wondering when he would next see the master of his ship. Finally they got him on board, but not before they had ballasted and were ready to go to the Chinchas Islands for another load of guano: The brig then made its way to the islands, they anchored, and the master went ashore to enter his ship and do the necessary formalities, before commencing to load. As might be expected, the Captain did not return until about 10 o'clock, when rather full of drink. William Ray, and the ship's steward, put their skipper to bed, but alas, it was to be 11 a.m. the following day before this jolly mariner could be aroused. When sober, however, this particular master was extremely capable, a capital seaman, and an excellent navigator but luck did not seem to be with him on this particular voyage.

After rounding Cape Horn, the *Rimac* made her long passage up the Atlantics, bound towards Queenstown for orders. When the brig eventually got near Ireland, and close to Cape Clear, the wind sprang up and prevented them getting around this cape and into Queenstown. At this point they then sighted land just to the southward of the river Shannon, but owing to the long passage they had experienced, they were now very short of provisions. All the pork and beef were finished, and the master and crew were now existing on bread and water. On the Friday night they took stock and discovered that even on short rations of bread, this would not last out beyond the following Wednesday. The Captain decided to wait until there was a fair wind to take them into Queenstown, but a deputation of the crew urged him to put into Galway, or some other Irish port, as they feared the provisions might run out before a favourable wind arose to take them into Queenstown. The master of the *Rimac* still felt it wiser to try and get into port at Queenstown – the wind would soon change he felt. Understandably however, pressure on him began to build up, until William Ray, and the 2nd Officer persuaded him it might be best to try and run the ship into the River Shannon and to anchor her at high water just above Kiloradam Point. They had to round this point to anchor in a little bay, but alas they ran too far before letting go the anchor.

In a very short time the *Rimac* began to heel on her side, the tide ran out leaving her high and dry. Low water found her lying well over on her side. The coastguards, stationed on that part of the coast, soon made their way to the vessel, but on boarding her assured the master and his crew that the ship was not in any immediate danger. She was however well and truly aground. Brocklebanks soon received news of the event, whereupon their Marine Superintendent made his way to the Shannon to inspect the ship. Eventually the brig was refloated, which I have no doubt pleased all of those at Brocklebanks who had served aboard this sturdy little vessel.

On the completion of his apprenticeship in 1860 young William Ellery was appointed third mate of the barque *Patriot King*, once commanded by Capt Wise. The *Patriot King* was now 28 years old, and had been taken out of the East Indies trade and put into the South American service under the command of Capt Lowden. In the near future William Ellery was destined to serve on the full-rigged ship *Arachne*, commanded at one time by Francis Wise. Related to this point in his career though, William Ellery has much of interest to tell us regarding the antics of typical Brocklebank apprentices aboard the barques *Lanercost* and *Patriot King*:

'Amusements of the Dog Watch – Here I may pause a minute to describe one way in which the apprentices on board the *Lanercost* and the *Patriot King* amused themselves during the dog watch. We called it "Follow the leader, and the devil take the hindmost," or "Shinning the backstays." This means shinning up the backstays on to the lower yards, then climbing up the leeches of the single topsails, along the yards again on to the stay, and then going hand-over-hand from one mast to the other. Very frequently the captain and officers were spectators of these athletic feats, and the thought that their eyes were on us stimulated the laggards and encouraged the more daring. Of course there was an element of risk in the "fun," as we considered it, but it braced up our nerves, gave us self-possession in trying situations, and so made us better sailors in working the ship. I never knew of any serious accident happening while we were exercising our muscles and nerves in this way.

Speaking generally of these times the discipline, though severe, was submitted to with the utmost willingness, and in despite of the heaviest weather. After shortening sail the crew were accustomed to tail along the halyards, keeping time to the strains of a chanty, such as "Oh Sally Brown, I love your daughter." But there was plenty of variety in the chanties, and all the sailors were conversant with them, so that the hardest work was made bright and cheery under all circumstances. Though a lump of sea would come over the bow drenching the men to the skin; it made no alteration in their good temper. After discharging at Callao we had to call at several small ports picking up cargo for the homeward passage, and the crew had to do all the necessary

90

The Whitehaven Herald

WHITEHAVEN, SATURDAY, OCT. 27.

ITALY AND THE GREAT POWERS.

WE have no intelligence of any further event likely to bring the question between the King of Naples and the Italians to a speedy conclusion. His Majesty still holds out in that corner of his dominions in which Garibaldi has penned him up, though the area covered by his troops is narrowed. It appears that he has abandoned the line of the Volturno, but only to withdraw within the compacter and more easily defended line of the Garigliano. The Liberator's forces hem him in on one side, with a barrier that cannot be broken; and the Piedmontese, in two columns, one of which is commanded by Victor Emmanuel in person, are approaching from the east and north, slowly drawing together the iron circle out of which there is no outlet. The Royalist position is blockaded from the sea, though we are not aware that the blockade is effectively maintained. Indeed, we suspect if the King took a fancy to go on board ship and escape, no opposition would be made to so convenient a solution of the difficulty. Garibaldi's object is apparently to win a bloodless victory by delay, and thus spare the Italians for the assault he scruples not to avow he meditates against Austria in Venetia in the coming spring.

The British brigade is now in position at Caserta. Garibaldi has acknowledged to them how much, from the beginning, the British nation has done for the Italian cause. "It has helped us," he said, "in every way, and to its powerful voice we owe it, in a great measure, that the principle of non-intervention has been upheld, which is our safety."

The progress of King Victor Emmanuel has been unaccountably slow, except on the supposition that the mountainous nature of the country has retarded the passage of his army. It is certainly time he were on the scene of action, unless he wishes to see the whole question pass into the hands of the diplomatists. He is expected at Naples to-morrow. The voting on the question of annexation to the Kingdom of North Italy has been proceeding this week, and no one entertains a doubt as to its result.

Advertisement in 'The Whitehaven Herald' for the barque Antigua *27th October 1860.*

work. Sharks abounded, we had to keep a sharp look out for them; and the heavy surf on the West Coast of South America made us expert in seizing opportunities. On Sunday afternoons we were generally allowed to go ashore. Some of us would bring home specimens of the Cacti which were growing on the sandy soil of the shore, while others would climb the foothills of the Andes, curious observers of the strange plants and trees. These occasional breaks were hugely enjoyed, and seldom abused.'

'Mutiny' on the Jefferson barque 'Antigua'

Most of the Crew Lists, and many of the Log Books relating to the voyages of Joseph Wise have survived. From these documents it is clear that most of his many passages across the Atlantic to the West Indies were relatively uneventful affairs, a notable exception to this being his voyage to Antigua and back, June to September 1861, in the barque *Antigua*. The ship's cook, Jan Kriezen, turned out to be an 'Old Slush', whilst several members of the crew refuse to attend to their duty – occupying the time thus saved in 'cutting and wounding' each other, and drinking Jefferson's cargo of rum! Extracts from the Official Log Book for this voyage therefore making fascinating reading:

JULY 12th	'7.55 p.m. St. John's Antigua. At 5.30 p.m. the Longboat came alongside of the ship with a full load of valuable produce. Frank Scory and Richard Squire A.B. at 5.55 p.m. refused duty and would not assist to discharge the Long Boat when requested by the mate to assist in discharging the boat. The answer given by the two men was as follows. If this is the way you are going to do it we will do no more.'
JULY 13th	'St. John's Antigua. Frank Scory A.B. and Richard Squire A.B. not to their duty, but down the Fore-Castle idleing their time, which is a very serious matter at this season of the year, the hurricane months, for these men to refuse duty. They deny the charge.'
JULY 15th	'At 2 p.m. Frank Scory A.B. and Richard Squire turned to their duty after making use of much improper language to the Captain.'
JULY 21st	'Jan Kriezen Cook – has proved himself incompetent to perform the duty of cook. This day ordered to provide a fry of fresh pork for breakfast, which he completely wasted and not fit for use, when questioned he threw the above pork over-board and refused to do further duty, but wished to have his discharge in the morning. Granted by Captain. Discharged by mutual consent, July 22 1861.'
AUGUST 2nd	'St. John's Antigua. Frank Scory A.B. Richard Squire A.B. Henry Jenkinson, Andrew Baxter A.B. James Robinson A.B. For riotous and disorderly conduct, and using knives, cutting and wounding each other in the Fore-Castle, they being the worse for spirits. Examined the Fore-Castle and found a bottle of Rum in it. Supposed to have been broached from the cargo.'
AUGUST 3rd	'Receiving that the cargo had been broached yesterday went down the hold and eventually examined the casks of rum, found one puncheon marked J YK S No. 8 holed in two places since being received on board of the ship, and having every reason that the casks were holed by some of the above men.'
AUGUST 5th	'St. John's Antigua. Frank Scory A.B. James Robinson A.B. sentenced to 14 days imprisonment with hard labour for riotous and disorderly conduct on board of the ship.'

AUGUST 13th '*Lat. 21.48 N Long. 63.45 W*. Richard Squire A.B. stating that he had a burning in his inside gave (him) a dose of calomile & Jalap.'

AUGUST 14th '*Lat. 24.50 N. Long. 63.45 W*. Having every reason to think that Richard Squire A.B. is not sick, called him on the quarter deck to ask him, what, if anything, was really the matter with him, his answer was that he had a pain in his belly (I gave him Castor Oil) – he said he wanted to get something to give him an appetite.'

AUGUST (   ) '*Lat. 27. 10 N. Long. 62.50 W*. Richard Squire A.B. not to his duty stating that he was very sick and not fit to come on deck (Now I saw him after dark in the night, that he is on the deck smoking his pipe and eating his victuals etc.)

AUGUST 18th 'No duty performed this day actually necessary for the navigation of the ship. Richard Squire A.B. on deck all day, and taking his meal with the rest of the crew – but did no further duty. Went below at 8 p.m. and remained in bed all night, I do declare he is not sick, but quite fit to do any work, but will not turn too.'

AUGUST 19th 'Richard Squire still below and will not turn to work, at 6 a.m. the chief mate ordered Richard Squire to work, his reply to the mate was, he would turn to when he thought fit. At 9 a.m. the Captain went down in the Fore-Castle and requested him to go on deck and return to his duty, he, Squire, would not do so, but made use of very aggressive language to the Captain, saying that he would make the Captain pay for all this when he got to Liverpool, and that he had got it all down .... (illeg.)'

(All above extracts signed by Joseph Wise, Master, John Ellison, Mate.)

Extract from the crew list relating to the above voyage of the *Antigua* – Liverpool to Antigua & back. 5th June 1861–13th September 1861

Joseph Wise, 26 Dexter Street, Liverpool, Master. Managing owner – Jefferson & Taylor, Liverpool.

Name	Age	Place born	Capacity	
Joseph Wise	40	Cumberland	Master	
John Ellison	31	Whitehaven	Mate	
Jan Kriezen	26	Hamburg	Stwd/Cook	
Frank Scory	27	Southampton	Seaman	
Andrew Baxter	30	Aberdeen	Seaman	
James Robinson	25	Longhope	Seaman	
Richard Squire	31	London	Seaman	
Henry Jenkinson	29	Leeds	Seaman	
George Dickinson	18	Liverpool	Ordy	
Joseph Oxford	32	London	Seaman	
John Owen	23	Hull	Seaman	
Hilton Davis	17	Antigua	Cook/Stwd	
William Spratly			Apprentice	Bound 16th May 1859
Henry Chas. Winters			Apprentice	Bound 6th Oct 1859
John Watson			Apprentice	Bound 12th Dec 1859

CHAPTER 11

1862–66 – Shipwrecks, Pirate Attacks and Jeffersons Build The 'Ehen'

The South China Seas in the 1860s continued to be plagued by pirates, the Brocklebank barque *Veronica* received their attention in January 1862. It was when the *Veronica* was about fifty miles south of Hong Kong, under the command of Capt Douglas, that the attack was mounted. Captain Douglas fired his rifle and fortunately brought down the pirate's mainsail. On arrival at Hong Kong the case was reported and the Government sent out a steamboat in hot pursuit. The pirates were captured and brought back to the colony; Capt Douglas and his crew being told upon the steamer's return that the twenty-two pirates involved would be hanged from a bough of a tree not more than four hundred yards from where the ship was lying at anchor. The formality of a trial seems to have been dispensed with, for sure enough next day, when *Veronica*'s bell was ringing noon the first pirate was strung up, and as fast as they could be lowered down, the noose was put round the neck of the next, until the whole lot were hanged.

January 1862 was an eventful month for the fleet of Thos. & Jno. Brocklebank, for whilst one of their ships was under attack by pirates in the Far East, another (their strangely, but perhaps aptly named craft the *Crisis*), was foundering off the coast of Ireland, the report regarding the incident reading as follows:

'Drogheda, 17th January 1862
The barque *Crisis* of and from Liverpool for Singapore struck on the Arklow Bank yesterday and foundered. Six men came ashore at Cloger Head in the pinnace. The master and the remainder of the crew left the vessel in the other boat but have not yet been heard of.'

It would seem though that Capt. Thompson and the remainder of the crew did survive this disaster, for a further report received from Newry on the 25th reported that a boat had been picked which was 'supposed belonged to the *Crisis* perhaps the missing one containing the master and the part of the crew.'

The next vessel to run into trouble off the Irish coast was the *Rimac*, a communication being received from Mr William Blair, underwriters agent at the port of Kilrush, south-

94

The Tenasserim *on the stocks at the Brocklebank shipyard, Whitehaven.*

west Ireland on the 28th February, which indicated that she had gone ashore near Kilrush. Mr Blair and the master, Capt Jenkins, worked together and eventually managed to organise the vessel's rescue; she was got off the bank and proceeded to Tayport Dundee with her load of Guano.

In the spring of 1862 William Ellery left the barque *Lanercost*, and after a stay ashore of only 48 hours sailed as third mate on the full-rigged Brocklebank ship *Arachne*, bound for Calcutta.

'As I said, the *Arachne* was bound from Liverpool to Calcutta, and carried a crew of 28 hands all told, the voyage taking about eight months there and back. It was an entirely new experience, my previous voyages having all been made to the West coast of South America. On the voyage out we carried a general cargo, and brought home jute, linseed, cotton, wheat and rice. When we had a new apprentice on board, on the outward voyage, the time honoured custom of Crossing the Line was invariably observed. During the dog watch a gruff voice would be heard hailing the ship, and asking if any of Father Neptune's sons were aboard for christening. On the reply "Yes, come along," Father Neptune and his barber appeared on deck. The former carried his trident, was crowned with a mass of seaweed, and wore a white flowing beard; the latter was wrapped in a sheet, and carried a piece of hoop iron to serve as a razor. Neptune then went to the quarter deck and asked permission of the captain to christen, which being granted the victim was marched to the strains of a chanty to the washdeck tub, abaft the windlass, where he was placed on a plank, the end of which rested on the tub. Neptune proceeded to catechise him, and as the helpless victim opened his mouth to reply, a wad of tar was thrust in every time. Then the barber stepped forward, and after freely "lathering" the victim's face with a mixture of grease and tar, proceeded to scrape it with the hoop iron. This part of the performance over, the plank was suddenly tilted, and the victim plunged into four feet of sea water, amidst the hearty laughter of all the spectators. Neptune, the barber, and all the hands then joined in a glass of grog, after which the chief actors in the comedy mysteriously disappeared.

This being my first visit to Calcutta I was much impressed with the natural beauty of "the City of Palaces." In after years I made many friends there, both among the Eurasian residents and Europeans, for it was my luck to be employed in the Calcutta trade for over thirty years, namely from 1870 to 1903. But at Calcutta I first became acquainted with the dreadful scourge of cholera and dysentry. It was quite a common thing to see bodies of hindoos floating with the ebb and flow of the tide past the ship as she lay at anchor, often fouling the moorings, and some of them giving off a most offensive stench. As our water supply was entirely drawn from the Hooghly, this contamination was a very serious matter, frequently causing outbreaks of cholera, dysentry, and fever while we were in port. Now the water is perfect.

On arrival in Liverpool from my first voyage in the *Arachne*, I was appointed second mate of the *Tigris*, a full-rigged ship of 456 tons register, and on returning was made first officer, remaining with the vessel till she was driven ashore at Manilla, in a cyclone which took place in September 1865. During my second voyage in her, on the passage from Liverpool to Batavia and Singapore, incidents occured of a most exciting character.'

In the 1860s the Prince's Dock Liverpool was filled with sailing vessels engaged in the India, South America, and West Indies trade, and it was here that one would be able to see the Indiamen of the Brocklebank fleet, the *Rajmahal*, *Aracan*, *Harold*, *Comorin*, and *Martaban*. One would also find there the ships of smaller owners, the barque *Antigua*, managed in Liverpool by Messrs James Poole and Company, being but one of many. The vessels discharged on the west side of Prince's Dock and loaded on the east side; on the walls of the dock and in the rigging of the ships, the owners would have notices hung giving details of the ship, its Master, the owner or agent's name and other details; a typical one would read:

> This well known Clipper ship, the *Rajmahal*, Clement Mossop
> commander, registered A.1. at Lloyds, will sail for CAL-
> CUTTA on the 12th of June.
> For terms of freight or passage apply to the owners,
>   Thos. & Jno. Brocklebank
>   13 Rumford Street.

At the south end of Prince's Dock was the George's Basin, a tidal basin through which ships going into the Prince's Dock had to enter. Sir William B. Forward, in his book 'Recollections of a busy life', recalls the scene there as it was in the 1860s: 'I remember seeing one of Brocklebank's Calcutta ships; the *Martaban* enter this basin under sail; it was done very smartly, and the way in which the canvas was taken in and the sails clewed up and

96

furled, was a lesson in seamanship.' Sir William continued, 'It was a joy to walk round the docks and admire the smart rig and shipshape appearance of the old sailing vessel. The owner and captain, and indeed, all connected with her, became attached to their ship and took a pride in all her doings. In those days the River Mersey was a glorious sight with probably half a dozen or more Indiamen lying to an anchor, being towed in or sailing in under their own canvas.

'The River Mersey, at all times beautiful with its wonderful alternations of light and its brisk flowing waters, has never been so beautiful since the old sailing ship days, when at the top of high water the outward bound fleet proceeded to sea, and the entire river from the Pier Head to the Rock Light was filled with shipping of all sizes working their way out to sea, tacking and cross tacking, the clipper with her taut spars and snow white canvas, and the smaller coaster with her tanned sails all went to make up a picture of wonderful colour and infinite beauty.'

On the 21st March 1863 Thomas & John Brocklebank sold their Brig *Kestrel* (commanded for so many years by Capt Abraham Vaux Wise) to Mr Frederick Gregory of Whitehaven. Capt William Cowman was later appointed master of the vessel by this owner. For most of her years afloat the *Kestrel* had been rigged as a barque, but 1863 found her re-rigged as a snow – this famous Cumberland built craft still had many years of service ahead of her as we shall see. The year 1863 saw not only the sale of one of Brocklebank's best known vessels, but the loss at sea of the Indiaman *Jumna*. The *Jumna* had been sold by the firm in 1856 to the Tay Whale Fishing Company of Dundee, which converted the old vessel into a steamer in February 1863. Shortly after her conversion she was sent on her first whaling expedition, but alas her role as a modern steamer was to be a brief one, for on the 6th July she was crushed in the ice whilst whaling in Melville Bay. The following snippet from the 'Cumberland Pacquet' of the 1st September puts the loss of this one vessel in 1863 into perspective.

'RECORD OF WRECKS: The number of ships reported wrecked during the past week is 34, making a total for the present year of 1,157.'(!)

On the 10th September Joseph Wise handed over command of the *Antigua* to Capt Joseph Morgan of Whitehaven, who was 39 years old, and had previously served as master of the Brocklebank built vessel *Irt*. Like his colleague Joseph Wise, the requirements of trade had also obliged Joseph Morgan to leave Whitehaven and set up home in Liverpool. 1863 found Capt Morgan living at 8 Galton Street, and his new vessel at this time being managed by Jefferson's Liverpool office, Jefferson & Taylor of London Chambers. The reason for this change of command was quite simple – Robert & Henry Jefferson were about to accept their latest ship from the builders, and as with the *Antigua* Joseph Wise was to be both part owner and first master of this new vessel.

The gently flowing River Ehen has its source in Ennerdale Water, which lies some eight miles to the east of Whitehaven, and Robert & Henry Jefferson decided to name their latest vessel after this beautiful lakeland stream. The *Ehen* was launched from the building yard of Lumley Kennedy and Co. of Whitehaven on the 1st December 1863, and registered at the port on the 17th. The *Ehen* was a larger vessel than the *Antigua*, her tonnage being just over 301; she measured 124 feet and was rigged as a barque. With the exception of eight shares held by Mr George Robinson of Carlisle, and a further eight held by Joseph Wise, all the shares of the *Ehen* were held by the Jefferson family.

Lumley Kennedy, the active partner in the firm which bore his name, was the son of a Whitehaven shipwright, and was himself, for almost 20 years manager at Whitehaven for Thomas & John Brocklebank. Lumley Kennedy left Brocklebanks in 1834, or 1835 to set up his own ship building firm – he launched his first vessel from this yard, the brig *Alciope* on the 24th October 1835. Apart from building Jefferson's brig *British Queen*, Joseph Wise's second command, he built at this yard some sixty-five vessels. The craft he produced included the clipper *John O'Gaunt*, the barque *Nile*, the Boadle ship *John Spencer*, down to the Jefferson sloop *Midge* launched in November 1840.

Seven days after the launch of the *Ehen* the following notice appeared in the 'Cumberland Pacquet': 'The long established firm of L. Kennedy and Co. being about to be dissolved by mutual consent, notice is hereby given that they are willing to treat for the disposal of their plant, and the letting (with the consent of the owner) of their premises, which are well adapted for either wood or iron ship building. Further particulars may be known by application at the building yard office at Whitehaven. Whitehaven 5th Dec 1863.' Despite this advertisement my great-grandfather's ship was not the last launched

Iron ship Baroda *built by Harland & Wolff, Belfast, 1864.*

from the Kennedy yard. On the 9th March 1864 Lumley Kennedy launched his last ship, the *Erato*, which we must assume was merely awaiting completion when it was decided to close the yard.

Lumley Kennedy himself was known and respected as a quiet, pleasant and retiring man who took little interest in the political life of the period. When his yard closed he moved from Whitehaven to the small and pleasant village of Beckermet which lies a few miles south of Whitehaven, and not far from the banks of the Ehen. The individual who responded to the above advertisement was a Kennedy Company employee, Mr Joseph Shepherd. Shepherd and Company operated from 1864 or 1865 to 1879 building in that time no less than seventeen vessels, the largest of which was the *Beckermet*, 229 tons.

In 1863 the now 93-year-old firm of Brocklebanks decided to place their first order for an iron vessel with Messrs Harland and Wolff of Belfast. This decision was to lead to the closure, two years later, of the Whitehaven yard, which had become out-dated and was totally unsuitable for the construction of the large iron vessels now required by the firm. Despite this move, the yard launched three more wooden vessels before it closed – the *Everest* in 1863, a 571-ton ship which traded for ten years to Hong Kong and Shanghai before being wrecked in 1873; and the *Bowfell* (1864) and the *Mahanada* (1865), both of them ships of just over 1,000 tons.

Harland & Wolff's first clients were Messrs Bibby & Company of Liverpool, but the order placed by Brocklebanks for their first iron sailing ship, the *Alexandra* is understood to be the second order received by the famous Belfast yard. In all Messrs Harland & Wolff were to build ten great sailing vessels for Brocklebanks – five pairs, as follows:

1863	*Alexandra*	1352	Tons
1864	*Baroda*	1364	Tons
1866	*Candahar*	1418	Tons
1866	*Tenasserim* (2)	1419	Tons
1874	*Belfast*	1865	Tons
1875	*Majestic*	1884	Tons
1885	*Zemindar*	2053	Tons
1885	*Talookdar*	2053	Tons
1887	*Sindia*	3007	Tons
1888	*Holkar*	3009	Tons

1864 – Ralph Brocklebank becomes a partner

On the 1st January Ralph Brocklebank Jnr., now aged 24, was made a partner in the firm of Thos. & Jno. Brocklebank. He was the son of Ralph Brocklebank Snr. of 'Annesley' Woodlands Road, Aigburth, who had by now been a partner in the firm for many years. Ralph Snr. was the son of John Brocklebank, and the grandson of the Reverend Ralph Brocklebank, the founder's brother.

For some years now Thomas Brocklebank had been living at 'Springwood', Allerton, Liverpool, but he retained the property of 'Greenlands' nr. Whitehaven as his Cumber-

Sir Thomas Brocklebank, 1814–1906. A copy of a portrait in 'Lancashire at the opening of the Twentieth Century', by W. Burnett Tracy, 1903.
(Photograph by Liverpool Public Libraries.)

land address. It was to this latter address that Edward Harrison, officer of Her Majesty's Court of Osborne House, Isle-of-Wight, wrote to Thomas Brocklebank on the 3rd February 1864. The letter was an important one in his life, for it informed this now forty-nine-year-old son of a Cumberland Mariner, that he had been appointed Sheriff of the County of Cumberland! The official letter penned by Mr Harrison on behalf of the Crown concluded with these words:

> 'These are therefore to require you to take the custody and charge of the said county, and duly to perform the duties of sheriff thereof, during her Majesty's pleasure, and whereof you are duly to answer according to law.'

While Thomas Brocklebank read the above lines in the month of February 1864 two ships prepared to leave the Prince's dock in Liverpool. One was the Jefferson barque *Ehen*, commanded by Capt Joseph Wise, the other was the Brocklebank Indiaman *Tigris*, once commanded by Joseph's brother George, but now commanded by Capt Miller. A long, but uneventful voyage lay ahead of my great-grandfather, whilst in contrast a long, but very exciting voyage lay ahead of Capt Miller and the officers and crew of the *Tigris*. The ship left Prince's Dock on the 22nd of that month, bound for Batavia and Singapore, and on board was William Ellery, newly promoted from 2nd to 1st mate. His story, of which we have already read extracts, continues with the vessel arrived in the East Indies:

> 'We had discharged our cargo at Batavia, and had taken stone ballast aboard, and when about two days out we were carried by the currents among reefs and shoals and ran aground, having been unable to take observations owing to the cloudy weather. I immediately launched the longboat and got the kedge anchor out, myself and four of the crew manning the boat. While running the warp out in the rough sea, the boat took a heavy sea on board and sank, all of us being thrown into the water. Three of the men managed to reach the ship, being expert swimmers, the fourth – a very fine young fellow – was never seen again, and I had an extremely narrow escape from drowning.
>
> I swam towards the vessel, was seen, and a rope with a bowline was thrown to me. I exclaimed, "What have you done?" and sank, being half unconscious. An apprentice jumped into the water, a rope was put around my body, and I was pulled on board, more dead than alive. The means taken to restore animation included the old-fashioned, but dangerous method of hoisting the body up by the feet, to let the water run out. To the captain's great joy I soon recovered consciousness, and resumed duty. Early the following morning a number of proas (Malay boats), each manned by ten men, and two or three larger covered-in boats, gathered round the ship, the natives to the number of considerably over a hundred swarming on board. Cutlasses, flint muskets, and pistols were quietly distributed among the crew, mustered on the quarter deck, our captain's object not being to provoke a fight, in which we must have been overwhelmed by numbers, but to show the pirates that we intended to sell our lives dearly if put to it.
>
> Of their piratical intentions there could be no doubt, for I noticed that the boats which were covered in contained big knives, other weapons and stink pots, and my suspicions were confirmed by the behaviour of our unwelcome visitors. They uncovered the hatches and discovered we were in stone ballast, began palavering and gesticulating, pointing at and appropriating our long boat, ropes, and kedge anchor, and other etceteras lying about. They then begged for some clothes to cover their entirely naked bodies. What is called a "tarpaulin muster" was made by the crew, resulting in a marvellously miscellaneous collection of old clothes, amongst which was a pair of sea boots and silk hat belonging to the captain.

101

The things were rapidly divided, and a comically grotesque scene ensued as one man took possession of the hat, another of the sea boots, others of trousers worn "stern foremost", waistcoats and jackets partly covering dark skinned bodies. They strutted proudly about the decks in their finery for some time, to our intense amusement, finally leaving the ship, but remaining near-by to take further advantage of our predicament in case we were unable to get off. Happily they were ignorant of the cargo in the after hold, and we ultimately freed ourselves and made the passage to Singapore, where the ship was hove down and repaired, by a small army of Chinese carpenters, there being no graving dock in those days.'

Voyage of the Jefferson clipper-barque *Antigua*, **Liverpool to Barbados under the command of Capt Joseph Morgan of Whitehaven. 20th August 1864**

Name	Place born	Age	Capacity	
Joseph Morgan	Whitehaven	40	Master	
Isaac Edmundson	Whitehaven	47	Mate	
James Braithewaite	Kendal	34	2nd Mate	
George Forrest	Edinburgh	27	Swd/Cook	
William Ward	London	25	A.B.	
Augus Robinson	Glasgow	22	A.B.	
John McNamara	Port Glasgow	25	A.B.	
James Spence	Salcombe	26	A.B.	
Joseph Morgan	Whitehaven	24	A.B.	
Joseph James Wise		14	Apprentice	Ind. 1 May 63
Edward Wood		16	Apprentice	1 Sep 63
John Hudson Spedding		15	Apprentice	4 Nov 62

Detail from Crew List of the *Antigua* held at the National Maritime Museum.

After having commanded the *Harold* for some five years, Capt Francis Wise returned to his old ship, the *Arachne* on the 13th January 1865. Francis Wise had last been aboard this ship in 1852 when he had served as 1st mate to Capt Roddock, the vessel's commander in that year. The *Arachne* carried a crew of twenty-nine all told; these being master, 1st, 2nd and 3rd mates, carpenter, steward, cook, 16 A.B.s and six apprentices. Francis was now living at 60 Windsor Street, Toxteth Park – the home of his sister Mary Foster, and Phillip Foster, river pilot. The crew for this voyage was signed on on the 13th, and she sailed for Calcutta some days later. On the 30th October the Indiaman *Arachne* appeared once more in the Mersey, having safely completed yet another 28,000 mile voyage to the Hooghly river and back.

This was to be Capt Francis Wise's only voyage as commander of this ship for on his return, after this voyage of 1865, he was appointed commander of a larger clipper, the *Comorin*, which beautiful vessel was aptly named after Cape Comorin – the southern-most point of the Indian sub-continent. Capt John Kennedy was now appointed master of the *Arachne*, and on the 13th February 1866 she left the Mersey, bound once again for the distant port of Calcutta. The port of Liverpool was to see the clipper ship *Arachne* no more, for whilst on her return passage she had to be abandoned in a sinking condition when some miles south of the Cape Verde islands in the Atlantic. Happily Capt Kennedy and his entire crew survived.

February 1865 found two Jefferson vessels, the *Antigua* and the *Ehen*, loading in the

Prince's Dock, Liverpool. The *Antigua*, now under the command of Capt Morgan was bound for the Island of Antigua, whilst the barque *Ehen* was loading for Buenos Aires. The first vessel to leave was the *Antigua*, this being on the 28th of the month, closely followed by the *Ehen* on the 1st March. My great-grandfather's mate for this voyage was Mr Benjamin Marshall Swaddle of Southwold. The *Ehen* carried four apprentices, these being Francis Spedding, William Brannigan, John Jackson, and Daniel Dickinson, all of them Cumberland lads. Daniel, now aged 15 was never to return, for on the 13th August he drowned at sea, the account of this tragedy taken from the log of the *Ehen* reading as follows:

'Sunday 13th August 1865, Lat 50. 47 S Long. 81.20 W. At 8 a.m. wind West to W.S.W. blowing heavy gale with high sea running, passing squalls of hail and sleet. All hands aloft reefing the mainsail, Daniel Dickinson apprentice, native of Cumberland, fell from the main yard overboard. Wore ship immediately round on starboard tack, and tried every means to save the boy, but could not do so, blowing heavy at the time. When we got the ship wore round we lost sight of him, when after a while we kept our course and proceeded on the voyage, with a continuance of heavy gales and high seas running.

(signed)   Joseph Wise   Master
Benjamin Marshall Swaddle   Mate
William Brannigan   Apprentice'

Following the normal custom and practice at sea young Daniel's effects were then listed and entered in the log. Judging from the large number of items thus entered against his name, it is clear that Daniel Dickinson came from both an affluent and caring home. One wonders just how many young apprentices, aspiring to be masters, ended their short sea-going careers by falling from yards, as did Daniel Dickinson, all those many years ago.

The *Tigris*, under the command of Capt Miller, and with William Ellery as first mate, left the Mersey, bound for Manila on the 20th March 1865. The pilot was discharged off the Bar, and she proceeded under all plain sail with a fresh breeze down from the N.E. She rounded Tuskar on the following day, encountering gales, and in due course the calm belt, with the variable airs, which marks the polar edge of the north-east trade winds, commonly known as the 'Horse Latitudes'. William Ellery continues his story from this point:

'Formerly vessels bound to the West Indies with a deck load of horses were often delayed so long in this calm belt of Cancer that for want of water the crew were compelled to throw some of the horses overboard; hence the name.
Having got beyond the tempestuous rotary gales of the high latitudes, we had a small spell of fine weather before us in the straight line winds of the Trades. Making the best of the light airs and calms of the present, all hands were employed in changing sails, that is, taking the newer and heavier canvas from aloft and replacing it by sails that had done good service in many a storm and were now side-seamed and re-roped for fine weather. In a few days we crept through the variables into the heart of the Trade winds, and with a free sheet and a flowing sail, studding sails set alow and aloft, we bounded away merrily to the southward. On the 25th April, cirrus, and cirro-stratus clouds began to form overhead, with nimbus to the southward, a sure sign that we were about to enter the "Doldrums."
We furled our sky-scrapers, and hauled down our studding sails. The word "Doldrum" is said to be a corruption of the Spanish word "dolorosa," or old Portuguese "dolorisa," equivalent in

nautical language to the English word "tormenting." And assuredly it is tormenting to all hands to be continually box-hauling the yards about, drenched to the skin for days together, vainly trying to cross the calm belt, while occasionally seeing another vessel coming up astern hand over fist with fair wind, and making as much headway in a few hours as we had done in as many days.

But Jack is in his element in the latitudes of the trade winds, he rarely seeks his berth in the watch below, and without he lies full stretch on deck, on the lee side of the spars amidship, and with a block for his pillow is soon in dreamland. His hobbies are also generally in evidence when off duty on the homeward voyage. Mats of wonderful shapes and designs are made for the folks at home, or his landlady; models and half-models of ships, with painted backgrounds and seas of putty, are made resplendent in all the colours of the rainbow, minature vessels, images, or crosses are mysteriously forced into narrow-necked bottles, with clever contrivances for pulling them into shape, the bottles then being filled with clear water, and hermetically sealed with pitch or wax.

Sailors are also very fond of tattooing each other with black and red Indian ink, pricked into the flesh with a group of needles. Many a breast, back or arm have I seen picturesquely adorned – or, more accurately, disfigured for life – with figures of dancing girls, anchors, ships, crosses or mottoes. When in authority I always used my influence to stop this practice, which is dying out.

Resuming the narrative of what proved to be the last voyage of the *Tigris*, we were joyful when a light breeze sprang up from the southward. The weather began to clear, and on the 28th April we observed a homeward bounder one point on our starboard bow. This afforded an opportunity of sending letters home. Signals were hoisted, courses hauled up, sails on the main mast hauled aback, and letters from officers and crew collected. It is one of Jack's greatest pleasures, and also of the afterguard, to write to sweethearts and wives leisurely when in the Trade winds, on the chance of meeting a homeward bounder on the equator. So here was our opportunity! The jolly boat was launched, manned by four men, with the second officer in charge, and not forgetting to take the latest newspapers, one or two pieces of corned beef, and a couple buckets of potatoes – so acceptable to a long-voyaged homeward bounder – our letters were duly transferred. Our boat soon returned alongside, for we cannot afford to waste precious time. Greetings by signal were exchanged, ensign dipped, sails trimmed and we proceeded on our way, feeling somehow a kind of afterglow which we delight to do down in our redletter book. The light southerly wind led to a fresh south-east Trades, and we crossed the Equator on the 25th day from Liverpool.

After the depressing Doldrums the effect of the trade winds of the South Atlantic is bracing and exhilarating to a degree, and with all plain sail well out and yards braced out on the port tack, we could not board tacks and sheets without the irrespressible chanty. One of the favourites was –

> O do my Johnny Boker,
> Come rock or roll me over,
> O do, my Johnny Boker, do.

Landsmen can have no idea how indispensable were these old chanties in the time of sailing vessels, some fifty years ago. We could not get the "pull together" at the right moment without them, hence their universal use. An old salt like myself may be pardoned for looking back with regret on the days of the chanties, which enlivened and made easy many a tough bit of work. In this spirit we bounded onwards, every man jack of us jubilant that he had worked off the deadhorse (meaning his month's advance), and was now earning good money again. I shall not trouble my readers with incidents concerning the rotary gales off the Cape, Trade winds in the

Indian Ocean, or monsoons in the China seas, but in the words of the chanty of an old Dutch sailor – it was the only one he knew – assure you that –

> In vindy veather, stormy veather,
> Ven the vind blows ve're all together.

Continuing our voyage in the light and moderate breezes of the China Seas, all hands were engaged in holystoning decks, painting ship alow and aloft, and making everything look spic-and-span for Manila. We were also mindful that August, September, and October are the worst months in the year for typhoons in these seas, so that we kept our weather eye lifting for any warning sky, undesirable ocean vagrants might give us through sea, sky, or barometer. The elements, however, were on their best behaviour, and on the 18th August we passed south of Corregidor Island, entered Manila Bay, and anchored in six fathoms water, two and a half miles off shore.

Manila, the capital of Philippines, under Spanish rule, is situated on the island of Luzon, at the mouth of the river Pesig. The bay has a circumference of 120 miles, and is far too large to afford adequate protection to ships. Vessels at the anchorage communicate with the shore by their own boats, and the loading and discharging of them in the bay is effected by means of lighters. In compliance with the rules of the port, we struck topgallant and royal yards, and had the second anchor over the bow, and cable ranged ready for letting go in case of bad weather. During the six weeks in which we were discharging general cargo, and loading a full cargo of sugar for Liverpool, we had fine weather throughout, everything worked smoothly and well. On the 25th September we began preparations for leaving port, homeward bound. Topgallant and royal yards were sent aloft, sails were bent, and everything done in sailor's language "ship shape and Bristol fashion."

The following day (our sailing date) dawned under a sultry and gloomy sky, with suspicious light airs. Captain Miller went early ashore to sign bills of lading and to clear the Customs, remarking that he would return about 2 p.m., and meanwhile we were to have the anchor hove short, with sails ready to proceed to sea. At noon however, storm signals were hoisted at the telegraph station, warning the shipping to prepare for bad weather; and I received a note from the captain directing me to strike royal and topgallant yards and masts. This was what sailors call "a tall order," but all hands buckled to, and all was at once bustle and hurry in dismantling. Soon after the captain came aboard, the second anchor was dropped, cable paid out, the ground tackling well attended to, and we awaited events with a singular mixture of curiosity and apprehension.

At 2 a.m. on the 27th September it was blowing a terrific hurricane, the wind vibrating between N.N.W. and N.N.E., and being accompanied by a deluge of rain and intensely vivid flashes of lightning. Even the thunder could not be heard owing to the tremendous roar of the wind and sea. Two hours later the ship commenced to drag her anchors, and we cut away the topmasts. The severity of the wind at this time was literally beyond description. It crushed everything. The bay was churned into liquid mud, tons of which were dashed over the bow, smashing the galley, and carrying all before it. Daylight revealed a terrible sight. Sea and sky seemed to be mixed up inextricably, and the drift and rain were so overpowering that we had to hang on for dear life. It was impossible to hear each other speak. Every man felt as if his last hour had come. Through the flying scud numbers of dismantled vessels dragging their anchors loomed up close to us. In this plight we drove under the bows of the ship *Sobrina*, and in the heavy sea she crashed down on our stern, carrying away taffrail and rudder, snapping her own cable at the same time, and was rapidly driven by the gale on the beach astern at Sangley Point.

We drove ashore about half-a-mile north of Cavite, striking the ground heavily, damaging the bilges, and the sea getting among the cargo mounted up to the 'tween deck beams. The gusts were still awful, and fearing the wind might shift and drive us into deep water, we cut away the fore and mizzen lower masts, leaving the main lower mast alone standing. It continued to blow hard all day with frightful gusts. Towards night the wind moderated and gradually subsided, enabling us for the first time to get rest and food. On the morning of the 28th the weather became normal, and we could see all around us evidence of the fearful havoc which had been wrought.

Fifteen vessels were ashore in a distance of about a mile and many others were lying dismantled in the bay – in fact, none had escaped damage. The Spanish Naval authorities notified us that if we did not remove our vessel within 24 hours they would blow us up, our reply being to hoist the Union Jack on the stump of the mainmast. The yards, sails, and spars were rafted on shore, and with the hull and cargo were sold by auction.'

Such then was the sad end of the Brocklebank ship *Tigris*; in her twenty-nine years service with the company she had sailed no less than 840,000 miles before being smashed in the port of Manila in 1865.

As well as losing the *Tigris* in 1865, Brocklebank also lost the *Tenasserim*, which vessel left the Mersey on the 23rd December, bound for Calcutta. Shortly after leaving port she ran into dense fog, and under these conditions then unfortunately ran aground on the Arklow Bank, Ireland, sadly three men were lost in this disaster. Apart from losing these two vessels, the firm almost lost the *Mindanao*.

After having served on George Wise's old ship the *Patriot King* and then the *Burdwan*, Capt William Ray assumed command of the *Mindanao* in 1864. Whilst homeward bound from Iquique to Liverpool in 1865 she developed a most serious leak when off Cape Horn. Captain Ray and his crew were unable to trace the leak from inside the ship, so, with great courage, his 1st mate volunteered to dive overboard in an attempt to locate the fault. He swam round the ship and discovered after repeated dives that at one point, several feet below the waterline, a bolt had fallen out of the structure. He eventually managed to drive a plug into the hole, and thus saved his ship. The *Mindanao* arrived safely at Liverpool on the 10th August, and sailed again on the 28th October – bound once more for Cape Horn, and the distant port of Callao.

The terrible hurricane of 1865 left William Ellery (and many other British seamen) stranded in the port of Manila without a ship. The young Brocklebank officer passed the time by making friends among the English speaking residents, finding the Spaniards in particular very kind and hospitable. They showed him many places of interest, a favourite one being the promenade, where a military band played most evenings after sunset. Eleven weeks of this idle shore-bound life however were enough for William Ellery and his fellow officer, Mr Barber. Unable to find berths as officers on a ship returning to the United Kingdom they decided to pay for a return passage via Australia. On November the 2nd 1865 Mr Ellery and Mr Barber went on board the barque *Catherine* bound for Sydney:

'Captain Low received us courteously, and in a short time we left the bay with a spanking breeze on our starboard beam. Passing Corregidor Island on the port hand we endeavoured to beat up north of Luzon and through the eastern passage into the North Pacific, but the wind blowing persistently from the N.E. we made very little progress. On our fourth day out the weather became threatening, and the wind increased to a strong gale from the northward, with a high sea.

It was exceedingly annoying, after wasting our days in trying to get to the northward, but there was nothing else for it, so the captain "up helm," and took the southern route via Sunda Straights. For a few days we made good progress, but light winds and calms followed, and our passage to Sydney proved long and tedious. We numbered twenty souls all told. Mr Alfred Jones, globe trotter and chess player was certainly a great acquisition. Whist, chess and draughts are all very well in their way, but months of enforced idleness grew very irksome. As a diversion I frequently took an airing aloft, sometimes giving the sailmakers a hand in repairing sails, or relettering lifebuoys and boats on occasion offered, our captain proving the most genial of men, and making the best of a long passage. On the 81st day out we put into Port Philip (Melbourne) for provisions and water, and resumed our voyage next day.

On the 27th January 1866 we entered the heads of Port Jackson, and proceeded to Sydney, a distance of about twelve miles. The lake-like expanse of water stretching inland from the heads, is dotted over with all kinds of craft, among them small excursion steamers and pleasure boats, cruising about from estuaries and coves; the scene being one of great beauty and animation. We moored at one of the wharves adjacent to Circular Quay, near the business centre of the city, and bidding adieu to all on board, I picked up my belongings and was soon in temporary lodgings at the Clarendon Hotel. Only those who have "gone through the mill" can realize the sensations of relief and pleasure which I felt at being once again among familiar scenes, and enjoying the simple luxuries of life.

My chief object being to obtain an officer's berth in any vessel bound for the United Kingdom, I made constant applications to shipping offices, and interviewed marine superintendants and others. Week after week passed, and still there was no vacancy. I had many a tempting offer on coasting steamers but I had domestic ties in England, and a strong desire to rejoin the service of the great shipping firm in which I had already passed nearly ten years of my life. At length I agreed to ship as boatswain on the Aberdeen clipper ship *Walter Hood*. She had been lying up for the wool season, and partly dismantled, but was now loading at Circular Quay for London. Two weeks more were spent in sending aloft the lighter masts and yards, setting up rigging and bending sails; and early in March we weighed anchor and proceeded to sea.'

Whilst the spring of 1866 found young William Ellery working his way home aboard the clipper *Walter Hood*, the same months found Francis Wise in command of his latest ship – Brocklebank's *Comorin*, some thousands of miles to the north; for the *Comorin* was now at Calcutta loading a return cargo for Liverpool. Calcutta, in that hey-day of the British Raj, was an amazing place – a city where ostentatious and extravagant displays of wealth merely served to spotlight the grinding poverty of most of the city's inhabitants.

The houses, shops, hotels, and offices of the merchants, officers and other wealthy citizens were lavishly staffed with Indian servants, and inside the houses immense 'punkahs' were swung constantly day and night, in a somewhat vain attempt to reduce the temperature.

From five to eight in the evening, prior to the evening's extravagant meal, was the great time in Calcutta, for then the rank and fashion would turn out in their own carriages, complete with Indian coachmen and other flunkeys, all trying to outdo one another in splendour and ostentation, driving up and down Calcutta's Strand, along the banks of the great Hooghly River. This nightly procession would often be miles in length – all the European ladies present being dressed in the height of fashion.

Captain Francis Wise remained at Calcutta, a modest part of this extravagant scene, until the 9th April; on that day he took on board the Calcutta Pilot, who then guided the *Comorin* down the long lower reaches of the Hooghly. The Brocklebank Indiaman was bound for the open seas once more, and a 14,000 mile passage to her home port of Liverpool, but without doubt Francis Wise would have spared a thought for another, now world famous, Cumberland mariner – Capt Richard Robinson – now master of the tea clipper *Fiery Cross*, lying at anchor in the Min River.

After serving with George Wise aboard the *Princess Royal*, Richard Robinson had been promoted by Brocklebanks to 2nd mate of Francis Wise's old ship the *Rimac*, before being promoted 1st mate of this vessel in August 1852. He left the *Rimac* in August 1854, and obtained his master's certificate at Liverpool on the 16th of the following month. On returning to service with Brocklebanks he obtained the position of 1st mate to Capt Kelly aboard the firm's barque *Hindoo*, which vessel had just been taken out of the East India service, and was now being traded to Bahia and Pernambuco. Captain Kelly noted at this time that Robinson was a smart officer, but one with a somewhat fiery disposition. Robinson's next ship was the *Herculean*, a full-rigger of 531 tons; the master of this ship was Capt J. Bell of Whitehaven. Captain Bell was more than pleased with his new 1st mate,

108

noting in the firm's records that Robinson was a very active officer. Of crucial importance to Robinson was the fact that Brocklebanks were trading the *Herculean* to China, experience of which trade was to prove invaluable to him in the very near future.

When, in 1860, the firm launched the barque *Veronica*, Richard Robinson was appointed commander and he made one voyage in this vessel, as it happens to Hong Kong, before leaving the firm in 1860 to take command of Messrs J. Campbell and Co's fine new ship *Fiery Cross* in 1861 – one month after the clipper's launch. He was to remain with this famous clipper until the completion of the great race in 1866.

The rules, if we can call them that, for Ocean Races were simple and basic – the first ship safely home and in dock at London was the winner! There was nothing at all in these 'rules' which prevented astute seamen, such as Capt Robinson, leaving Foo Chow Foo ahead of other ships, by loading only a part cargo. At the conclusion of the long passage, there was again nothing in the rules which prevented a ship being towed half-way up the English Channel by a powerful steam tug. George Wise's old ship-mate, Richard Robinson, was clearly a man who had taken both these factors into consideration. Nevertheless the *Fiery Cross* was a fine ship, and Richard Robinson one of the world's greatest sailing masters.

Bearing the above factors in mind the Tea Clipper race of 1865 was a most interesting one. The *Fiery Cross* and the *Serica* left the Pagoda Anchorage Foo Chow Foo on the 28th May – both clippers being bound for London. The race was an extremely close one, the vessels sighting each other several times during the race. After a passage of 106 days the *Fiery Cross* and the *Serica* sped up the English Channel on 10th September, making their signals off St. Catherines, Isle-of-Wight within seconds of one another. They continued up channel running before a light westerly wind. By the time the clippers had reached Beachy Head the *Serica* had gained two miles on the *Fiery Cross*, but it was here that Capt Robinson had the good fortune to sight the tug sent out to meet him; the master of the *Serica* had no such luck. Captain Robinson reached the London Docks one tide ahead of his rival and the *Fiery Cross* was declared the winner and awarded the prize – a premium of 10 shillings per ton on the cargo. The *Taeping*, another participant in the 1865 race did not obtain a full cargo until some days after the *Serica* and the *Fiery Cross* had left the Min river, but made the 16,500 miles passage to the Downs in 101 days. Understandably the 'rules' relating to this annual event led to a good deal of unpleasantness between the respective masters. The excitement generated by this great race of 1865 led to the world-wide interest in the race of 1866. Robinson did not win the race of 1866 – but to participate in this, the greatest ocean race of all times, was to gain a place in world maritime history.

William Ellery's dream whilst aboard the 'Petchelee'

After an absence of over 14 months, caused by the loss of the *Tigris*, William Ellery at last found himself back in Liverpool, happy to find things well at home, and anxious to rejoin Brocklebanks without delay. At Rumford Street he applied to the firm's genial marine superintendent, the well known Capt McWean, and was highly gratified with his promise that he should have the first vacancy. Captain McWean was as good as his word, for young William Ellery's short home visit was brought to a close when he was promptly appointed chief officer of the barque *Petchelee*, 393 tons register, Capt Owens then being in command. The *Petchelee* was loaded at London and sailed for Singapore on the 20th August 1866. William Ellery made three voyages in the *Petchelee* before making his final voyage in the capacity of chief officer, this being in 1869 on the ship *Aracan*, serving under Capt Henry Jones, on a long voyage from Liverpool to Shanghai. According to William Ellery nothing of any great interest occurred to him whilst serving aboard the *Petchelee*, with the exception of one remarkable dream he had, and a related incident:

'A remarkable dream I had in the *Petchelee*, which I am persuaded saved the ship from a great disaster. We were homeward bound from China, and were approaching the East coast of Cape Colony during the stormy season. I had the first watch below, 8 p.m. to midnight. In my sleep I dreamt that the ship was struck by a violent squall and thrown on her beam ends, the masts going by the board, and part of the crew being swept into the sea. While the vessel was in this perilous position I dreamed that I clutched the weather rail with one hand and seizing the captain with the other hand, held on to him by his coat collar. Hanging on for dear life at a big angle, the weight of the captain seemed to be pulling my arms out of their sockets, and I called out "I shall have to let go sir." At that instant I was startled out of my dreams by an apprentice calling "Eight bells sir." I sprang out of my berth and without waiting to dress was on deck in an instant, the exciting impression caused by the dream being still upon me. The night was pitch dark, and big splashes of rain were falling. I found the second mate, a smart able officer, was busy with his watch bracing up the foreyards on the starboard tack, but there was very little wind. Away to windward in the north-west, just above the horizon an arched squall, with lightning issuing from it, was tearing down on us, and lashing the seas into a white foam. Realising our dangerous plight, sailing as we were under full canvas, I directed the helm hard a starboard, and, raising the top of the after skylight, I sang out to the captain below and he came running up. All hands were now engaged in letting fly top-gallant and topsail halliards and shortening sail. Peak and throat halliards of spankers were let rip, bringing the gaff and sail crashing on deck. In a few minutes the squall was upon us striking the ship on the starboard beam, and laying the lee rail under the raging sea, exactly as pictured in my dream. All hands then sprang on the weather rail and clung to the rigging, powerless to do anything more. The jib blew to atoms, and the boom carried away; the sails on the main were split and shaken to ribbons, but the foresail fortunately held on. The ship, being now relieved of after sail, responded to her starboard helm, payed off and brought the wind dead aft, and righted, and with the wind in this direction we ran before it for hours, making all as snug as circumstances permitted. We then hove to on the port tack, and were saved from further trouble.

This violent squall was the forerunner of a heavy north-west gale and wild sea lasting 30 hours. These vagrants of the ocean which come so suddenly, are frequent in the Mozambique Channel, and off and around the Cape of Good Hope, but they usually give timely warning by a sudden fall in the reading of the barometer. Unfortunately the glass tube in our mercurial barometer had been accidentally broken early in the passage through the steward clearing out a locker and thoughtlessly placing some boxes so near the bulb of the barometer as to interfere with its free swing, consequently it collided and broke the tube, scattering the mercury all over the place. It was subsequently collected by the steward, the tube was refilled and inadvertently corked up to 30 inches, the defective bulb or cup being hidden by the ornamental brass covering. Hence we were caught napping.

The handsome dummy occupied its usual place in the cabin, and was probably some consolation

110

to the steward for the slating he received for his stupidity at the time of the accident. Nevertheless, the accident to the barometer, which it was impossible to repair, proved a source of great anxiety to the navigating staff of the ship in these stormy latitudes. In due course, however, spare sails were bent, damages aloft were made good, new jibboom rigged out, and favoured by wind and weather we rounded the Cape shortly after, little the worse for our bitter experience and narrow escape in the Mozambique Channel.'

CHAPTER 12

Tea Clipper Races and the Opening of Suez

The number of vessels in the fleet of Thomas & John Brocklebank remained static at thirty throughout the year 1867, no vessels being launched, bought, sold or lost during this twelve month period. 1866 had seen the launch of the iron ships *Candahar* and *Tenasserim* (2) at Belfast, which vessels were immediately placed in the Calcutta service, the former vessel under the command of Capt Mossop, the latter under the command of Capt Ponsonby; both vessels returned safely from their maiden voyages in 1867.

Joseph Wise remained in command of the *Ehen* and his brother Francis remained with the *Comorin*. The *Ehen* left the Princes Dock, Liverpool bound for Antigua on the 21st January, his mate for this voyage being a young Cornishman from Penzance – Mr John Jewel, aged 24. The full crew for this voyage numbered 13, which included four apprentices, all from Whitehaven – Francis Spedding, William Braunson, Tyson Jackson, and Graham Bingham. One of the seamen on this voyage was a Mr Carl Jamieson, aged 24, from Norway, who deserted while the *Ehen* was at St. John's, Antigua on Wednesday the 15th May.

The 25th June found both the *Ehen* and the *Comorin* lying in the Prince's Dock; the *Comorin* had in fact arrived back from Calcutta on the 6th June, and she sailed again for the same place on the 20th July, 'a stranger', Mr A. M. Haldane, acting as first mate to Francis Wise on this voyage. It is interesting to note here that despite the fact that Mr Haldane had already served two voyages as mate of Brocklebank's *Tigris*, George Wise's old ship, served as 2nd mate on Abraham Wise's ship the *Kestrel* – acted as 2nd mate on the *Princess Royal*, served as mate on the *Patriot Queen*, and was now serving as first officer on the *Comorin*, he was *still* listed in the firm's documents as a 'stranger.' It clearly took considerable time, effort, and service to become fully accepted by the ancient firm of Thos. & Jno. Brocklebank.

The Clipper 'Everest'

In the opinion of some writers the Brocklebank clipper *Aracan* was the finest (and fastest) ship ever owned by the firm, but others are clearly of the view that the *Everest* – a much smaller vessel of only 571 tons, against the *Aracan*'s 864 – was the best they ever produced; in fact they were both very fine ships. The *Everest*, built by the firm in 1863, was traded exclusively to China, her first voyage being under the command of Capt Curwen; Capt Clarke took command in 1865 and remained in this capacity until the vessel's loss in 1873. The year 1868, however, found the vessel at Foo Chow Foo, lined up with some of the clipper ships that had competed in the great race of 1866. The following interesting article related to the scene at the Chinese port in the year 1868, appearing in the columns of the 'Liverpool Telegraph and Shipping Gazette' on the 29th August –

'According to advices received here from China, the clipper tea race promises to be as exciting as ever. All the vessels had sailed at their appointed dates. The *Ariel*, *Sir Lancelot*, and *Taeping* left Foo Chow together, on the 28th May; the *Spindrift* on the 29th; the *Lahloo* on the 30th; and the *Black Prince* on the 31st. The *Serica* sailed on the 1st of June, the *Fiery Cross* on the 2nd, and the *Zuba* on the 3rd, the *Chinaman* on the 4th, the *Yangtze* and the *Delana* on the 7th, the *Deerfoot* on the 10th, the *Gresham* on the 17th, the *Achilles* (SS), (from Hong Kong) on the 18th, the *Eleanor* on the 20th, and the *Ada* on the 20th. The *Dilkhoost* on the 22nd, *Albert Victor* on the 25th, and the *Chusan* on the 3rd of July.
All the above vessels with the exception of the *Everest*, which is destined for the Mersey, are bound to the Thames. It is quite possible that some of the first named clippers may reach the Thames before the *Achilles*. Intelligence was received in this port yesterday to the effect that that the *Ariel*, *Tapeing* and *Sir Lancelot* had passed the Gaspar Straits under full canvas, on the 21st June.'

The 'Liverpool Telegraph & Shipping Gazette' noted on Thursday 8th October:

St. Helena Shipping (Arrived)

'*Everest*. Ship, (of Liverpool) 571 tons, Clarke, from Foo Chow for Liverpool 84 days, 6th September, and left same day, – did not anchor.'

The *Everest*, arrived in the Mersey on October the 17th, her passage from St. Helena to Liverpool alas taking half as long as her entire passage from China to this Atlantic island. In passing it is worth noting here that Capt Richard Robinson, late of *Fiery Cross* was now in command of the famous *Sir Lancelot*, mentioned above. He remained in command of this ship until October 1869 when he became commander of the *Lord of the Isles*. If the *Everest* did not do very well in this particular race, she did far better in 1870, when she took 11 days less than the celebrated clipper *Wylo* on her passage down the China seas to Anjer, this run being achieved in company with the clipper *Chinaman*.

The *Everest* was not the only Brocklebank clipper participating in the Foo Chow Foo trade in 1868, their other vessel engaged in this trade at this time being their famous ship the *Maiden Queen* – now commanded by Francis Wise's ex-apprentice, William Ray. The *Maiden Queen*, a vessel of 814 tons, had completed her previous round voyage between London – not Liverpool – and Foo Chow Foo, under the command of Capt George Foster, on the 10th January 1868. William Ray assumed command on the 15th February and sailed on that date for Hong Kong and Foo Chow Foo, returning this time from the tea port to Liverpool which was reached on the 8th December 1868.

Meanwhile at Liverpool...

Whilst the ships of the Brocklebank Line raced across the oceans, Ralph Brocklebank continued to concern himself more with Liverpool affairs. As always he remained active in running the Liverpool Sailors Homes, first established in the Strand in 1844; however, one of his main interests was with the training ship *Conway*, which was run by the Mercantile Marine Association, Ralph Brocklebank being an honorary member of this organisation. On this training vessel Ralph Brocklebank offered to take apprentices without premium, thus enabling many working class lads to become ships' officers.

Apart from the above his other main interest was with the Liverpool Dock Board, for it was here that he served as Chairman for many years. The Board met weekly, and the proceedings were usually well reported in the local press, in particular the 'Liverpool Telegraph & Shipping Gazette'. The following short extracts, taken from the pages of this paper, give one an interesting insight into the nature and content of these meetings:

October 2nd 1868

> 'Mr Ralph Brocklebank presided at the weekly meeting of this board held yesterday, the other members present being Messrs Smith, Job, Paton, Nicholson, Langton, Fletcher, Steele, Hubback, Bold, Maxwell, Littledale, and James Holme. Mr Job in moving the confirmation of the marine committee's proceedings, stated that the Trinity House had given their sanction to the marine surveyor to improve the lighting and buoying at the approaches to the river.'

November 13th 1868

> 'The usual weekly meeting of the Mersey Docks and Harbour Board was held yesterday. Mr Ralph Brocklebank presiding.... A long discussion arose upon the old question of anchoring vessels in the track of the Ferry steamers. It was urged that the most stringent rules should be enforced upon pilots, and that vessels should not be anchored immediately opposite the stages at the caprice of shipowners who were desirous that their vessels might be seen.'

The 'Shipping Telegraph' also carried many reports given to the paper by ships' captains, the column being headed by the caption 'SHIPS REPORTS' – Capt Joseph Joughlin, master of the Brocklebank Lines *Rajmahal* submitting the following for inclusion:

Thursday October 15th 1868

> 'SHIPS REPORTS:– Report of the *Rajmahal*, Joughlin, from Calcutta, at this port: sailed 21st June. With the exception of a gale from the W of a few hours duration to the eastward of the Cape of Good Hope, had mostly light calms and very fine weather throughout the passage. From latitude 26 to 29 N. in the Atlantic, the winds were very light, and for the most part from NNE to NE, with a very large sea from the same direction, and a current of from 20 to 30 miles per day to the SSW.
>
> Saw a great quantity of homeward-bound vessels since passing the Cape of Good Hope. In lat 19 40 N, long 34 49 W, saw a schooner with only a mainmast set, and looked as if abandoned; run towards her, when she made all sail and stood to the southward and westward.'

Brocklebanks sold three ships in 1868, these being the barques *Patriot King*, George Wise's old ship, and the *Aden*, the latter vessel being sold to Messrs Cochran & Co. of

Liverpool, who reduced her to a three-masted schooner. The most noteworthy sale however was that of the *Patna*, for this celebrated ship which had now been traded by the Brocklebank Line exclusively to China for over a quarter of a century, was sold to Messrs Robert & Henry Jefferson of Whitehaven, the last ship ever purchased and traded by this ancient Company. The *Patna* completed her last voyage for Brocklebanks to Foo Chow Foo on the 13th May 1868, this being under the command of Capt Henry Jones. At Jeffersons following her purchase she was placed under the command of Capt Joseph Morgan, late master of the *Antigua* (1863–68). She was traded by Jeffersons to the West Indies for some four years only, this before being sold to the well known Whitehaven firm of W. R. Kelly.

Suez

By November 1869 the opening of the newly constructed Suez Canal was only a matter of weeks away. This development was to have a most profound effect on shipping, shipbuilding, and trade throughout the world. Already steam was beginning to gain on sail – at least on the shorter sea routes, and even to a limited extent on the long hauls to the East Indies and China. Steamships were now to be found competing with sail at Foo Chow Foo, Hong Kong, Calcutta and Manila, but the cost of providing fuel for these exceptionally long voyages around the Cape of Good Hope remained a very real problem.

The Liverpool shipowners engaged in the East Indies trade noted that Suez development with keen interest; those engaged in the steamship trade prepared eagerly to participate in the expected trade bonanza resulting from the development. Surprisingly owners such as Brocklebanks did not respond to this development by building steamers, but ultimately responded by building bigger and better sailing vessels, and despite Suez Thos. & Jno. Brocklebank were to remain with sail for many more years. Whilst Thos. & Jno. Brocklebank displayed attitudes of disdain for both steam and Suez, the Merchants' Trading Company of Liverpool eagerly filled the steam vessel the *Brazilian* with an exceptionally large cargo, destined for India via a canal that was still not open to traffic.

The *Brazilian* left the Mersey early in November 1869 with instructions to proceed to Alexandria, and as soon as the Canal be declared open, to pass through on her route to Bombay. 'The *Brazilian* is a very fine vessel' stated a Liverpool shipping reporter – 'in fact a more suitable vessel could not have been selected by the Merchants Trading Company to inaugurate the trade between the port of Liverpool and the East by way of the Suez Canal. The *Brazilian* is upwards of 400 feet long – in fact, we believe, she is the longest vessel that ever left the Mersey – and as the requirements and rules connected with the Suez Canal Company are of a very stringent nature, notwithstanding her splendid steaming power, it will take her two days before she can get over the 100 miles of Canal – that is providing she adheres to the regulations, which limit the steaming power to not more than four or five nautical miles per hour. The *Brazilian* will not draw more than 20 feet when she enters the Canal, and will leave it with the same draft of water. In connection with the above matter, we may state that one of the principal steamship companies in Liverpool are having several vessels built especially for the Suez Canal traffic.'

The Brockebank Ships and Masters 1868

Movements of the Brocklebank Fleet recorded at Rumford Street Liverpool

Ship	Arrived	From	Master	Left	For	Master
Maiden Queen	Jan 10th	(At London) ex Foo Chow	George Foster	Feb 15th	H. Kong	William Ray
Robert Pulsford	Jan 13th	Calcutta	Thomas Richardson	Apr 16th	Manila	W. Forsyth
Lanercost	Jan 14th	Lima	W. Forsyth	July 17th		J. Clements
Bowfell	Jan 16th	Calcutta	J. Balderstone	Feb 26th	Calcutta	Jas. Balderstone
Sumatra	Feb 5th	Calcutta	Geo. Fletcher	Mar 27th	Calcutta	Thomas Beattie
Veronica	Feb 17th	Hong Kong	Caleb Brown	May 2nd	Hong Kong	A. M. Haldane
Juanapore	Feb 22nd	(At London) ex Shanghai	(Late) J. Wilson	Mar 29th	Shanghai	Caleb Brown
Patriot King	Apr 17th		John Clements	(SOLD)		
Harold	Mar 11th	Calcutta	Thos. Beattie	Apr 4th	Calcutta	Thomas Steele
Cormorin	Jan 22nd	Calcutta	Francis Wise	Apr 20th	Calcutta	Francis Wise
Chinsura				May 21st	Calcutta	Geo. Fletcher
Alexandra	Apr 28th	Calcutta	William Kelly	June 24th	Calcutta	William Kelly
Princess Royal	May 8th	Calcutta	Robert Cragg	June 9th	Calcutta	Robert Cragg
Patna	May 13th	Foo Chow Foo	Henry Jones	(SOLD TO JEFFERSON'S)		
Petchelee	May 18th	Whampoa	Richard Owen	Aug 6th	Singapore	Richard Owen
Aracan	June 25th	Calcutta	Thomas C. Potts	July 19th	Calcutta	Henry Jones
Thomas Brocklebank	July 9th	Calcutta	P. Graham	(SOLD) 1869		
Tenasserim	July 13th	Calcutta	J. Ponsonby	Aug 22nd	Calcutta	Thos. C. Potts
Aden	July 30th	Junin	Thomas Brown			
Baroda	Sept 1st	Calcutta	Thomas Tully	Oct 5th	Calcutta	Thomas Tully
Cambay	Sept 23rd	Calcutta	Chas. Howe	Nov 6th	Calcutta	Chas. Howe
Mahanada 1	Sept 24th	Calcutta	John Kenworthy	Nov 17th	Calcutta	John Kenworthy
Valparaiso	Oct 10th	Callao	(Late) A. Murray			
Rajmahal	Oct 14th	Calcutta	Jos. Joughlin	Feb 1st 1869	Calcutta	Jos. Joughlin
Martaban	Oct 17th	Calcutta	D. M. Williams	Nov 25th	Calcutta	David M. Williams
Everest	Oct 17th	Foo-Chow-Foo	J. Clarke	Nov 14th	Shanghai	John Clarke
Candahar	Oct 25th	Calcutta	Clement Mossop	Dec 2nd	Calcutta	Clement Mossop
Bowfell	Nov 5th	Calcutta	R. J. Balderstone			R. J. Balderstone
Burdwan	Nov 8th	(At London) ex Shanghai	William Douglas	Dec	Shanghai	W. Douglas
Sumatra	Nov 22nd	Calcutta	Thomas Beattie	Feb 1st 1869	Calcutta	Thomas Beattie
Maiden Queen	Dec 8th	Foo-Chow-Foo	William Ray			William Ray
Patriot Queen	Dec 21st	Manila	Thomas Southward			T. Southward

Early days in the Suez Canal.
(Photograph from P&O archives.)

Whilst the heavily laden *Brazilian* made her way towards Alexandria excitement related to the opening of the Canal rose to fever pitch in Egypt. Despatches from Port Said dated November 16th indicated that 'The fetes in inauguration of the Suez Canal were commenced by religious ceremonies in the open air, and concluded by a speech and benediction from Baner, Almoner of the Empress Eugenie, the Emperor of Austria, the Princes of Prussia, Holland, and Hesse, and the diplomatic representatives of all nations, as well as an immense concourse of distinguished visitors.' On November the 17th the Imperial yacht *Aigle*, with the Empress Eugenie on board led a convoy of over 40 ships through the canal; the British vessel *Psyche* taking the English Ambassadors and a full Admiral through as representatives of Great Britain. The great convoy carrying it's precious cargo of nobles and dignitaries through the new waterway arrived at Ismailia from Suez on the afternoon of the 17th. The Khedive and his royal guests arrived only hours later – at which point great festivities and rejoicing took place. The desert town of Ismailia being splendidly illuminated to match both the dignity of the occasion and the doubtless happy condition of its guests.

But to return now to the Merchant Trading Company ship *Brazilian*. Some weeks after leaving Liverpool she arrived safely at Port Said, but alas on arrival it was found that it would be impossible for the Liverpool vessel actually to pass through the canal. She was grossly overladen! Almost half of the *Brazilian*'s cargo had to be discharged at Port Said before she could pass through, and even then it took her five days to reach Ismailia – this being on or about December 11th. No doubt all of this caused some amusement in the offices of Thos. & Jno. Brocklebank at Rumford Street, Liverpool.

Suez was now open, but the great Indiamen of the Brocklebank Fleet continued to do what they had done for generations – make the long passage round the Cape. On the 4th June 1870 Capt Francis Wise completed his first voyage as master of the *Cambay*, the firm's vessel named after the Indian city situated at the head of the Gulf of Cambay. The 1,000 ton *Cambay* was now some nine years old, having been built in 1861 when Francis Wise was serving as master of the *Harold*. The *Cambay* had now been commanded in turn by Capts Kelly, Joseph, Joughin and George Wise's old mate in the *Aracan*, Charles Howe. On the voyage of 1869/70 Capt Wise's 1st officer had been Mr Harry Rigby of Runcorn, an experienced man who had now seen service on the firm's ships *Burdwan* and *Aden* before returning to the *Cambay* as mate. On this occasion the *Cambay* remained in the port of Liverpool for less than one month, sailing once again for Calcutta on the 2nd July. All told the *Cambay* carried a crew of thirty-one, which figure included a sailmaker, carpenter and bosun. Also included in the above figure were five apprentices, and amongst these for the 1870/1 voyage of this ship was listed 15-year-old James Robert C. Joughlin – who, one suspects, may well have been related to Capt Joughlin, formerly master of this Indiaman.

Less than three months after Capt Francis Wise left the port of Liverpool, Capt William Ellery was appointed master of the *Bowfell*, Capt J. Balderston then commander of this clipper having been appointed to the *Rajmahal* a vessel of some 1,302 tons. The *Rajmahal* carried a crew of 33, and had now been engaged in the Calcutta trade since her launch at Bransty in 1858. September 1870 found both ships loaded for Calcutta and lying in the Prince's Dock, Liverpool awaiting instructions to sail. These instructions eventually came, and both ships sailed down the Mersey, bound for Calcutta on the afternoon of September 27th. Inevitably Capts Ellery and Balderston decided to make a race of it, which no doubt did much to relieve the monotony of what would otherwise have been just another long, and rather tedious voyage to the distant port of Calcutta – 'RACE OF OVER 14,000 miles. And a busy day it was! I retain a perfect mental picture,' wrote William Ellery, who continued –

'The shore gang of riggers worked the ship from the dock into the river, and having hauled the *Bowfell* from her loading berth into the locks were now standing by. The crew commenced their work on the sailing day, and at noon they came along with their dunnage, one or two lots at a time, in various stages of exalted inebriation, but always with the sailor's instinct, and ready for their work. The more provident seamen had their well-stored sea chests, the less thoughtful found moderate sized canvas bags large enough for their possessions. One hour before high water, and the pilot on board, all hands are at their stations. The mate takes charge of the top gallant forecastle, with the third mate to assist him, and the second mate attending to the warps

118

aft. The dock gates are then swung open, a hawser is passed to the tug in attendance, and away we are towed from the Prince's basin into the river, amidst the cheers of the crowd who usually gathered at the pierhead to hear the chanties, and to which there was a hearty response by the sailors from the forecastle.

'We kept in company with the *Rajmahal* for some hours but in the mist and darkness of the night we lost sight of her off the Skerries. Headwinds kept us tacking in the Irish Channel for two or three days, when the wind veered to the northward, and under full sail we were glad to face the breezy ocean once again, and to see the blue waters dance and frolic in the bright sunshine.

'We made a good passage to the Cape de Verdes, but were much bothered in the Doldrums. We crossed the Equator on the 33rd day from Liverpool, and the meridian of the Cape of Good Hope on our 60th day out. We ran our easting on the fortieth parallel, and made good progress in what Lieutenant Maury calls "the brave west winds of the southern Ocean." Passing St. Paul's island on the 16th December, a sail was reported on the port beam. We edged towards here, and the vessel proved to be our friend the *Rajmahal*. She bore down to us within signal distance, and greeted her warmly. Then, bearing away to the northward in a crisp south-westerly wind, we ran together neck-and-neck for five days, with as much canvas as we could carry in the strong wind, but became separated again in the murky weather which set in on the southern edge of the trade winds.

'On arriving at the Sandheads, and getting our pilot on board, on evening of the 14th January, 1871, we learnt that the *Rajmahal*, in tow of a tug, had been supplied with a pilot only an hour previously, and was still in sight. At midnight we anchored alongside our spirited competitor in Saugor Road. The following day we were towed up the Hooghly, reaching our moorings at the same time as the *Rajmahal*, each vessel having covered the distance of 14,260 miles (north-east Monsoon) in 110 days. In the opposite Monsoon the route is more direct the distance being 12,670 miles. It was a marvellous finish to as tight a race as ever I engaged in.

'Nothing very material has to be recorded respecting the return passage of the *Bowfell* from Calcutta to Liverpool. I remained with her as master for nearly five years. During that period the *Bowfell* made many successful passages, the most notable being one of fifty-nine days from Calcutta to the Equator in the Atlantic, but it was somewhat discounted by an annoying experience of the equatorial calms to the north of the equator. Nevertheless we arrived in Liverpool in ninety-two days – a very excellent run. A great deal was then thought of the *Bowfell*, and a well executed model made of her in full sail, was exhibited in the Walker Art Gallery in August 1907, on the occasion of the Liverpool Pageant, and I believe is now in the possession of the firm.'

In 1871 Thomas & Jno. Brocklebank sold two well-known ships, these being the Indiaman *Princess Royal* and the *Petchelee* – the former vessel having been in company service for some 30 years. She was sold to Messrs T. Cookson & Company of Liverpool, and was to remain afloat for another seven years. The *Petchelee* built in 1850 was sold to W. Killey & Company, also of Liverpool. These two sales left the firm with a fleet of 19, employed now almost exclusively in the Calcutta and China trades.

On the 2nd March Francis Wise brought the *Cambay* back from Calcutta, thus completing his final voyage as a master of Cumberland-built wooden ships. In August he took command of the only iron ship ever sailed in by any of the Wise brothers, and incidentally the only ship built at Birkenhead for the firm of Thomas & Jno. Brocklebank. The vessel was the famous *Chinsura* named after the town situated some miles to the north of Calcutta. The *Chinsura*, launched from the building yard of Messrs Grayson, Rollo, and

The Brocklebank Chinsura *(seen here as the Polish training ship* Lwow.

Clover at Birkenhead in April 1868 was a vessel of some 1,266 tons; she remained in company service for 15 years before being sold. The *Chinsura's* first commander was Capt Fletcher, who was succeeded by Capt Frederick Lathom, who brought the vessel back to Liverpool on the 21st July prior to Francis Wise assuming command. Captain Lathom was then appointed master of the firm's smaller ship *Sumatra*; he remained with this ship until the vessel's sale in 1876.

As always, Ralph Brocklebank remained active in Liverpool affairs; on the 11th September he laid the foundation stone of the Liverpool Seamen's Orphan Institution, Newsham Park. The assembly was then addressed by the 15th Earl of Derby, 'in his usual clear and sensible style'. This was followed by a speech made by the Dean of Ripon, Dr Hugh M'Neile – a man noted more for his eloquence and vigour than for his support for radical causes, one of the good Doctor's main claims to fame being that he had 'triumphed' some 30 years prior to this date in the rout of the radicals! J. A. Picton attended this ceremony and noted at the time that though the Dean's powerful style of address had mellowed, he was still a man capable of exercising a powerful sway over his audience. Ralph Brocklebank gave generously to this particular cause.

On the 15th September 1871, four days after the above ceremony, Capt Joseph Wise handed over command of the Jefferson barque *Ehen*, then loading at Liverpool, to Capt Albert Henry Hulme, thus ending 37 years service with Messrs Robert & Henry Jefferson, most of these years having been served as master. Joseph Wise and the Jeffersons were parting company, but Wise, now aged 50, had no intention of parting company with the sea. . . .

On the 26th June 1872 he assumed command of the Devon built barque *William Graham*, a vessel of 276 tons built originally for the man whose name she bore – William Graham of Newport, by Messrs Cox and Sons of Bideford – one of many ships built at this yard. In 1872, at the time when Joseph Wise became Captain of the barque she was one of three ships belonging to George Gray McAndrew of Liverpool, the other two ships in his small fleet being the *Rosalie* and the *Westwood*.

Little is known about my ancestor's life as a McAndrew master, apart from the fact that Lloyds List of the 16th November 1872 reported that '(At) Queenstown, 15th November, noon – The *Wm Graham* (barque), from London to Liverpool, has arrived off here with loss of bowsprit, from collision on 13th Nov., off the Land's End with an Italian barque.' Which report coincides with a note on Joseph Wise's own record regarding the above collision.

Joseph Wise was soon to become the master of another ship – the *Marengo*, whilst the *William Graham* remained the property of George McAndrew until the 22nd August 1887, when she was sold to Richard Atkinson of Liverpool. She ended her days trading out of Port-of-Spain, Trinidad, renamed the *Columba*, and owned by Antonio Jose Sotilla. She was still afloat in 1893.

CHAPTER 13

The Loss of the 'Aracan' – The Building of the Windjammers

In 1873 Brocklebanks sold the *Martaban* and the *Veronica*, they also lost one of their finest ships, the *Everest*. The clipper *Everest*, under the command of Capt Thomas Jones left Manila, bound for Cork or Falmouth with a full cargo of hemp and sugar on the 24th August 1873. Sadly she became stranded on the notorious Danger Reef in the China Seas, on the 5th September; she quickly became a total wreck, but fortunately no lives were lost in this disaster. At the time of her loss the 571-ton clipper had been in service ten years, and during that period had achieved some remarkable runs.

On the 22nd January 1874 Capt Francis Wise brought the *Chinsura* into the Mersey and in so doing ended the Wise family's connection with the firm of Thomas & John Brocklebank. Francis Wise, only 49 years old and at the peak of his career, was terminally ill; he was never to sail again, but his last command, the *Chinsura*, sailed again for Calcutta under the command of his colleague, Capt William Roberts on the 5th March.

On the 4th March 1874 the clipper *Aracan* sailed from London, bound for Hong Kong, her commander for this voyage being Capt Charles Harwood, and the first mate Mr Robert Nelson. The *Aracan* passed through the Downs without incident and proceeded down Channel. By the evening of the 9th March the *Aracan*, sailing fast under a full press of canvas, was some 16 miles off Portland; visibility had become poor when at five minutes past ten o'clock the steamer *American* bound from the Cape for Southampton appeared across the clipper's bows. Nothing could be done to avoid the steamer. The bows of the *Aracan* sliced through the iron upper plates of the *American* like a knife through butter, the debris from the impact being driven into the steamer's saloon, and all her port bulwarks and stanchions being smashed. Both vessels were crippled, they drifted apart, and at 10.45 p.m. the *Aracan* sank. Captain Harwood and his crew all escaped, for at 10.30 the Union Company's steamer *Syria* had taken on board the full crew of the *Aracan*. Both the *American* and the *Syria* came into dock at Southampton the following afternoon.

The year 1874 saw many changes at Brocklebanks; apart from losing the *Aracan* the firm also lost the *Mindanao*, which vessel foundered. The *Mindanao*, it will be remembered, had been built in 1854 not by Brocklebanks but by Williamson and Sons, of Harrington. The firm sold the 14-year-old barque *Veronica* to Anderson and Company of London, and the *Juanapore* was also sold in the year to a London firm, Messrs T. Davies & Co. The *Maiden Queen* also built by Williamson & Sons at Harrington in 1864 was sold to German owners and renamed *Betty*, all of which reduced the number of vessels in the fleet to 12. The launch of the great windjammer *Belfast* however brought this figure up to 13.

At Jeffersons their fleet had now been reduced to two vessels, these being the *Antigua* and the *Ehen*. The *Patna*, bought from Thomas & John Brocklebank in 1868 was sold in 1873, Capt Morgan, the *Patna*'s commander at the time being given command of the *Ehen* on the 28th March 1874. The *Ehen* was to remain under Capt Morgan's command until the 17th May 1878 when the vessel was sold to Mr Lewis Evans. Since the 18th March 1872 Joseph Wise's old ship the *Antigua* had been commanded by Capt Francis Trannock Calf, born in County Wicklow in 1832. Francis Trannock Calf remained with Jeffersons until the sale of the ship to H. S. Van Gauten of Holland on the 15th October 1880. This sale marked the end of the Jefferson Company's history as ship owners – but not the end of the firm of Robert & Henry Jefferson, who are still in existence today, over a century later – but selling wine, not sailing ships.

The year 1874 found Joseph Wise alive and well, and still afloat. He assumed command of the Sunderland built vessel *Marengo* at Cardiff on the 12th August 1873, the ship's previous master being Capt William Speck. The *Marengo* was a barque of 326 tons, built at Sunderland by Messrs John Haswell in 1860, to the order of Messrs Tindall & Co. of Scarborough, her first master being Capt Charles Nicholl. Joseph Wise traded the vessel to Bahia, for Lloyds list of November 7th 1874 states that on the 6th November, the *Marengo*, under his command, arrived at Queenstown at 11.30 a.m. The weather was calm, but foggy, and Joseph Wise had on board his barque a cargo of sugar that he had brought from Bahia. It is with this rather dramatic image of Joseph Wise, bringing the *Marengo* into port on a foggy autumn day in 1874 that the story of his life at sea must end. However, the Shipping Registers show that Joseph Wise remained master of this vessel until the 11th February 1875, at which point he handed over command to Capt Peter Taylor whilst the barque was at Hull.

The story of the great sailing fleet of Thomas & John Brocklebank continues, for many years were still to pass before they were to leave sail and turn to steam. William Ellery continues that story in 1876....

'After a short holiday I was appointed to the command of the ship *Baroda*, 1,364 tons, built by Messrs Harland & Wolff, in 1864. We sailed on the 28th October, 1876, and made two successful voyages, when I was transferred to the ship *Majestic*.
During the short holiday referred to above an incident occured of a somewhat exciting character. I had resolved on a visit to my native place in Cornwall, and for that purpose took a passage in the screw steamship, *South of England*, bound from Liverpool to London, intending to land at Falmouth. A dense fog prevailed while the steamer was in the channel, and she struck on the Smalls Rock, near the Lighthouse. The engines were backed full speed, and she was got off in a few minutes, and proceeded on her voyage. It was soon discovered however, that the water in the hold was rapidly increasing, and the 29 passengers and crew, numbering 20, took to

1873/4   Arrivals and Departures Recorded at the Offices of Thos. & Jno. Brocklebank

Ship	Arrived	From	Master	Left	For	Master
Veronica (At London)	Jan	Hong Kong	Thos. Jones	SOLD	Hong Kong	William Forsyth
Maiden Queen	Jan 22	Foo Chow Foo	William Forsyth	Feb 13	Calcutta	R. J. Balderstone
Rajmahal	Jan 23	Calcutta	R. J. Balderstone	Feb 28	Calcutta	Joseph Joughlin
Alexandra	Jan 29	Calcutta	Joseph Joughlin	Mar 14	Calcutta	Fred. Lathom
Sumatra (at London)	Feb 1	Hong Kong	Frederick Lathom	May 16	Anjer	Charles Harwood
Aracan (at London)	Feb 25	Shanghai	Charles Harwood	Mar 17	Anjer	Thos. C. Potts
Tenasserim	Mar 9	Calcutta	Thos. C. Potts	Apr 26	Calcutta	Francis Wise
Chinsura	Mar 31	Calcutta	Francis Wise	May 10	Calcutta	William Roberts
Comorin	Apr 27	Calcutta	William Roberts	May 25	Calcutta	Thomas Tully
Baroda	June 14	Calcutta	Thomas Tully	July 16	Calcutta	John Kenworthy
Mahanada	June 26	Calcutta	John Kenworthy	Aug 8	Calcutta	Wm. M. Selkirk
Mindanao	July 27	Iquique	James Wright			
Cambay	Aug 25	Calcutta	Wm. M. Selkirk	Sept 13	Calcutta	William Ellery
Mariaban	Sept 1	Calcutta	John F. Ainscow	Oct 24	Calcutta	Joseph Joughlin
Bowfell	Oct 1	Calcutta	William Ellery	Nov 20	Calcutta	John F. Ainscow
Candahar	Oct 23	Calcutta	Joseph Joughlin	Nov 29	Calcutta	R. J. Balderston
Alexandra	Oct 29	Calcutta	Allan McKenzie	Jan 19	Calcutta	Thos. C. Potts
Rajmahal	Nov 29	Calcutta	R. J. Balderston	Jan 21	Calcutta	Allan McKenzie
Tenasserim	Dec 3	Calcutta	Thos. C. Potts			
Maiden Queen	Jan 13	Calcutta	Wm. Forsyth	SOLD		
Comorin	Jan 21	Calcutta	William Roberts	Mar 21	Calcutta	Charles Harwood
Aracan (at London)	Jan 17	Shanghai	Charles Harwood	Mar 4	Calcutta	William Roberts
Chinsura	Jan 22	Calcutta	Francis Wise	Mar 5	Calcutta	

(To January 22nd 1874 only)

the boats, but stood by the vessel until she sank some hours later, after which passengers and crew were safely landed at Milford. The passengers were good enough to speak highly of the services which I was able to render on the occasion. I had the misfortune to lose nearly all my travelling effects, but was thankful there was no sacrifice of life.

Here it will not be out of place to refer to the excellent business spirit of Messrs T and J Brocklebank, as shown especially in their sailing letters. Three of these are before me as I write. The first relating to the *Baroda*, bears the date 28th October, 1876; and the others, dated respectively 25th October, 1878; and 22nd June 1880, refer to the ship *Majestic*. The instructions laid down are explicit and comprehensive. The captain is expected to make as good passages as vessels sailing at the same time, and to take every precaution to ensure safety. "Stow your cargo carefully, have your ship well loaded, and attend to ventilation." "For your crews you will, of course, have a proper consideration and we hope you will give your apprentices some instruction during the voyage, and thus, as well as making them good seamen, develop a taste for the scientific part of the profession in which you take so much interest." The above are extracts from the *Baroda* letter. On assuming command of the *Majestic* I am reminded:– "The rules you have hitherto practised, to guard against accident, and to make rapid passages, obviously require to be more sedulously put in force in a larger than in a smaller vessel. The use of the lead, good lights, and every precaution, as well in mid-ocean as off the land you will carefully adopt." The previous instruction regarding apprentices is repeated, "and we desire you will mark Sunday in some way that may seem expedient to you." The third letter says – "As regards your ship, her cargoes, and her navigation, we trust you will continue to practice the care, vigilance, and precautions that have hitherto made you successful, and have been satisfactory to us." Each concludes with a wish for good health and a prosperous voyage. I look upon them as models of what sailing letters ought to be.

The ship *Majestic*, 1,884 tons register, was built by Messrs Harland & Wolff, Belfast, in 1876. Her dimensions were length, 273 feet; 40 feet beam: and 24 feet depth of hold. She was among the famous beauties in the East India trade. Her shapely bow would literally cleave the waves, instead of hitting them, and retarding the passage of the hull through the water; and her fine lines and rise of floor enabled her to glide through the water with a minimum of resistance. When fully laden with 2,800 tons of Calcutta cargo, her mean draught was 22 feet 7 inches. Her complement was 36, all told; and under full sail she would spread 11,000 running yards of canvas.

On the death of the commander in 1878, the well-known and energetic Captain T. C. Potts, the commodore of the line, I succeeded, and retained command of the *Majestic* until August 1885, when I was transferred to Messrs T & J Brocklebank's new ship *Talookdar*, then nearing completion at Belfast. The *Majestic* made excellent passages and my third voyage in her may be deemed worthy a place in these incidents:– We left Liverpool for Calcutta (laden with 2,692 tons of salt, draft 22 feet 10 inches aft, 22 feet 4 inches forward) on the p.m. tide, 22nd June, 1880, and were off Tuskar at 4 p.m. the following day. We had light head winds in the channel, but on the third day the wind veered to the northward and freshened, leading us into the N.E. trades, and we crossed the Equator in long 25 deg. 7 min. W., on our 25th day out. We had fresh S.E. trades, which we carried beyond the tropic of Capricorn, and reached the latitudes of the brave west winds without a calm. I elected to run our eastings down on the 39th parallel, and had very unsettled weather, with much lightning, after passing the meridian of the Cape of Good Hope. Meeting on the 6th of August with an increasing south-westerly gale, and resumed our course to the eastward as the wind drew to the westward. In this manner we kept within the northern quadrant of the gale and had strong fair winds, the gale eventually running ahead of the ship, and leaving us on the 11th inst., the wind meanwhile veering S.W. and South.

125

We made 1,219 knots (or 1,403 statute miles) during the continuance of the gale, which was very good considering the heavy seas we ploughed through. Moderate westerly winds followed, taking us into brisk southeast trades, and, braced sharp on the starboard tack, the lower yards on the backstays and upper yards braced well in, we did excellent work to latitude 4 deg. south, when the wind fell away and the weather became unsettled, indicating that we had reached the equatorial belt of calms and variable winds. The doldrums were, however, of short duration, lasting only two days, when a heavy westerly squall, with thunder, lightning, and torrents of rain, lapsed into a steady topgallant breeze, sending us flying into the Bay of Bengal and into the heart of the south-west Monsoon. This proved, on its last legs, and as we proceeded to the northward the wind fell light and veered to the eastward. In a very few days we crept up to the Sandheads, received our pilot, and anchored at Saugor at 3 a.m. on the 6th September, after a remarkably rapid passage of 74 days 11 hours from Tuskar.

This voyage was rendered notable from the fact that all our competitors from the United Kingdom made long passages – none being under three figures. When we arrived the South-west

Thomas Brocklebank and Capt Wm Ray aboard the Bolan.
(Photograph from Merseyside County Museums.)

126

monsoon was on the decline, and after the middle of September vessels entering the bay had a very tedious passage to the Sandheads, particularly those that were to the westward of long 90 deg. east, as calms and light easterly winds winds prevail. Gales and cyclones are also frequently met with during the change of monsoons, of which appearances and a fall in the reading of the barometer should give timely warning.'

Throughout the years 1877, 1878, and 1879 the ships in the Brocklebank fleet numbered 12, all of them engaged almost exclusively in the Calcutta trade. During this three year period no ships were bought, sold, launched or lost. The number was increased to 13 in 1880 by the 1,967 ton ship *Kyber*, which was built to the order of Thomas & John Brocklebank by the Liverpool builders, W. H. Potter & Son. In 1882 the fleet was increased to 14, the additional vessel being the *Bolan*, an iron ship of 2,003 tons built for the firm by Oswald Mordaunt & Co. of Southampton. The *Bolan* was in fact one of two ships built for the firm by Messrs Mordaunt & Co., the other being the *Bactria*, a vessel of similar tonnage built some years later in 1885. As will be noted, the number of vessels in the Brocklebank sailing fleet had now been reduced drastically, but as the following table will indicate the tonnage of each individual ship had increased dramatically:

Brocklebank Fleet 1882

Ship	Tonnage	Rig	Mat.	Built by
Rajmahal	1,302	Ship	Wood	Brocklebank's, Whitehaven
Cambay	1,000	Ship	Wood	Brocklebank's, Whitehaven
Burdwan	803	Ship	Wood	Brocklebank's, Whitehaven
Alexandra	1,352	Ship	Iron	Harland & Wolff, Belfast
Baroda	1,364	Ship	Iron	Harland & Wolff, Belfast
Bowfell	1,002	Ship	Wood	Brocklebank's, Whitehaven
Mahanada	1,003	Ship	Wood	Brocklebank's, Whitehaven
Candahar	1,418	Ship	Iron	Harland & Wolff, Belfast
Tenasserim	1,419	Ship	Iron	Harland & Wolff, Belfast
Chinsura	1,266	Ship	Iron	G. R. Clover, Birkenhead
Belfast	1,865	Ship	Iron	Harland & Wolff, Belfast
Majestic	1,884	Ship	Iron	Harland & Wolff, Belfast
Khyber	1,967	Ship	Iron	W. H. Potter & Son, Liverpool
Bolan	2,003	Ship	Iron	Mordaunt & Co., Southampton

Loss of the 'Rajmahal', and the Fisher family brig 'Kitty'

In the autumn of 1883 the Brocklebank Indiaman *Rajmahal* sailed from Birkenhead bound for Bombay under the command of Capt H. Williams. The vessel had now been in Company service for no less than a quarter of a century, voyaging exclusively to Calcutta, and on this, her last voyage, she carried a full cargo of coal. She was spoken on the 20th October, in Lat. 30 S. Long. 0.11 W, but Capt Williams and his crew were never seen again, the final fate of this ship remaining a mystery. In December another Brocklebank built vessel was lost, this being the schooner *Fairy*, built by the firm in 1848. In 1883 her owners were G. Pluck of Bray, County Wexford; she sailed from Wexford for Glasgow on the 11th

1877 Arrivals and Departures Recorded at the Offices of Thos. & Jno. Brockebank, Rumford Street

Ship	Arrived	From	Master	Sailed	For	Master
Bowfell	Feb 15	Calcutta	James Connell	Mar 17	Calcutta	James Connell
Tenasserim	Mar 11	Calcutta	R. J. Balderston	Apr 17	Calcutta	R. J. Balderston
Chinsura	Mar 27	Calcutta	Jos. C. Joughlin	Mar 27	Calcutta	J. C. Joughlin
Belfast	Apr 23	San Francisco	Caleb Brown	June 14	Calcutta	Caleb Brown
Alexandra	June 1	Calcutta	Jno. F. Ainscow	July 11	Calcutta	J. Kenworthy
Rajmahal	July 7	Calcutta	Hugh Campbell	Sept 6	Calcutta	H. Campbell
Mahanada	July 16	Calcutta	A. G. Marley	Aug 15	Calcutta	A. G. Marley
Baroda	July 29	Calcutta	William Ellery	Sept 20	Calcutta	Wm. Ellery
Burdwan (At London)	Aug 4	Singapore	Henry B. Brown	Sept 13	Anjer	H. B. Brown
Candahar	Sept 17	Calcutta	Allan McKenzie	Oct 25	Calcutta	A. McKenzie
Majestic	Oct 16	Calcutta	Thos. Crosby Potts	Dec 6	Calcutta	T. C. Potts
Cambay	Oct 20	Calcutta	Walter S. Holmes	Dec 20	Calcutta	Edmund Toden
Bowfell	Dec 9	Calcutta	James Connell	Jan 18 1878	Calcutta	James Connell
Tenasserim	Dec 22	Calcutta	R. J. Balderston	Feb 2 1878	Calcutta	R. J. Balderston
Chinsura	Dec 24	Calcutta	Joseph Forshaw	Feb 18 1878	Calcutta	J. F. Ainscow

December 1883 under the command of Capt Beans, but alas was never seen again. Many Cumberland built craft, such as the *Fairy*, reached a ripe old age before being lost or taken out of service, but none to my knowledge ever reached the age of the famous Fisher family brig *Kitty*, commanded for eight years by my ancestor John Glover.

The sailing vessel *Kitty* was one of the best known, and certainly most interesting, vessels ever to be built and registered at the port of Whitehaven. She was built in 1765 by the well known shipbuilder William Palmer, a man responsible for building at least ten ships, and probably many more. He was born in 1702, and died about the close of 1778. William Palmer built the *Kitty* on the site of the Whitehaven Patent Slip – upon which construction she was attended to on many occasions.

The *Kitty* was constructed to the order of Capt B. Fisher, her first master, whom we may perhaps assume was related to Capt Wilson Fisher, ancestor of the present Brocklebank family. Captain B. Fisher remained in command of the *Kitty* for 21 years, but died suddenly whilst in command of his vessel on the 24th May 1786, whilst on passage from Dublin to Whitehaven. He was 70 years of age.

The *Kitty* was remarkable, amongst other things, for the very few captains she had since she was launched; and for the fact that she remained for all her many years afloat, the property of the Fisher family of Whitehaven.

She was repaired and renovated many times during her long life, but in 1860 she underwent a thorough overhaul in the same yard where she was originally built, at which

The Kitty, *first command of Capt John Glover.*

time she had 12 feet added to her length. The addition being made to her aft caused her to have a very narrow stern – a most noticeable feature of the ship in her later years. The staunch old *Kitty* was said to be a remarkably successful money-making ship; John Glover commanded her from 1816 until 1824, which term of service certainly enabled him to amass sufficient capital to buy his own ship, the *Massereene*. Apart from this aspect of the *Kitty* she was also a remarkably safe vessel to sail in, for it is said she never met with a single casualty of any importance up to the time she was lost. Writing about her in the early years of this century, Joseph Wear, who served his time aboard the *Kitty* had this to say about her:

'I was always interested in the old brig, so I joined her as an apprentice, to serve five years for the princely wage of £40 for that period. That was in 1865, and she was then 100 years old. She was a splendid sea-going ship. Her registered tonnage was 137 tons; but after the additon made to her she carried about 250 tons.
I well remember my first voyage. We left this port along with a large fleet of vessels which had been lying wind-bound, and the old *Kitty* was the second ship to anchor on Cardiff mud, the first being the brigantine *Excel*, a vessel built some 60 or 70 years after *Kitty*. We had a mixed crew of eight. The master (Captain M. Shealor) was a Dutchman; the mate, an Irishman; cook, a Manxman; three able-seamen, two Irish and one Dutch; an Irish apprentice belonging to Drogheda, and myself (English).'

The brig was lost when she was 118 years old. On November 18th 1883, she loaded a cargo of 244 tons of flint and 11 tons of whiting at Dieppe, France, for Runcorn, and sailed with a crew of six hands. On December 3rd, owing to stress of weather, she put into Falmouth, leaving the latter place on December 12th. This was the end of the poor old *Kitty*! She foundered, and was never seen again.

The year 1883 which had seen the loss of the *Rajmahal* also saw the sale of the *Mahanada* and the *Chinsura*, these sales reducing the fleet to 11 vessels. In 1884 the firm also sold the *Cambay* to Norwegian owners, and then on the 16th August 1885 the firm's 23-year-old vessel *Burdwan* was proceeding through the Gaspar Straits, under the command of Capt H. Woodward when she was wrecked at Pulo Leat, in the Macclesfield Channel. Captain Woodward and his crew were, thankfully, all saved. With this loss, the fleet was further reduced to nine ships, but the number was brought up to 12 by the addition of the *Bactria*, *Zemindar* and *Talookdar*, Capt William Ellery being appointed commander of the latter vessel in August 1885.

On Friday the 21st May 1886 a telegram was received at the Liverpool offices of Thomas & John Brocklebank bringing news of the loss of the *Bowfell*. The telegram, from Batavia, stated that the s.s. *Tambora* had picked up a boat containing five hands from the wreck of the British ship *Bowfell*, which struck on Discovery Shoals, E.S.E. of Milliton.

The *Bowfell* had left Manila bound for Liverpool with a cargo of sugar, and the steamer *Tambora* belonging to the Netherland-India Steam Navigation Company picked up the Captain and five of the crew soon after the vessel struck. Captain Smith reported that two other boats had left the *Bowfell* containing a further 16 men, and that he feared that they were lost, but happily he was wrong for the following day both boats came into Batavia. The *Bowfell* was not altogether a very lucky ship, for only a few years previous to this she had been in collision with the Wallasey ferry steamer *Gem*. This collision occurred during dense fog, and unfortunately several persons lost their lives.

Departures 1886			
Ship	Master	Sailed	For
Baroda	J. Healy	May 22	Calcutta
Bolan	H. Campbell	Mar 8	Calcutta
Alexandra	Daniel Cochran	June 17	Calcutta
Tenasserim	Alex. J. Orr	Apr 21	Calcutta
Candahar	Wm. D. Peterkin	May 5	Calcutta
Zemindar	Allan McKenzie	July 16	Calcutta
Kyber	Chas. J. Russell	Aug 28	Calcutta
Belfast	A. G. Marley	Oct 18	Calcutta
Talookdar	Wm. Ellery	Oct 29	Calcutta
Majestic	Alex. J. Orr	Dec 13	Calcutta
Bactria	R. J. Balderston	Dec 28	Calcutta

'Early yesterday morning a most disastrous collision occured in the Mersey, resulting in the sinking of the fine iron ship *Baroda* belonging to Messrs T. & J. Brocklebank of this City. From the information we have received it appears that the *Baroda* was inward bound from Calcutta in tow of the tug *Kingfisher*, and the iron ship *Buccleuch* outward bound in tow of the steamtug *Ranger*. When near the South Battery, north wall, they collided with the above result. The *Buccleuch* struck the *Baroda* on the starboard side and in about 20 minutes, the *Baroda*, which was loaded with wheat, linseed &c. sank. The *Buccleuch* anchored near to the wreck, and it was observed that she had sustained some serious damage, her bows being stove in, and fore-compartment full of water.

The *Buccleuch* docked with the afternoon's tide at Birkenhead. Fortunately no lives are reported as having been lost. The *Baroda* is an iron sailing ship of 1,364 net tonnage, built in Belfast, by Messrs Harland & Wolff in 1865 and commanded by Capt. Healy.

The *Buccleuch* is also an iron sailing ship and was built at Liverpool by Messrs T. B. Royden & Sons in 1885 having a net tonnage of 1,991. Her owners are Messrs W. H. Ross and Co. and she is commanded by Captain Grose. This collision makes the third as having occured in the River Mersey during the last week, the others being the *Ajax*, and the *Qui Vive*, and the *Comeragh* and the *Iowa*. Two of the *Baroda*'s masts only are visible, the other having been smashed.'
(From Liverpool 'Journal of Commerce' – Monday 21st November 1887)

The 'Sindia' and the 'Holkar' the Last of Brocklebank's Sailers

Both the great 'windjammers' *Sindia* and *Holkar* were built at Belfast by Messrs Harland & Wolff, the former in 1887, and the latter in 1888, the *Sindia* being a vessel of 3,007 tons, and the *Holkar* two tons larger at 3,009. At the time of their launch they were amongst the largest sailing vessels the world had ever seen, for both of these great Brocklebank vessels carried a cargo of some 5,000 tons deadweight. These ships were built of steel, not iron, they had steel spars, double topsail and topgallant yards; both were fitted with the latest contrivances for working the ships, and for their loading and discharging.

131

The *Sindia* sailed from Liverpool on her maiden voyage to Calcutta on the 1st February 1888, under the command of Capt Allan McKenzie, whilst the *Holkar* was despatched from the Mersey to the Hooghly on her first voyage on the 8th June 1888, her master for this voyage being Capt William Ellery. This voyage was specially notable for Capt Ellery since it brought to a close his sailing ship experience of over 32 years. On the completion of this voyage he handed over command of the *Holkar* to his colleague, Capt Charles J. Russell. Writing in 1912 about his days as commander of the *Holkar* Capt. Ellery wrote as follows:

'The sailor always finds it pleasing to see the British shore rising above the horizon after a voyage, and I felt this genuine thrill in the good ship *Holkar*, as under a pressof canvas in a stiff Nor' wester, she bounded up channel in February 1889, at her best speed, the Tuskar lighthouse meanwhile flashing her welcome from the Irish coast. Passing the Skerries the following

Entrance to Prince's Dock, c 1874.

132

morning, it is also delightful to take the bearings of the old familiar landmarks leading to the Pilot Station at Point Lynas. Then with home flag, ensign, and signals hoisted and fluttering in the breeze, we round to the wind and with the sails on main and mizzen aback and the ship stopped, the pilot climbs on board. With a broad smile, a hearty hand shake, and a cheery welcome home he hauls out the inevitable pocketful of crumpled newspapers, probably about a week old, but nonetheless precious, as conveying tidings of the dear homeland. "Up helm" is then the word, and we square away and head for the North West Light Ship. Sail is gradually reduced and with a crisp northerly breeze, and the tide two hours ebb, we pass New Brighton and proceed to the Sloyne, where we anchor. Soon afterwards the tug comes alongside with the docking order, and at night we are safely berthed at the Herculaneum Dock, after a pleasant passage of precisely 100 days from Calcutta.'

1893 Arrivals and Departures (Sailing Vessels) Recorded at the Offices of Thos. & Jno. Brocklebank, Rumford Street

Ship		Arrived	From	Master	Sailed	For	Master
Holkar	(At London)	Mar 9	Calcutta	William Peterkin	May 2	Calcutta	Wm Peterkin
Zemindar	(At Dundee)	Apr 4	Calcutta	William V. Graham	May 12	Calcutta	W. V. Graham
Majestic	(At London)	May 26	Calcutta	J. J. Nicholson	Aug 11	Calcutta	J. J. Nicholson
Belfast	(At Dundee)	Sept 3	Calcutta	John Smith	*Oct 11	Calcutta	John Smith
Bactria	(At London)	Sept 24	Calcutta	Walter Cornish	*Oct 29	Calcutta	W. Cornish
Sindia	(At London)	Dec 11	Calcutta	Daniel Cochran	*Feb 4 1894	Calcutta	D. Cochran

* ex Middlesboro'

CHAPTER 14

From Sail to Steam

In the year 1889 the ancient house of Brocklebank purchased the steamer *Ameer*, built to their order by Messrs Harland & Wolff. She was a ship of 4,000 tons gross with a deadweight capacity of 6,450 tons. Despite Brocklebanks' late move into steam the *Ameer* was amongst the finest and most advanced ships of her day; she had a triple expansion engine and could maintain a useful speed of ten knots, and at the time of her construction she was one of the largest vessels passing regularly through the Suez Canal.

In order to facilitate the change over to steam, Brocklebanks' Marine Superintendent and a few senior captains were sent on cruises in steam vessels belonging to other firms. When the *Ameer* first left for Calcutta on the 27th October 1889 she was under the command of Capt William Ray, the firm's Superintendent – the man once apprenticed under Capt Francis Wise on the brig *Rimac*. As she sailed down the Mersey on that historic day the ship's company was as follows:

Capt William Ray	Master
Capt William Ellery	1st Mate
Capt Allan McKenzie	2nd Mate
J. G. Simpson	3rd Mate (Master's Certificate)
J. Cooke	4th Mate (Master's Certificate)
Chief Engineer	
Engineer Officers	
Two Stewards	
Two Cooks	
One Donkeyman	
Fourteen greasers, firemen and trimmers	
Twelve A.Bs	

The *Gaekwar* of similar design and tonnage was purchased from the famous Belfast yard in 1890, but in our long story which deals with the history of the Brocklebank Line, and Messrs Robert & Henry Jefferson's of Whitehaven, the first voyage of the *Ameer* has a particular significance, which we should mention at this point. When she returned to London from Calcutta on the 2nd December 1891 she was under the command of Capt W. D. Peterkin – close friend of Capt William Ray. Captain Peterkin's 2nd mate however was none other than Mr Henry Jefferson of Whitehaven, direct descendant of Capt Henry

134

Jefferson – founder of the ancient firm of Robert and Henry Jefferson of Whitehaven. He was however a young man who was destined to play a more significant role in the development of the Brocklebank Line than that of 2nd mate to Capt Peterkin!

Whilst 1889 was clearly a year of great significance in the history of the Brocklebank Line, it was not to be one without loss. The *Bolan* with a crew of 34, including six apprentices, under the command of Capt W. P. Hughes, left the Hooghly bound for London on the 27th April. On the 5th July she was spoken in position 33 S and 32 E – but alas was never to be seen again! It would seem that shortly afterwards very bad weather was reported off the Cape of Good Hope, and a number of large vessels in the vicinity disappeared without trace – which number we must assume included the *Bolan*.

With the launch of the *Ameer* in 1889 the days of sail for the Brocklebank fleet were at long last drawing to a close – but as might be imagined with the Brocklebank Line, the transitional period between moving from sail to steam was spread over a number of years. Clearly it could only have been with some reluctance that the Line broke with its one and a quarter century tradition of trading in sail.

Shortly after obtaining the *Ameer* and the *Gaekwar* from the Belfast yard of Harland & Wolff, another order was placed with this firm for the twin screw *Pindari*, which was launched in 1891, followed by the launch of the *Mahratta (1)* at Belfast in 1892 – a ship of 5,679 tons. However, from this date no other steamers were built to the order of Thos. & Jno. Brocklebank until Messrs Gourley Brothers of Dundee built for the Line the 5,659 ton ship *Marwarri (1)* in 1900, and the *Bengali* in 1901. From this date there was a significant break in launches until 1905–6, when the firm returned once more to Messrs Harland & Wolff in Belfast, who built for them the *Mahronda (1)* and the *Malakand (1)* in 1905, and the *Manipur (1)* and the 7,654 ton *Matheran (1)* in 1906. The period when the Brocklebank Line was trading in sail and steam lasted for over a decade – from the launch of the *Ameer* in 1889, to the sale of the *Holkar* in 1901. Thus we find that the firm was trading seven sailing ships – the *Holkar, Zemindar, Majestic, Belfast, Bactria, Sindia,* and *Khyber,* and only four steamers – the *Ameer, Gaekwar, Pindari,* and *Mahratta.* The balance was not to swing in favour of steam until 1898/9. In the former year the sailers *Khyber, Bactria,* and *Zemindar* were sold, which was followed by the sale of the *Belfast* in 1899; all of which left the firm with a fleet of seven ships in 1899 – four steamers and three sailers.

In the mid 1890s however the Mersey rarely saw the great windjammers of the Brocklebank fleet for although ships such as the *Sindia* made her first four voyages from the Mersey, increasingly the sailing ships of the fleet would now return to London from Calcutta, load at Middlesbrough, or Dundee, and never visit the Mersey. For a short period in 1901 the great windjammer *Holkar* was the firm's only sailing ship – until her sale later in that year; Capt Dunning having the honour of commanding the last sailing ship of the world's oldest shipping Company!

The sale of the *Holkar* however has a particular significance for this interrelated story of two shipping companies, and a family of 19th century mariners, and their colleagues; for the first commander of this ship had been Capt William Ellery, a man now aged 62, who had once served on ships such as the *Patriot King* and the *Tigris*, ships once commanded by Capt George Wise – a man whose father had been born at Cockermouth in 1784! Ellery

135

was to survive and leave us a written account of his many adventures – which account he published in the 'Wallasey and Wirral Chronicle' in 1912 – and which I have used in this work. He died in September 1924, the Chronicle writing about him in these terms:

'There were laid to rest at Anfield cemetery Liverpool on Wednesday the remains of a well known and highly respected resident in the person of Capt. W. Ellery of "Holkar" Orrell Road, who passed away on Monday at the advanced age of 85 years. The deceased gentleman, who settled in Wallasey on his retirement from Sea Service in 1903 had an unique distinction of having been forty seven years in the services of Brocklebank & Co. Ltd., in the early days of sailing ships and later in command of steamers of that Line. Some years ago Capt. Ellery contributed a series of articles to the Chronicle giving in an interesting and racy style his experiences of adventures from the first day he stepped onto the barque *Hindoo* 265 tons register, for a voyage to the Brazils in 1856 as an apprentice, until the year 1903 when he handed over the command of the steamer *Marwarri* on his retirement. The articles attracted considerable attention and were widely read.'

The old generation were now giving way to the new – Ralph Brocklebank Snr., partner in the firm for over 43 years, and a much respected citizen of Liverpool died in 1892. He was 89 years old. The 'Liverpool Courier' summed up the feelings of many when they published the following obituary:

'... While Mr Ralph Brocklebank for many years guided this great mercantile enterprise, and was consequently a busy man, he nevertheless found time to labour advantageously in the cause of public and benevolent undertakings. For over thirty years he was one of the most active and judicious members of the bodies administering the affairs of the Mersey Docks – first the old Dock Committee of the Corporation and then the Mersey Docks and Harbour Board which superseded it – and he worked assiduously and successfully to promote such dock improvements and extensions as growing ships and development necessitated.... In the sphere of philanthropy, too, Mr Brocklebank was as earnest as in other enterprises. Though he gave liberally, while unostentatiously, to various charitable undertakings – and especially those provided for seafarers and their bereaved families – he was not content with merely loosening his purse strings, but took an active and personal interest in the various institutions.'

Sir Thomas Brocklebank retired from the business on the 31st December, 1894, handing over his shares to his sons, Thomas and Harold, who had become partners in the early eighties. Sir Thomas had been a partner for 51 years, and was Senior Partner for 49 years, taking over that position from his uncle Thomas Brocklebank, who died in 1845, and who previously held that position for 45 years, so that the control of the firm was in the hands of these two men for the astonishing period of 94 years. If Daniel Brocklebank's period of control of 31 years is added to this figure it makes a total of 125 years for these three individuals. In the year of Sir Thomas Brocklebank's retirement the firm was still mainly in sail. The fleet numbered 11 ships, and seven of these were sailers.

Sir Thomas Brocklebank, the only son of Capt Wilson Fisher, died at Springwood, Woolton on Friday the 8th June 1906, in his 92nd year, and was buried at Halewood Church, near Liverpool. His activities had overspanned the Victorian era at both ends. Blessed with a fine physique the deceased Baronet had hardly in the course of his long life known a day's illness, and up until a few years before his death he took riding exercises daily. His successor in the Baronetage was his eldest son, Mr Thomas Brocklebank of Irton Hall, Cumberland, and the Hollies, Woolton, Liverpool.

When Sir Thomas Brocklebank died in 1906 the firm were trading ten ships – all of them steamers, these vessels being the *Ameer*, *Gaekwar*, *Pindari*, *Mahratta*, *Marwarri*, *Bengali*, *Mahronda*, *Malakand*, *Matheran*, and the *Manipur*. This tonnage constituted a surplus to requirements on the Calcutta service, and in view of this situation the firm started a new service, in which some of the fleet were traded from Antwerp to Singapore, China and Japan.

In 1911 the firm's famous Marine Superintendent, Capt William Ray – once a lively young apprentice serving his time aboard the Cape Horn brig *Rimac* with Capt Francis Wise – retired from his post. As fate would have it he was succeeded by Capt Henry Jefferson, descendant of Capt Robert Jefferson, founder of the still existent firm of Robert & Henry Jefferson of Whitehaven! Jefferson who had served on the sailing vessels *Kyber*, *Talookdar* and *Bactria*, and had been master of the *Ameer*, joined the Royal Navy in 1895, but returned to Brocklebanks after attaining the rank of Commander R.N.

The following year Brocklebanks purchased the Calcutta Conference rights of the Anchor Line and four of their ships. This firm had now been running ships to Calcutta for almost 30 years, all the ordinary shares of the Line being held by Cunard, and both Sir Alfred Booth and Lord Royden being at this time directors of both the Cunard Line and the Anchor Line. The interests of the three firms began to draw together – but the complete incorporation of the Brocklebank Line into Cunard-Brocklebank was not formally ratified until 1940.

During the first decades of this century the firm's steamer fleet began to grow in a manner redolent of the increase of their sailing fleet in the early years of the last century. However, the First World War dealt the firm a heavy blow, no less than five ships being lost to enemy action in 1917, and a further vessel the following year.

In the autumn of 1918 it was agreed that the Cunard Line would buy the shares held by the Brocklebank and Bates interests, the remaining 40 per cent shareholding being held by the Anchor Line, which were not to be bought until 1940. These financial moves however made little difference to the day-to-day management of the firm, Sir Aubrey Brocklebank remaining as Chairman. After his death in 1929 he was succeeded as Chairman by Colonel Dennis Bates.

On the 28th April 1926 Capt William Ray, late Marine Superintendent of the oldest shipping company in the world, died at his home, Hallgarth, Brynaston Road, Birkenhead. He was in his 88th year. His mortal remains were laid to rest at a small country churchyard in the Wirral. Amongst those present at the moving ceremony were many master mariners of the Brocklebank Line – notably his old friend and colleague, Capt Peterkin, once commander of the great windjammers *Sindia* and *Holkar*. Also present at this ceremony was the old mariner's grandson – Mr J. H. Ray, who today, in the 1980s, helped me locate material on the Brocklebank Line used in this work. Captain Ray was held in such high regard by the Company that at the time of his death the house flag over the Brocklebank offices and on their ships around the globe were lowered to half-mast.

In 1929 the Polish Government pensioned off their Merchant Marine Training Ship – the sailing barque *Lwow*, which vessel had in fact been built at Birkenhead in 1868 as the

Brocklebank Indiaman *Chinsura* – the last command of Capt Francis Wise. And so it was that the long and romantic history of the great sailing fleet of Thomas & John Brocklebank finally came to a close.

At the outbreak of the Second World War the Brocklebank fleet numbered 25 vessels, but the fleet were to suffer terrible losses during this war. It clearly goes beyond the scope of this book to detail this aspect of the Brocklebank history, but it can be noted that no less than 16 vessels were lost during the period of hostilities.

In 1948, soon after the Second World War, the Brocklebank Line were trading 21 ships; this firm founded by Capt Daniel Brocklebank was soon to become known as Cunard-Brocklebank, for it was destined to become an integral part of the world's most prestigious shipping line – Cunard, owners of the world's most luxurious ocean liner – the *Q.E.2*. If only time could be distorted and we could allow the ancient mariners of the Brocklebank Line a glimpse of this great ship – the successor of such vessels as the tiny *Castor*, *Swallow* and *Westmorland*! But I wonder how they would react to such a manifestation – would they be filled with admiration and awe, or would they merely be reduced to a state of terror and shock?

Today, in the closing decades of the 20th century, we certainly wonder at the undoubted beauty of ships such as the *Q.E.2*, and ponder upon the skill of our present day craftsmen who can create such vessels. But the brigs and brigantines and barques of yesteryear, with their towering masts and snow white sails were uniquely beautiful, and a magnificent tribute to the skill of the craftsmen who produced them. It is certain that mankind will never forget these ships – the 'Wandering Beauties' of yesteryear – in the great days of sail.

It is perhaps even more certain that mankind will never forget the skilled and courageous mariners of the Brocklebank Line, and Jeffersons of Whitehaven. Men who endured almost unimaginable hardship whilst navigating their tiny vessels to the farthest points of the globe – quite literally – from Cumberland to Cape Horn. It is to their collective memory that I dedicate this modest record.

> In the still watches of the tropic night,
> When meditation throws the years behind,
> I see again the old remembered sight
> Of towering canvas in the wind.
> But time's relentless hand has turned a page:
> The lovely ships have faded like a dream,
> Discarded with the debris of an age,
> On evolution's ever-flowing stream.

(From Voices from the Sea, by
kind permission of the Marine Society)

THE END

Appendix A

Fleet List of Sailing Vessels Owned and/or Built by Brocklebanks

Notes: 1. The numerical sequence includes – at Nos. 100 and 124 – two paddle steamers, the only such vessels built by Brocklebanks.

          2. Both the Brocklebank and the Jefferson Fleet Lists have been compiled by reference to a variety of sources, which sometimes offer contradictory information. This is particularly true of the rigs attributed to various vessels – for instance brig or brigantine. In some cases this is because the vessel in question actually underwent a change of rig during its lifetime; in others it may be due to the fact that then – as now! – opinions differed as to the correct classification of certain sail-plans.

1–4. 'The first four ships'
Built 1770–75 by Daniel Brocklebank at Sheepscutt
It is known that four ships were built at Sheepscutt by Daniel Brocklebank between 1770 and 1775, but no conclusive evidence has been found regarding their size, rig or tonnage. There are indications however that these may have been the *Minerva*, *Hector*, *Nestor* and *Jane*.

5. *Castor* (1) (1775)
20 gun brig
220 tons
Built at Sheepscutt.
The last ship to be built in America by Capt Daniel Brocklebank, who brought the vessel back to Whitehaven in 1775. The vessel was later commanded by Capt Williamson. The *Castor* was in service six years, and traded to New York and the West Indies. She was wrecked at Jamaica in 1781.

6. *Pollux* renamed *Precedent* (1780)
6 gun ship
Built by Spedding and Co., Whitehaven
301 tons
94 ft 11 ins × 27 ft 4 ins × 18 ft 0 ins
The *Precedent* was traded to America by Capt Brocklebank and Capt Williamson. In 1787 she was placed in the Greenland whaling trade and commanded by Capt Benn and then by Capt Wise; she was wrecked off the coast of Ireland in 1791 whilst under the command of Capt Wise.

7. *Castor* (2) (1782)
18 gun ship
343 tons
Built by Spedding & Company, Whitehaven
103 ft 6 ins × 28 ft 9 ins × 18 ft 6 ins
Commanded by Capt Daniel Brocklebank until 1786, then commanded by Capts Richardson and Storey. Traded to Philadelphia, the West Indies and New York. Sold in 1789. In service seven years.

8. *Cyrus* (1786)
   6 gun brig
   Built by Spedding & Co., Whitehaven
   81 ft 6 ft × 23 ft 0 ins × 14 ft 0 ins
   Commanded by Capt Harrison. Traded to America, Jamaica, St. Petersberg and Ireland. Sold in 1797 after being in Company service for 11 years. Last recorded owner Bell & Co. Liverpool. Whilst on passage from Liverpool to the Bahamas in 1814 was condemned at Bermuda as being unseaworthy.

9. *Zebulon* (1787)
   187 tons
   Built by Henry Stockdale & Co. at Whitehaven
   79 ft 8 ins × 23 ft 8 ins × 15 ft 8 ins (Brig)
   This vessel remained in Company service for eight years, being sold in 1795. She was traded by Brocklebanks to Carolina, New York, Virginia, London, France and Ireland. Capt Hodgson was her commander.

10. *Dolphin* (1788)
    75 tons
    Built by Henry Stockdale & Co. at Whitehaven
    55 ft 10 ins × 18 ft 4½ ins × 10 ft 3 ins (Brig)
    In service eight years, traded to Chester, Ireland and Europe. First commander Capt Kelsick, followed by Capt Brocklebank (1789–91), the last Company commander being Capt Fleming. (The *Dolphin* was jointly owned by Daniel Brocklebank and William Atkinson.)

11. *Perseverence (1)* (1788)
    155 tons
    Built by Daniel Brocklebank at Whitehaven
    No other details known.

12. *Hero* (1788)
    Brig
    174 tons
    Built by Daniel Brocklebank at Whitehaven
    77 ft 6 ins × 23 ft 6 ins × 14 ft 0 ins
    Sold in 1796, in service eight years, during that period commanded by Capt Stewart, traded to Virginia, St. Petersburg, Ireland, and coastally.

13. *Mackerel (1)* (1790)
    Cutter
    12 tons
    Built by Daniel Brocklebank at Whitehaven
    30 ft 10 ins × 10 ft 10 ins × 4 ft 3 ins
    Daniel Brocklebank was the sole owner of this cutter, no partners being involved. The vessel's master was John Kneale, she remained in service until the 4th April 1795, on which date she was seized and condemned by the exchequer and broken up.

14. *Castor (3)* (1790)
    Brig
    197 tons
    Built by Daniel Brocklebank at Whitehaven
    82 ft 0 ins × 24 ft 3 ins × 15 ft 10 ins
    The *Castor* (3) was built for Capt J. Storey, being sold to him upon completion. This brig was afloat for 42 years, but was wrecked in 1832. Daniel Brocklebank retained a share in this vessel after its sale to Capt Storey, the sole owners being Daniel Brocklebank, John Storey, and John Sargent. (Next sale was to Capt Sims – 1797.)

15. *Rockliff* (1790)
    Brig
    127 tons

Built by Daniel Brocklebank at Whitehaven
No records found, but usually listed as a Brocklebank vessel.

16. *Scipio* (1) (1790)
    Brig
    180 tons
    Built by Daniel Brocklebank at Whitehaven, later rebuilt by Shepherd & Co., Whitehaven
    78 ft 5 ins × 24 ft 0 ins × 15 ft 5 ins
    First registered on the 24th Dec 1790, jointly owned by Daniel Brocklebank, John Richardson and Nich. Thompson. Commanded by Capt William Birkett. In service until the 27th Feb 1795, when she was sold and re-registered at Dublin.

17. *Hope* (1788)
    Brig
    151 tons
    Built at Whitby
    70 ft 11 ins × 21 ft 10½ ins × 14 ft 0 ins
    Bought by Daniel Brocklebank, and re-registered at Whitehaven on the 16th April 1791. Made one voyage for the Company under the command of Capt Thomas Sherlock, and was then sold and re-registered at Liverpool on the 26th August, just over four months after being bought. End not known.

18. *Castor* (4) (1791)
    Brig
    247 tons
    Built by Daniel Brocklebank at Whitehaven
    88 ft 8 ins × 28 ft 0 ins × 16 ft 6 ins
    Registered at Whitehaven, May 12th 1791. Owners being John Curwen & Co., the brig's commander however being Capt Daniel Brocklebank Jnr. She was traded to Virginia, Halifax, and Ireland, no doubt on joint Curwen/Brocklebank account. Lost near Galway in Ireland in March 1794.

19. *Ann* (1791)
    Brig
    65 tons
    Built by Daniel Brocklebank at Whitehaven
    Sold upon completion to W. Glover, Leith. Last recorded owner Oswald and Co. Made voyages to Danzig and Dublin.

20. *Nestor* (1792)
    6 gun ship
    233 tons
    Built by Daniel Brocklebank at Whitehaven
    88 ft 11 ins × 25 ft 0 ins × 15 ft 10 ins
    Traded to Cork, Philadelphia, Pillau and Lubeck. First commander Capt Birkett (1791–94), then by Capt Thompson (1795). The vessel was captured by the French whilst under the command of Capt Thompson in 1795. In service three years.

21. *Grampus* (1792)
    Brig
    87 tons
    Built by Daniel Brocklebank at Whitehaven
    62 ft 2 ins × 18 ft 5 ins × 10 ft 6 ins
    Registered on the 14th July 1792, the owners being Messrs. Thompson and Richardson. The master was Capt William Clague. She was lost off Plymouth on the 20th August.

22. *Triton* (1793)
    Brig
    204 tons
    Built by Daniel Brocklebank at Whitehaven
    Features on some lists as a Brocklebank vessel, but no details traced.

141

23. *Irton* (1793)
    10 gun snow
    201 tons
    Built by Daniel Brocklebank at Whitehaven
    82 ft 0 ins × 24 ft 2 ins × 16 ft 0 ins
    Jointly owned by Daniel Brocklebank and Capt Isaac Thompson. Sold by them and re-registered at Liverpool on the 1st April 1794. Whilst under the command of Capt Wanlace she was lost near Orfordness, Dec 1815, whilst on passage from London for Shields.

24. *Jupiter* (1793)
    Ship
    207 tons
    Built by Daniel Brocklebank at Whitehaven
    82 ft 6 ins × 24 ft 10 ins × 16 ft 2 ins
    Traded to Waterford, St. Petersburg etc. In service three years, sold in 1796 (Nov 10th) to new owners at Newcastle.

25. *Mary Ann* (1794)
    Brig
    155 tons
    Built by Daniel Brocklebank at Whitehaven
    70 ft 6 ins × 21 ft 0 ins × 14 ft 0 ins
    Registered 1st July 1794, first commander being Capt John Johnston. Sold to Messrs Wood and Company, then to Mitchell & Co. Made voyages to Sardinia, Ireland, America and Quebec. Out of registers 1823.

26. *Dispatch* (1795)
    Brig
    102 tons
    Built by Daniel Brocklebank at Whitehaven
    70 ft 0 ins × 18 ft 6 ins × 10 ft 6 ins
    Commanded by Capt Brocklebank and traded to Spain and Libau. Sold in 1796, lost in 1802.

27. *Jane* (1795)
    Brig
    124 tons
    Built by Daniel Brocklebank at Whitehaven
    69 ft 0 ins × 20 ft 7½ ins × 12 ft 0 ins
    First registered at Whitehaven on the 16th April 1795 by the sole owner, Daniel Brocklebank, Capt William Larkin being placed in command. In service only until the 31st Oct 1796, when sold and re-registered at Liverpool.

28. *Jane & Sarah* (1795)
    6 gun snow
    158 tons
    Built by Daniel Brocklebank at Whitehaven
    79 ft 4 ins × 22 ft 6 ins × 14 ft 6 ins
    Sold upon completion to Steele & Co. Whilst under the command of Capt Brown bound for St. Andrew's, New Brunswick, was rammed and sunk at sea on 25th Oct 1810; crew picked up by the *Clothier*, and landed at Philadelphia.

29. *Cavereene* (1795)
    Brig
    127 tons
    Built by Daniel Brocklebank at Whitehaven
    61 ft 6 ins × 20 ft 6 ins × 12 ft 8 ins
    No further details known.

30. *Carrier* (1795)
   Brig
   127 tons
   Built by Daniel Brocklebank at Whitehaven
   69 ft 0 ins × 20 ft 8 ins × 12 ft 0 ins
   Sold in 1797, wrecked at Whitehaven in 1830. Whilst in service made voyages to Danzig under the command of Capt Folder.

31. *Alert* (1796)
   Brig
   85 tons
   Built by Daniel Brocklebank at Whitehaven
   57 ft 2 ins × 18 ft 9 ins × 10 ft 0 ins
   Traded to Libau in 1797 under the command of Capt Barrow. In service two years, sold in 1798.

32. *Alfred* (1796)
   2 gun ship
   314 tons
   Built by Daniel Brocklebank at Whitehaven
   95 ft 0 ins × 27 ft 0 ins × 17 ft 0 ins
   In service two years but sold in 1798. Afloat 51 years, crushed in the ice, Davis Straights 1847. The first commander of this ship was Capt Danl. Brocklebank Jnr. In 1798 she was commanded by Capt J. Ward.

33. *Scipio* (2) (1797)
   16 gun brig
   242 tons
   Built by Daniel Brocklebank at Whitehaven
   85 ft 0 ins × 25 ft 4 ins × 16 ft 10 ins
   Traded to Martinique, Carolina, and Wilmington, under the command of Capt Brocklebank. In service two years, sold in 1799.

34. *Duncan* (1798)
   16 gun ship
   239 tons
   Built by Daniel Brocklebank at Whitehaven
   85 ft 0 ins × 25 ft 4 ins × 16 ft 10 ins
   Sold the year following her construction (1799). She was afloat for 13 years but was lost whilst on passage from Jamaica for Dublin on the Cayman Islands in 1810.

35. *Earl of Lonsdale* (1) (1798)
   Smack
   61 tons
   Built by Daniel Brocklebank at Whitehaven
   51 ft 0 ins × 16 ft 11 ins × 8 ft 8 ins
   This vessel was a 'square sterned smack', her subscribers being Isaih Greenlow, Daniel Brocklebank, and Edward Penny. Her 'non-subscribers' included William Penny and Samuel Potter – all Whitehaven Merchants. The smack's first master was the above 'subscriber' Isaih Greenlow. The vessel was sold at Liverpool on the 2nd Aug 1799.

36. *Ceres* (1798)
   Brig
   93 tons
   Built by Daniel Brocklebank at Whitehaven
   66 ft 3 ins × 18 ft 1 in × 10 ft 5 ins
   Daniel Brocklebank was the sole owner of this vessel, Capt Francis Hutchinson was the master. Taken by the French and sunk on the 29th June 1799 whilst on passage from Whitehaven to Hull and when about four leagues from Duncans Head.

143

37. *Montgomery* (1799)
   12 gun ship
   190 tons
   Built by Daniel Brocklebank at Whitehaven
   84 ft 0 ins × 22 ft 9 ins × 15 ft 5 ins
   Named after her master, Capt John Montgomery, first registered by Daniel Brocklebank on July 16th, re-registered at Belfast on 20th Aug 1799.

38. *Ariel* (1) (1800)
   14 gun ship
   238 tons
   Built by Daniel Brocklebank at Whitehaven
   86 ft 6 ins × 25 ft 3 ins × 16 ft 6 ins
   Commanded by Capt Fox who made one voyage to Virginia for the firm before the ship was sold in 1801. Afloat for 39 years.

39. *Active* (1800)
   Brig
   134 tons
   Built by Daniel Brocklebank at Whitehaven
   70 ft 0 ins × 20 ft 0 ins × 13 ft 4 ins
   First commander was Capt David Merrie, sole owner at first registration being Daniel Brocklebank. Re-registered at Whitehaven 7th April 1808 (No. 32).

40. *Cumberland* (1800)
   Ship
   340 tons
   Built by Daniel Brocklebank at Whitehaven
   100 ft 0 ins × 28 ft 2 ins × 18 ft 6 ins
   Last ship to be built by Daniel Brocklebank at Whitehaven before his death. Sold upon completion to Messrs Hartley & Co., then to Buchanan. Made voyages to Jamaica. Whilst under the command of Capt J. Thomas, from Jamaica to Greenock, was becalmed off Rathlin Island, 21st June 1815, and drifted onto a rock just off that place and went to pieces the next day. Crew saved by a Revenue Cruiser.

41. *General Hunter* (1801)
   Ship
   217 tons
   Built by Thomas & John Brocklebank at Bransty, Whitehaven
   85 ft 0 ins × 23 ft 6 ins × 15 ft 6 ins
   First ship to be built by founders sons, the partners Thomas & John Brocklebank. Sold upon completion, but eighth interest retained in vessel. Carried Brocklebank cargoes. Whilst under the command of Capt W. Smith from Mirimachi for Liverpool was taken and set on fire by an American privateer about ten miles south-west of Baltimore, 12th Aug 1814. Taken in tow by fishermen, beached in a creek, then burned to waters edge.

42. *Matty* (1801)
   Brigantine
   163 tons
   Thos. & Jno. Brocklebank at Bransty, Whitehaven
   76 ft 0 ins × 21 ft 6 ins × 13 ft 6 ins
   Sold upon completion to Messrs Hutchinson, made many voyages to Quebec, Dublin, Libau, New Brunswick, etc. Still in Registers in 1826.

43. *Dryad* (1) (1801)
   4 gun ship
   256 tons
   Thos. & Jno. Brocklebank at Bransty, Whitehaven
   90 ft 4 ins × 25 ft 4 ins × 16 ft 3 ins

Registered on the 24th Dec 1801, Capt John Jenkinson being the master. Traded to the West Indies. Sold and re-registered at London on 21st Nov 1805.

44. *Experiment* (1802)
Schooner
89 tons
Built by Thos. & John Brocklebank at Bransty, Whitehaven
62 ft 3 ins × 18 ft 3 ins × 9 ft 10 ins
This schooner's first master was Capt Jonathan Hodgson. Sold in 1807 to Messrs Barker & Co, then to Lyee – Capt Christianson. (When sold to Messrs Richard Barker & Co. in 1807 she was re-rigged as a brigantine.)

45. *King George* (1803)
Ship
264 tons
Built by Thos. & Jno. Brocklebank at Bransty, Whitehaven
89 ft 2 ins × 26 ft 6 ins × 17 ft 10 ins
Remained in Brocklebank service two years under the command of Capt Caffey. Sold in 1805 to Rodie & Co. Other owners include Shand & Co., Horsfall, Livingston, and Tobin & Co.

46. *Volunteer* (1803)
12 gun ship
353 tons
Built by Thos. & Jno. Brocklebank at Bransty, Whitehaven
100 ft 6 ins × 28 ft 6 ins × 18 ft 6 ins
Sold upon completion to J. Hartley & Co., Whitehaven, then to Messrs Wallace. Whilst under the command of Capt J. Ashley, on passage from Liverpool for Bahia in 1813, this ship was taken by the American frigate *Chesapeake* and carried into Portsmouth (America).

47. *Queen Charlotte* (1804)
Snow
211 tons
Built by Thos. & Jno. Brocklebank at Bransty, Whitehaven
82 ft 0 ins × 24 ft 4 ins × 16 ft 0 ins
Recorded voyages include Cork, Cadiz and Antigua. Recorded Brocklebank commanders include Capts Fearon and Nicholson. Sold in 1812. Wrecked on the Scillies on the night of Jan 27th 1815, whilst under the command of Capt W. Rayside. Four people drowned from the ship, also two pilots engaged in rescue attempts.

48. *Beaver* (1804)
Brigantine
81 tons
Built by Thos. & Jno. Brocklebank at Bransty, Whitehaven
55 ft 6 ins × 18 ft 0 ins × 9 ft 4 ins
In Brocklebank service for five years, Capt R. Brocklebank master in 1805. Recorded voyages whilst in Company service to Ross, Drogheda, Dublin and Alicante. Sold in 1809 to W. Forrest.

49. *Hercules* (1805)
6 gun ship
301 tons
Built by Thos. & Jno. Brocklebank at Bransty, Whitehaven
93 ft 10 ins × 27 ft 2 ins × 18 ft 0 ins
From 1807 to 1817 in Government service to Malta and the Cape under the command of Capt Caffey. Later commanded by Capts Kneale, Power, Lennox, and Kerr. Voyages made to New Brunswick, Savannah, Bahia, Charleston, New Orleans etc. Run down at sea in 1825.

50. *Swallow* (1) (1806)
6 gun brig
114 tons

Built by Thos. & Jno. Brocklebank at Bransty, Whitehaven
70 ft 5 ins × 19 ft 3 ins × 11 ft 7½ ins
Traded to the Baltic and Ireland for the firm. Sold to Capt Wilson Fisher, Whitehaven, merchant, and son-in-law of Daniel Brocklebank. Command given to Capt Abraham Vaux Wise (Sept 1809), who remained in command of this brig until Sept 1810, when he was given command of the Fisher/ Brocklebank brigantine *Maranham*. Re-registered at Montego Bay 1816.

51. *Brown* (1807)
8 gun snow
220 tons
Built by Thos. & Jno. Brocklebank at Bransty, Whitehaven
84 ft 8 ins × 23 ft 5 ins × 16 ft 2 ins
First registered on the 26th Feb 1807, the owners then being Richard and Wm. Whiteside, with Thos. & Jno. Brocklebank retaining a share in the vessel. The vessel's first master was Capt Wilson Fisher, the father of Thomas Fisher – who became by a name change at a later date, Thomas Brocklebank.

52. *Ariel* (2) (1807)
10 gun brig
204 tons
Built by Thos. & Jno. Brocklebank at Bransty, Whitehaven
82 ft 6 ins × 23 ft 11 ins × 15 ft 3 ins
Only in service two years. Recorded voyages to Cork. Captured by the French in 1809.

53. *Dryad* (2) (1808)
6 gun brig
220 tons
Built by Thos. & Jno. Brocklebank at Bransty, Whitehaven
85 ft 0 ins × 23 ft 6 ins × 16 ft 3 ins
In service two years, voyaged to the West Indies and Newfoundland. Whilst under the command of Capt J. Gunston was wrecked in St. Mary's Bay, Newfoundland, in mid-August 1810; two boys drowned.

54. *Maranham* (1809)
Brigantine
154 tons
Built by Thos. & Jno. Brocklebank at Bransty, Whitehaven
74 ft 1 in × 21 ft 10 ins × 13 ft 6 ins
Sole owners, Thomas & John Brocklebank, till Sept 1810. Wilson Fisher and others, incl. Jno. Brocklebank Jnr. then became owners. Capt Abraham Vaux Wise then given command of this brigantine until Feb 1814. Capt John Holliday then given command. Capt W. Osborne given command 6th Dec 1814. Wrecked Isle-of-Man 16th Dec 1814.

55. *Balfour* (1809)
10 gun brig
310 tons
Built by Thos. & Jno. Brocklebank at Bransty, Whitehaven
96 ft 10 ins × 27 ft 0 ins × 18 ft 6 ins
This vessel was in service for 41 years, being traded to the West Indies, New Orleans, Bahia etc. In her final years of service was traded exclusively to Bombay under the command of Capt Overend. Sold in 1850. Wrecked in 1865.

56. *Caroline*
French built schooner – 10 guns
Bought at auction
87 ft 10 ins × 24 ft 11 ins × 17 ft 1 in
Some ambiguity in records regarding this vessel. First master under Brocklebank ownership – Capt Gregg. Thought to have been sold and bought back by firm. Later masters c 1820–26 Captains Brown and Cowman. Traded to Savannah, Bahia, Pernambuco, Tarragona, etc. Wrecked on the Atlin shoals, nr Maranham; 29th Oct 1826. Crew saved.

146

57. *Nimble* (1810)
6 gun brig
139 tons
Built by Thos. & Jno. Brocklebank at Bransty, Whitehaven
76 ft 0 ins × 20 ft 3 ins × 12 ft 1 in
Traded to Jamaica & Demerara by Brocklebanks, under the command of Capt Lawson. Sold in 1816 to Thompson, then to McKenzie, followed by Messrs Creighton.

58. *Watson* (1810)
Brig
162 tons
Built by Thos. & Jno. Brocklebank at Bransty, Whitehaven
76 ft 2 ins × 22 ft 2 ins × 13 ft 11 ins
Sold to Capt J. Roper, owner and commander, who traded the brig to Dublin, Demerara, Brazils, Newfoundland, Prince Edward Island, Riga etc. The brig was wrecked off the Isle-of-Man in 1830.

59. *Bransty* (1) (1811)
Brig
104 tons
Built by Thos. & Jno. Brocklebank at Bransty, Whitehaven
68 ft 0 ins × 18 ft 8 ins × 10 ft 3 ins
In service eight years. Master in 1817 Capt Edmonson. Wrecked Ireland in 1819, whilst on passage from Whitehaven to Newport was driven on shore on the 9th Jan between Rush and Skerries, and went to pieces.

60. *London* (1812)
10 gun ship
351 tons
Built by Thos. & Jno. Brocklebank at Bransty, Whitehaven
101 ft 8 ins × 28 ft 1 in × 19 ft 5 ins
In service for 43 years. 1812–33 mainly traded to Virginia, West Indies, Savannah, New Orleans etc. Commanded by Capt Robert Wise 1820–21. From 1834–46 voyaged exclusively to Calcutta. Commanders in this trade being Captains McLean, Hoodless, King, Adamson, Benn and Michael. Sold in 1847 – afloat over 43 years.

61. *Mary* (1) (1812)
2 gun brig
208 tons
Built by Thos. & Jno. Brocklebank at Bransty, Whitehaven
82 ft 3 ins × 24 ft 2 ins × 15 ft 9 ins
Sold soon after completion to Capt H. Benn & Company. Later sold to Wilson & Co. Made voyages to Martinique, Brazils, Buenos Ayres, Quebec etc. for these owners. Wrecked at Mirimachi 1834.

62. *William* (1812)
Brig
237 tons
Built by Thos. & Jno. Brocklebank at Bransty, Whitehaven
86 ft 0 ins × 25 ft 3 ins × 17 ft 1 in
Sold to Capt Richardson in 1814, later sold to Capt Fraser; both men commanded the brig. The *William* made voyages to Berbice, New York, Jamaica, New Brunswick, Antigua etc. Whilst on passage from Porto Rica for Gibraltar was taken by a pirate on the 1st Jan 1825. The master arriving at Gibraltar on Feb 26th. Brig seized and condemned in U.S. in 1828.

63. *Cossack* (1813)
8 gun brig
172 tons
Built by Thos. & Jno. Brocklebank at Bransty, Whitehaven

147

81 ft 0 ins × 21 ft 6 ins × 14 ft 0 ins
In service 11 years. Made voyages to Jamaica, Bahia, St. Domingo, Pernambuco, Buenos Ayres etc. Whilst on passage from Liverpool for Buenos Ayres, under command of Capt Kerr she struck the Orhez Bank nr. B.A. and sank in 5 fathoms of water. The mate drowned. The date of this disaster being 19th March 1824.

64. *Margaret & Francis* (1813)
Brig
98 tons
Built by Thos. & Jno. Brocklebank at Bransty, Whitehaven
63 ft 9 ins × 18 ft 1 in × 10 ft 0 ins
First owners Thos. & Jno. Brocklebank, and Capt John Welsh, mariner of Calcutta, her first master being Capt Hugh Welsh. Registered be-novo at Liverpool 19th June 1815. Owners Taylor & Co. Later owned by W. Phillips & Co. Used in Med. trade also made voyages to Canada.

65. *Westmorland* (1) (1813)
Brig
168 tons
Built by William Wilson & Co. Whitehaven
76 ft 1 in × 22 ft 9 ins × 13 ft 11 ins
The brig's owners were Daniel Bird, John Brown (Snr.), John Brown (Jnr.) and Thomas Brocklebank. Capt William Morrison was the master. 'This vessel was taken by the enemy the 13th Sept 1813 – The Danes'.

66. *Aimwell* (1813)
2 gun brig
257 tons
Built by Thos. & Jno. Brocklebank at Bransty, Whitehaven
90 ft 6 ins × 25 ft 4 ins × 17 ft 8 ins
Sold upon completion to L. Bouch & Co. Made voyages to West Indies, Jamaica, St. Thomas, New Brunswick, Antigua, Dominica etc. Afloat for 26 years – wrecked in 1839.

67. *Mary* (2) (1781)
Brig
144 tons
Built at Liverpool
72 ft 10 ins × 22 ft 5 ins × 14 ft 0 ins
Bought by Thos. & Jno. Brocklebank in 1813. In service 12 years. Made voyages to Demerara, Limerick, St. Lucia, Bahia, Quebec, Nova Scotia etc. Commanded by Captains Wilson, Fell, and Cowman. Afloat 44 years. Wrecked 1825.

68. *Tobago* (1813)
6 gun brig
268 tons
Built by Thos. & Jno. Brocklebank at Bransty, Whitehaven
93 ft 9 ins × 25 ft 6 ins × 15 ft 6 ins
In service 5 years, made voyages for firm to St. Petersburg, Virginia, and Antigua, her commander at Brocklebanks being Capt Christopherson. Sold in 1818 to Hartley and Company. Other owners include Spence and Co. and Young and Company. Out of registers 1840.

69. *Westmorland* (2) (1814)
2 gun brig
195 tons
Built by Thos. & Jno. Brocklebank at Bransty, Whitehaven
85 ft 2 ins × 22 ft 10 ins × 15 ft 4 ins
In service for 43 years and afloat for 56 years. At Brocklebanks traded to Pernambuco, Newfoundland, Rio, Bahia etc. Commanded by Captains Warner, Airey, Dixon, Harrison, Mann, Hunter, Fulton,

Conway, Fisher, and Halliday. Sold about 1850 to Owen & Co., Portmadoc, and put into Quebec trade. Broken up in 1870.

70. *Duke of Wellington* (1814)
Brig
139 tons
Built by Thos. & Jno. Brocklebank at Bransty, Whitehaven
74 ft 11 ins × 20 ft 7 ins × 13 ft 10 ins
Sold to Capt A. Kerr and Co. in 1814, who commanded the vessel. Recorded voyages made to Lisbon and Brazil. Whilst under the command of Capt Kerr, on passage from Liverpool for Bahia, she was driven ashore near Rio Real on the 6th Sept 1821; crew saved. Most of the cargo taken out and landed at Bahia.

71. *New Triton* (1814)
Sloop
55 tons
Built by Thos. & Jno. Brocklebank at Bransty, Whitehaven
56 ft 10 ins × 16 ft 1 in × 8 ft 2 ins
Sold upon completion to Capt Hugh Beedon and others, first registered on the 21st Oct 1814.

72. *Jamaica* (1815)
Brig
215 tons
Built by Thos. & Jno. Brocklebank at Bransty, Whitehaven
84 ft 0 ins × 24 ft 4 ins × 16 ft 4 ins
Sold to W. Fisher upon completion; bought back in 1824. In service 30 years. West Indies and Brazil trader, making many voyages to Bahia in particular. Masters at Brocklebanks – Harvey, Cowman, Matterson, Weston, Perry, Pritt, Lawson, Selkirk, Sharp and Fletcher. Lost on Jan 1st 1854.

73. *Princess Charlotte* (1815)
22 gun ship
514 tons
Built by Thos. and John Brocklebank at Bransty, Whitehaven
119 ft 3 ins × 31 ft 2 ins × 18 ft 6 ins
East Indian trader, voyages mainly to Calcutta, then Bombay. In service 30 years. Capt McKean master 1815–27. In 1845 sold to Willis and Company, Scarborough; re-sold to East Coast Scottish Whalers; was lost on 14th June 1856.

74. *Antigua Packet* (1815)
20 gun ship
272 tons
Built by Thos. & Jno. Brocklebank at Bransty, Whitehaven
95 ft 4 ins × 25 ft 4 ins × 18 ft 0 ins
Sold upon completion to Messrs Dawson & Co., voyages made to New Brunswick, Antigua, Barbados etc. for this owner. Afloat for 48 years. Wrecked off Workington in 1863.

75. *Prince Leopold* (1816)
Brig
111 tons
Built by Thos. & Jno. Brocklebank at Bransty, Whitehaven
70 ft 10 ins × 18 ft 11 ins × 12 ft 0 ins
Traded to Pernambuco, Bahia, Dominica, Maranham, Newfoundland, Rio etc. Nearly lost in 1817 (18th Jan) going on shore at Whitehaven Harbour; lost her masts, boats, bulwarks etc. Hold filled with 7 ft of water, but was saved. Sold in 1839. Owner in 1847: Messrs Dower of Drogheda. Out of registers 1848.

76. *Shammon* (1816)
Brig
161 tons
Built by Thos. & Jno. Brocklebank at Bransty, Whitehaven
73 ft 6 ins × 22 ft 6 ins × 13 ft 10 ins

149

Sold to Hales & Company; voyages made to Waterford, Tobago, New Brunswick, Quebec, Maranham etc. for this owner. Wrecked in 1845.

77. *Dryad* (3) (1816)
Brig
231 tons
Built by Thos. & Jno. Brocklebank at Bransty, Whitehaven
88 ft 8 ins × 24 ft 4 ins × 16 ft 4 ins
In service 14 years; commanded by Capts Fell and Power, voyages made to Waterford, Tobago, Demerara, Maranham, Lisbon, Rio, and Pernambuco. Lost at sea in 1830.

78. *Constellation* (1817)
Brig
187 tons
Built by Thos. & Jno. Brocklebank at Bransty, Whitehaven
83 ft 5 ins × 22 ft 8 ins × 14 ft 6 ins
Traded to Demerara and West Indies; wrecked New Brunswick 1819.

79. *Doris* (1818)
Brig
133 tons
Built by Thos. & Jno. Brocklebank at Bransty, Whitehaven
72 ft 10 ins × 20 ft 7 ins × 13 ft 5 ins
Sold soon after completion to Robert & Henry Jefferson, Whitehaven. Voyages made to Brazils, Charente, Malta etc. Whilst on passage from St. Domingo for Falmouth was lost on Haneaga (Bahamas) on 15th April 1825. Capt White was in command at the time of this disaster; the crew and some of the materials were saved.

80. *Santon* (1) (1819)
Brig
169 tons
Built by Thos. & Jno. Brocklebank at Bransty, Whitehaven
76 ft 11 ins × 22 ft 8 ins × 14 ft 6 ins
Subscribers – William Gaitskell, mariner Whitehaven. John Brocklebank and Daniel Bird. Lost in Nov 1821 on the coast of the Isle-of-Man. (The brig's master was Capt William Gaitskell.)

81. *Perseverence* (2) (1819)
18 gun ship
513 tons
Built by Thos. & Jno. Brocklebank at Bransty, Whitehaven
123 ft 0 ins × 30 ft 5 ins × 21 ft 8 ins
In service 10 years, almost entirely employed in the East Indies trade; most voyages made to Calcutta. Her commanders were Capts Mounsey, Benn, and Brown. She was wrecked at Madras in 1829.

82. *West Indian* (1819)
Sloop
44 tons
Built by Thos. & Jno. Brocklebank at Bransty, Whitehaven
47 ft 9 ins × 15 ft 0 ins × 7 ft 7 ins
First registered at Whitehaven on the 24th Nov 1819, T. & J. Brocklebank being the sole owners. The master of this sloop was Jeremiah Corran. She was sold and re-registered at Grenada on the 23rd Oct 1821. Lost in the West Indies in 1839.

83. *Candidate* (1820)
Brig
225 tons
Built by Thos. & Jno. Brocklebank at Bransty, Whitehaven
85 ft 0 ins × 23 ft 6 ins × 16 ft 3 ins
In service three years, being traded to Rio, Gibraltar, Pernambuco, Bahia, and Buenos Ayres, under the

150

command of Capt J. Bacon. Whilst on passage from Cape Verdes with salt, went aground near Buenos Ayres, 12th June 1823 and was bilged and abandoned. Capt Bacon and his crew arrived at Buenos Ayres five days later.

84. *Ariel* (3) (1820)
Brig
154 tons
Built by Thos. & Jno. Brocklebank at Bransty, Whitehaven
81 ft 4 ins × 21 ft 1 in × 12 ft 7 ins
In service for 25 years; traded to Valparaiso, Arica, Lima, Pernambuco, etc. Amongst her masters were Capts Cragg, Lowden, Mann, and Crockett. Later sold to T. Rigby, Liverpool, and traded to Brazil. Out of registers 1851.

85. *Crown* (1821)
8 gun barque
297 tons
Built by Thos. & Jno. Brocklebank at Bransty, Whitehaven
98 ft 11 ins × 26 ft 8 ins × 18 ft 8 ins
1821–25 mainly employed in the West Coast South America trade. 1826–48 traded mainly to Calcutta then Bombay. Most famous commanders, Capts Craig, Pinder, and Ponsonby. Sold about 1848 to Hatton & Co. Liverpool. Lengthened, and tonnage increased to 430 tons. Traded to Africa. Condemned 1859.

86. *Globe* (1) (1822)
Brig
212 tons
Built by Thos. & Jno. Brocklebank at Bransty, Whitehaven
89 ft 8 ins × 23 ft 6 ins × 16 ft 6 ins
In West Coast South America Trade for 13 years under the commands of Captains Pinder, Kneale, Dixon, Wilson, Storr, and Mann. Wrecked off Bahia in 1835.

87. *Swallow* (2) (1822)
Brig
141 tons
Built by Thos. & Jno. Brocklebank at Bransty, Whitehaven
77 ft 6 ins × 20 ft 8 ins × 12 ft 5 ins
Mainly employed in the West Coast South America trade, her commanders being Capt Nicholson 1822–26, and Capt M'Kean, 1827–37. She made several voyages – including her last one – to Newfoundland, at which place she was crushed in the ice in 1837.

88. *Telegraph* (1823)
Schooner
111 tons
Built by Thos. & Jno. Brocklebank at Bransty, Whitehaven
71 ft 6 ins × 19 ft 2 ins × 10 ft 9 ins
In service only two years. Whilst on passage from Alvarado, under the command of Capt Dixon, she was lost near Havana, April 1825.

89. *Andes* (1823)
Brig
216 tons
Built by Thos. & Jno. Brocklebank at Bransty, Whitehaven
90 ft 2 ins × 23 ft 7 ins × 16 ft 0 ins
In service for 29 years; from 1823–33 she was commanded by Capt King, under whose command she was mainly engaged in the South America trade, but did make two voyages to the East Indies. Later voyages mainly to Bahia and Pernambuco. Capt Brocklebank in command 1839–43. Wrecked at Inschelling in 1852.

90. *Whitehaven* (renamed *Bolivar*) (1824)
    Brig
    214 tons
    Built by Thos. and Jno. Brocklebank at Bransty, Whitehaven
    90 ft 2 ins × 22 ft 9 ins × 15 ft 1 in
    Sold upon completion – afloat until 1855.

91. *Bransty* (2) (1824)
    Schooner
    130 tons
    Built by Thos. & Jno. Brocklebank at Bransty, Whitehaven
    75 ft 2 ins × 19 ft 10 ins × 10 ft 5 ins
    This schooner was in service for only six years, 1825–27 traded to Vera Cruz and Havana; 1828–29 made voyages to Tampico under the command of Capt Brocklebank – wrecked at Yucatan in 1830 whilst under the command of Capt Dixon.

92. *Manchester* (1824)
    Brig
    163 tons
    Built by Thos. & Jno. Brocklebank at Bransty, Whitehaven
    82 ft 8 ins × 21 ft 3 ins × 13 ft 10 ins
    In service for 28 years, and afloat for 49 years. Mainly traded to Pernambuco, Bahia, Newfoundland etc. Second commander was Capt Dixon late of the *Bransty 2*. Sold in 1852 to Capt Armstrong of Working-ton; who was still the master in 1870, but the vessel was then owned by Lamport & Co. of Workington. Broken up in 1873.

93. *Affleck* (1825)
    Brig
    237 tons
    Built by Thos. & Jno. Brocklebank at Bransty, Whitehaven
    88 ft 8 ins × 24 ft 8 ins × 16 ft 8 ins
    Sold upon completion to Capt Fell of Whitehaven, traded between London and the West Indies. In 1841 Capt Fell remained the owner, but the vessel was now commanded by Capt Chester. Last recorded voyage – London to Demerarra – 1841 – wrecked on this voyage.

94. *Grecian* (1825)
    Armed brig
    235 tons
    Built by Thos. & Jno. Brocklebank at Bransty, Whitehaven
    88 ft 8 ins × 24 ft 8 ins × 16 ft 8 ins
    Sold upon completion to Capt Bouch of Whitehaven, who placed Capt W. Sharp in command; the vessel then made voyages to India with Brocklebank cargoes. Last recorded voyage was from Liverpool for Rio, under the command of Capt Bouch; this being in 1831, when the vessel was wrecked in the Mersey.

95. *Superior* (1825)
    Brig
    240 tons
    Built by Thos. & Jno. Brocklebank at Bransty, Whitehaven
    90 ft 0 ins × 24 ft 6 ins × 16 ft 6 ins
    Sold upon completion, but made voyages for Brocklebanks, one such being to Singapore in 1829. Owned in 1850 by Bell & Co. Whitehaven, traded to Havana under command of Capt Crowther. Lost in 1864 when owned by Messrs Riley & Co. of London, and commanded by Capt G. West.

96. *Gazelle* (1826)
    Brig
    240 tons
    Built by Thos. & Jno. Brocklebank at Bransty, Whitehaven
    89 ft 10 ins × 24 ft 8 ins × 16 ft 6 ins

Sold upon completion to Capt Benn of Whitehaven. Traded from Liverpool to the West Indies. By 1841 Capts Ashbridge and Crighton were involved with the vessel, but Capt Benn remained the owner. Foundered in 1850 whilst on a voyage from Liverpool to Bahia, under the command of Capt Ramsey.

97. *Courier* (1) (1826)
Schooner
142 tons
Built by Thos. & Jno. Brocklebank at Bransty, Whitehaven
75 ft 3 ins × 20 ft 7 ins × 12 ft 6 ins
In service 19 years, mainly traded to Valparaiso, Callao, Pernambuco etc. Masters at Brocklebanks, Capts Storrs, Robinson, Nelson, Huntress, and Elliot. Sold in 1845; owner and master in 1850, Capt Curry of London. In 1852 Capt Curry was employing Capt Blagdon to command this schooner. Recorded voyage for that year – London–Spain. Out of register 1855.

98. *Meteor* (renamed *Helvellyn*) (1826)
Barque
240 tons
Built by Thos. & Jno. Brocklebank at Bransty, Whitehaven
90 ft 2 ins × 24 ft 8 ins × 16 ft 6 ins
Built for the Boadle Brothers of Whitehaven, but part owned by Brocklebanks. Under this joint ownership she made a number of voyages to Australia and Tasmania. In 1856 the *Helvellyn* was owned by L. Harker of London, and commanded by Capt P. W. Kidd, when on her last recorded voyage – Newcastle for Rio, she was lost.

99. *Lady Shaw Stewart* (1827)
Brigantine
181 tons
Built by Thos. & Jno. Brocklebank at Bransty, Whitehaven
85 ft 5 ins × 22 ft 1 in × 14 ft 1 in
Sold upon completion to Robert & Henry Jefferson of Whitehaven, most of her voyages being to Antigua. Commanded by Capt Joseph Wise, 5th July 1842–14th June 1846. From this date owned by Messrs Buckingham & Co., who traded her between Liverpool and California, under the command of Capt G. Roper. Last year in the registers – 1850.

100. *Countess of Lonsdale* (1827)
Paddle steamer
241 tons
Built by Thos. & John Brocklebank at Bransty, Whitehaven
127 ft 0 ins × 20 ft 0 ins × 13 ft 0 ins
The vessel was a 120 h.p. Paddle steamer, built for the Whitehaven Steam Navigation Company, in which firm Thomas & John Brocklebank had an interest. The *Countess* sailed between Whitehaven, the Isle-of-Man, and Liverpool.

101. *Oberon* (1827)
Brig
150 tons
Built by Thos. & Jno. Brocklebank at Bransty, Whitehaven
80 ft 0 ins × 20 ft 0 ins × 12 ft 1 in
In service 18 years, traded to Valparaiso, Callao, Bahia, Newfoundland, Arica, etc. Abraham Vaux Wise Jnr. mate to Danl. Brocklebank Jnr. voyage to Bordeaux, Feb 1839, and other voyages. Commanded in 1842 by Capt Hoodless. Sold in 1845 to Fairee & Company, Liverpool; Capt Tasker master. Missing on voyage Liverpool to Africa in 1846.

102. *Herculean* (1) (1828)
Barque
317 tons
Built by Thos. & Jno. Brocklebank at Bransty, Whitehaven
105 ft 3 ins × 26 ft 1 in × 18 ft 6 ins

In service 25 years, almost all her early voyages to Calcutta, then from 1839 to Bombay. Her masters included Captains Battersby, M'Kean, Grindale, Overend, and Mounsey. Sold in 1853 to J. Mondel of Liverpool. Condemned at Mauritius, 17th July 1855.

103. *Gleaner* (1828)
Sloop
50 tons
Built by Thos. & Jno. Brocklebank at Bransty, Whitehaven
56 ft 0 ins × 14 ft 3 ins × 6 ft 2 ins
In service 7 years, traded in the Irish Sea and commanded by Capt Edmondson. In Feb 1835 totally wrecked during a gale near Ardwell Bay, Capt Edmondson and his crew being drowned.

104. *Irt* (1828)
Barque
215 tons
Built by Thos. & Jno. Brocklebank at Bransty, Whitehaven
92 ft 6 ins × 22 ft 11 ins × 16 ft 1 in
First commander was Capt Hoodless, who made voyages to Valparaiso, Cadiz, Calcutta, Rio etc. for the firm. Later commanded by Capts Ludlow, Grier, and Young, then traded mainly to Bahia, Pernambuco, and Newfoundland. Sold to Lumley Kennedy in 1849. Re-sold 1846 to Alcock & Co., Sunderland, for Baltic & Med. trade. Broken up in 1884.

105. *Dash* (1828)
Schooner
86 tons
Built by Thos. & Jno. Brocklebank at Bransty, Whitehaven
66 ft 3 ins × 17 ft 3 ins × 10 ft 2 ins
Mainly traded to Tampico, Cadiz, Bahia, and Newfoundland, particularly the latter place. Commanded by Capt Brocklebank 1835–36. Sold c 1851 to Martin & Co. Liverpool; then traded coastally. Commander in 1855 – Capt J. Usher. Out of registers 1856.

106. *Buoyant* (1828)
Schooner
130 tons
Built by Thos. & Jno. Brocklebank at Bransty, Whitehaven
76 ft 10 ins × 19 ft 10 ins × 11 ft 8 ins
Traded to Tampico, Vera Cruz, Newfoundland, Pernambuco etc; also made several voyages to Gibraltar. Sold in 1838 and lost in 1839.

107. *Esk* (1828)
Barque
217 tons
Built by Thos. & Jno. Brocklebank at Bransty, Whitehaven
92 ft 7 ins × 22 ft 11 ins × 16 ft 0 ins
In service 27 years, traded mainly to South America. Voyages made to Batavia and Singapore (Capt Ponsonby) c 1835. Also made one voyage to Australia in 1854. Commanded by Capt George Wise, Dec 1847 – to close of 1851, who made voyages to Pernambuco, Trieste, and Bahia for the firm.

108. *Maypo* (1828)
Barque
173 tons
Built by Thos. & Jno. Brocklebank at Bransty, Whitehaven
84 ft 8 ins × 21 ft 9 ins × 13 ft 4 ins
In South American trade for 17 years, main commander – 1829–35 Capt Cragg. Sold about 1846 to Messrs Tasker & Co. Liverpool, traded by them under Capt Bishop to Africa; resold later to Owner-Master, Capt Thompson of Liverpool, who took the vessel from London to Australia in 1854 – wrecked in 1855.

154

109. *Mite* (1) (1830)
Sloop
54 tons
Built by Thos. & Jno. Brocklebank at Bransty, Whitehaven
57 ft 4 ins × 14 ft 10 ins × 7 ft 0 ins
The master of this sloop was Capt J. Little, the vessel was used for coastal work and was in service three years – she was reported missing in 1833.

110. *Avoca* (1830)
Barque
256 tons
Built by Thos. & Jno. Brocklebank at Bransty, Whitehaven
94 ft 6 ins × 24 ft 10 ins × 16 ft 0 ins
Built for the Boadle brothers of Whitehaven. Brocklebanks retaining a small share in this barque. At first traded to Bombay, the Cape, and Madras. In 1840 commanded by Capt L. Boadle – London–Sydney trade. In 1850 Capt T. Ridley in command, and voyages made to Panama. 1855 commanded by Capt Crowder. Out of registers 1858.

111. *Bonanza* (1830)
Schooner
176 tons
Built by Thos. & Jno. Brocklebank at Bransty, Whitehaven
85 ft 6 ins × 21 ft 8 ins × 13 ft 2 ins
Mostly employed in the South American trade, but made about three voyages to China; two of these being in 1846/7 when Francis Wise was First Mate to Capt Mossop. In service 26 years, but was sold to J. Mondel in 1856. Sent on a voyage from Liverpool to the West Indies, she never returned, being lost on the 7th Oct 1856.

112. *Tampico* (1830)
Brig
129 tons
Built by Thos. & Jno. Brocklebank at Bransty, Whitehaven
76 ft 9 ins × 19 ft 10 ins × 11 ft 9 ins
In service 9 years – traded mainly to Vera Cruz, Tampica, Callao. First Master, Capt Sproule, followed by Capts Weston, Robinson, and Chrighton. Abraham Vaux Wise finished his apprenticeship on this vessel Aug 1834–Apr 1836, serving under Capt Robinson. Sold in 1839, lost the following year.

113. *Hindoo* (1831)
Barque
266 tons
Built by Thos. & Jno. Brocklebank at Bransty, Whitehaven
96 ft 2 ins × 24 ft 11 ins × 16 ft 11 ins
In service 33 years; first master Capt Pinder; traded exclusively to Calcutta until 1854, then placed in South American trade. Sold c 1864 to T. Carter of Liverpool (Capt Norfolk) Africa–West Indies trade. In 1878 owned by J. Irvine of Liverpool (Capt Bistrup) out of registers 1880.

114. *Mackerel* (2) (1831)
Cutter
23 tons
Built by Thos. & Jno. Brocklebank at Bransty, Whitehaven
40 ft 9 ins × 11 ft 6 ins × 6 ft 7 ins
Very few records; thought to have been sold in 1850, owners in 1890 – Messrs J. A. Ross, Isle-of-Skye. Broken up 1899, afloat 68 years.

115. *Mazeppa* (1831)
Brig
134 tons
Built by Thos. & Jno. Brocklebank at Bransty, Whitehaven

78 ft 1 in × 19 ft 11 ins × 12 ft 4 ins

In service 16 years. Mainly employed in the South American trade. Also made voyages to Gibraltar, Newfoundland, St. Petersburg, and Riga. Commander in 1837, Capt Brocklebank. Sold in 1847 to Fairie & Co. Liverpool; traded to Africa. Master in 1849, Capt Atkinson. Lost 1862.

116. *Bransty* (3) (1832)
Schooner
99 tons
Built by Thos. & Jno. Brocklebank at Bransty, Whitehaven
70 ft 8 ins × 18 ft 1 in × 10 ft 10 ins
1832–34 traded to Gulf of Mexico and coastally, also made voyages to Hamburg, Newport etc. Abraham Vaux Wise Jnr. served part of his apprenticeship on this craft (1832–34) under Capt Wilson. Sold to J. Wood, Whitehaven about 1847, Capt Wood being the master and owner. Owner in 1881 – W. Nulty, Whitehaven. Wrecked off Tyrella, Co. Down 7th Feb 1881 – crew of four saved.

117. *Patriot King* (1832)
Barque
338 tons
Built by Thos. & Jno. Brocklebank at Bransty, Whitehaven
108 ft 1 in × 26 ft 8 ins × 18 ft 11 ins
Traded almost exclusively to Calcutta until 1853, notably under Capts Clarke, Roddock, and Fletcher. 1852–55 traded to Bombay under command of Capt George Wise. Vessel then placed in South American trade, under Capts Lowden, Cragg and Brown. Sold in 1868.

118. *Lord Althorp* (1832)
Brig
233 tons
Built by Thos. & Jno. Brocklebank at Bransty, Whitehaven
91 ft 2 ins × 24 ft 1 in × 16 ft 2 ins
In service 27 years, at first mainly traded to the Far East. From 1847 put into the South American trade. Sailed from Pernambuco for Liverpool on the 19th Jan 1859. A derelict vessel fitting her description sighted by the ship *Mary Simmond* on the 10th Feb. What happened to the crew of this abandoned brig remains a mystery.

119. *Mary Gordon* (1832)
Sloop
55 tons
Built by Thos. & Jno. Brocklebank at Bransty, Whitehaven
52 ft 7 ins × 15 ft 9 ins × 8 ft 1 in
At first owned by Messrs Bird, and later by McGowan. She was employed on coastal work, and in particular made voyages to Londonderry. Capt C. Conning (or Canning) being the master. Whilst on passage from Londonderry for Whitehaven she was abandoned off Blackhead in a sinking condition 22nd Mar 1840.

120. *Jumna* (1833)
Ship
364 tons
Built by Thos. & Jno. Brocklebank at Bransty, Whitehaven
111 ft 10 ins × 27 ft 9 ins × 18 ft 11 ins
Employed in the East India trade for 23 years – voyages mainly to Calcutta. Sold in 1856 to the Tay Whale Fishing Company, Dundee, who converted her into a steamer. She was crushed in the ice in Walvis Bay (75.10 North) on the 6th July 1863.

121. *Rimac* (1834)
Brig
214 tons
Built by Thos. & Jno. Brocklebank at Bransty, Whitehaven
90 ft 6 ins × 23 ft 2 ins × 15 ft 6 ins

West Coast South America trader, making many voyages to Valparaiso and Callao. Capt Francis Wise master – Nov 1855–58. In service 30 years. Sold in 1864 to Nutal & Co. Liverpool, then to Nicholson & Co. Liverpool. Last owner/master – Capt W. Heron of Liverpool. Wrecked 12th Dec 1874 near North Somercotes.

122. *Earl Grey* (1834)
Brig
242 tons
Built by Thos. & Jno. Brocklebank at Bransty, Whitehaven
94 ft 6 ins × 24 ft 2 ins × 16 ft 2 ins
At first placed in West Coast South American trade, but then traded to the far East, mainly under Capts Adamson, Mawson, and M'Wean. Then put back into American trade – 1846–60, her masters then being Capts Sproule, Chesters, Sharp, Curwen, Bell, and Woof. Sold 1860, lost in 1873.

123. *Ituna* (1834)
Brig
221 tons
Built by Thos. & Jno. Brocklebank at Bransty, Whitehaven
87 ft 8 ins × 24 ft 2 ins × 15 ft 8 ins
Sold upon completion to Bell & Company, Whitehaven. (Capt Sanderson) In West Indies trade. Circa 1853 owned by Wheelwright & Co. – in Dundee–Australia trade under Capt J. Braithewaite. Later owned by Kelly & Company, Whitehaven. Foundered in Atlantic 1874.

124. *Earl of Lonsdale* (2) (1834)
Paddle steamer
239 tons
Built by Thos. & Jno. Brocklebank at Bransty, Whitehaven
125 ft 4 ins × 20 ft 1 in × 13 ft 4 ins
A vessel of 120 h.p. built for the Whitehaven Steam Navigation Company, in which Brocklebanks had an interest. Steamed between Liverpool and Whitehaven, via the Isle-of-Man.

125. *Tigris* (1836)
Ship
422 tons
Built by Thos. & Jno. Brocklebank at Bransty, Whitehaven
115 ft 2 ins × 28 ft 2 ins × 20 ft 6 ins
Traded to the East – mainly Calcutta for 29 years. Commanders at Brocklebanks being Capts Tethering-ton, Robinson, McGill, Mawson, Patrickson, Selkirk, George Wise (June 1855–March 1856), Fletcher, and Miller. Wrecked at Manila 1865.

126. *Globe* (2) (1836)
Brig
252 tons
Built by Thos. & Jno. Brocklebank at Bransty, Whitehaven
95 ft 0 ins × 23 ft 3 ins × 15 ft 9 ins
Mainly traded to Valparaiso, Callao etc. Masters at Brocklebanks, Capts Cragg, Ward, Huntress, Crowder, Bell, Mossop, Penrice, and Chambers. Sold in 1861, but was still afloat and in service in 1910 – 74 years after being built! Her long life came to a close when she caught fire in Strangford Loch in 1910.

127. *Dryad* (4) (1837)
Brig
251 tons
Built by Thos. & Jno. Brocklebank at Bransty, Whitehaven
96 ft 2 ins × 23 ft 5 ins × 16 ft 0 ins
The brig on which Francis Wise served his time under Capt Rickerty. Traded mainly to Valparaiso, Callao, etc. but made several voyages to the Far East. Sold in 1862 to Lowden of Whitehaven (Capt W. Osborne). Later re-sold to W. R. Kelly of Whitehaven, c 1883 – Master at this time, Capt Anderson. Wrecked Nov 1894. Afloat 57 years.

128. *Fairie* (1837)
Schooner
80 tons
Built by Thos. & Jno. Brocklebank at Bransty, Whitehaven
66 ft 8 ins × 15 ft 9 ins × 9 ft 4 ins
In service 11 years, first Brocklebank master being Capt Welch. Owned by G. Pluck of Co. Bray in 1883. She sailed from Wexford for Glasgow on 11 Dec 1883, under the command of Capt Beans, and was never seen again.

129. *Mite* (2) (1837)
Smack
61 tons
Built by Thos. & Jno. Brocklebank at Bransty, Whitehaven
60 ft 0 ins × 15 ft 9 ins × 7 ft 9 ins
In service only three years. Recorded owners in 1858, O'Connor of Wexford. Master – J. Barrey. Traded from Wexford to Gloucester. Burnt in 1865.

130. *Patriot Queen* (1838)
Ship
547 tons
Built by Thos. & Jno. Brocklebank at Bransty, Whitehaven
124 ft 2 ins × 29 ft 5 ins × 20 ft 2 ins
In service 31 years, almost entirely traded to Calcutta. Masters being Capts Hoodless, Adamson, Roddock, Ponsonby, Bell, Fletcher, Richardson, and Williams. George Wise 1st Mate Nov 1845–Dec 1847. Sold c 1869. Owners 1880s P. Sutherland Jnr. of Liverpool. Master for these owners 1889, Capt J. Harper – burnt in that year.

131. *Horsburgh* (1838)
Barque
320 tons
Built by Thos. & Jno. Brocklebank at Bransty, Whitehaven
106 ft 6 ins × 22 ft 6 ins × 17 ft 1 in
South American trader – mainly to Valparaiso. Masters – Capts Askew, Cragg, Rickerty, Smith, and Carr. In service 17 years. Wrecked at Valparaiso in 1855.

132. *Susanna* (1838)
Schooner
65 tons
Built by Thos. & Jno. Brocklebank at Bransty, Whitehaven
59 ft 9 ins × 15 ft 9 ins × 8 ft 2 ins
Few records regarding this vessel. Sold upon completion – and placed in N. Atlantic and Mediterranean trades, c 1852–53. Lost in 1887.

133. *Santon* (2) (1839)
Barque
345 tons
Built by Thos. & Jno. Brocklebank at Bransty, Whitehaven
106 ft 6 ins × 22 ft 6 ins × 17 ft 3 ins
Made four voyages to Calcutta under Capt W. Huxtable; whilst homeward bound was driven ashore in very bad weather on the Irish coast, near Wexford in Jan 1843. Three men being lost.

134. *Aden* (1839)
Barque
339 tons
Built by Thos. & Jno. Brocklebank at Bransty, Whitehaven
107 ft 3 ins × 22 ft 6 ins × 17 ft 2 ins
In service 29 years – traded mainly in Canton, Hong Kong, and Singapore trade until 1862; from this date until sold in 1868 on voyages to South America. Francis Wise serving as Mate to Capt Smith – 1851.

Owners from 1868, Cochran and Co. Liverpool. Reduced to three-masted schooner. Out of register 1878.

135. *Swallow* (3) (1839)
Brig
236 tons
Built by Thos. & Jno. Brocklebank at Bransty, Whitehaven
95 ft 0 ins × 23 ft 6 ins × 16 ft 0 ins
In service only one year. The brig's commander was Capt Nelson. Under his command the brig sailed from Guayaquil on the 15th July 1840 – Capt Nelson and his vessel were never seen again.

136. *Kestrel* (1840)
Brig
231 tons
Built by Thos. & Jno. Brocklebank at Bransty, Whitehaven
95 ft 0 ins × 24 ft 5 ins × 14 ft 9 ins
In service for 23 years, voyages mainly to Valparaiso and Callao. Capt Abraham Vaux Wise being the brig's commander from Nov 1841 till his death aboard the vessel in Jan 1855. First master was Capt Farrell, Peter Bowman, mate, took over command on Abraham's death, followed in 1859 by Capt Potts. Sold to Cowman, then to Kelly etc. Wrecked Kings Cross Point, Arran Firth of Clyde, 4th Jan 1885.

137. *Industry* (1840)
Schooner
63 tons
Built by Thos. & Jno. Brocklebank at Bransty, Whitehaven
63 ft 6 ins × 17 ft 5 ins × 8 ft 0 ins
In service only one year, but afloat for 21. Lost in 1861.

138. *Princess Royal* (1841)
Ship
579 tons
Built by Thos. & Jno. Brocklebank at Bransty, Whitehaven
133 ft 8 ins × 29 ft 3 ins × 21 ft 1 in
Traded exclusively to Calcutta for thirty years, under the commands of Capts D. Robinson, Wm. Hoodless, Clarke, Adamson, Mawson, Selkirk, Howe, Kenworthy, and Cragg; George Wise serving as 2nd Mate to Capt Hoodless 1843–Nov 1845. Sold in 1871 to T. Cookson, Liverpool. Broken up 1877.

139. *Valparaiso* (1841)
Barque
317 tons
Built by Thos. & Jno. Brocklebank at Bransty, Whitehaven
102 ft 2 ins × 22 ft 6 ins × 17 ft 5 ins
Traded mainly to Valparaiso and Callao, under the commands of Capts Dixon, Whiteside, Joughan, Peters, Curwen, Murray, and Stephens. Sold in 1869 to A. Sutherland, Valparaiso. Had several other changes of ownership, and was still in the registers in 1893.

140. *Callao* (1842)
Brig
170 tons
Built by Thos. & Jno. Brocklebank at Bransty, Whitehaven
84 ft 7 ins × 19 ft 3 ins × 13 ft 5 ins
Traded mainly to Callao, but made one voyage to Calcutta in 1845, under the command of Capt Whiteside. Sold in 1860 to Hodgson of Whitehaven, still afloat under this ownership until broken up in 1890 – 48 years afloat.

141. *Lanercost* (1842)
Barque
318 tons
Built by Thos. & Jno. Brocklebank at Bransty, Whitehaven

159

100 ft 8 ins × 22 ft 6 ins × 17 ft 4 ins
Traded mainly to Valparaiso, Callao etc., but made one voyage to Hong Kong in 1847 under the command of Capt Gibson. Sold in 1869. Missing 1872.

142. *Patna* (1842)
Barque
362 tons
Built by Thos. & Jno. Brocklebank at Bransty, Whitehaven
113 ft 0 ins × 25 ft 1 in × 17 ft 5 ins
Traded exclusively to China under Capts Ponsonby, Clarke, Mann, Robinson, Rorison, Smith, Rogers, Pole, and Lewis. Sold in 1868 to Robert & Henry Jefferson of Whitehaven, Master at Jeffersons – Capt Joseph Morgan, who made voyages for the firm to the West Indies. Later sold to Kelly & Co., then to G. H. Jones. Broken up at Plymouth 1886.

143. *Camana* (1842)
Brig
185 tons
Built by Thos. & Jno. Brocklebank at Bransty, Whitehaven
89 ft 7 ins × 19 ft 5 ins × 13 ft 6 ins
In service 18 years, mainly traded to Callao and Valparaiso etc., but made two voyages to Calcutta – 1844–46, under Capt Hoodless. Sold to Hodgson of Whitehaven in 1860, who traded her to the West Indies. Lost 25th May 1863.

144. *Robert Pulsford* (1844)
Ship
593 tons
Built by Thos. & Jno. Brocklebank at Bransty, Whitehaven
130 ft 0 ins × 26 ft 5 ins × 21 ft 1 in
Traded almost exclusively to Calcutta, under Capts D. Robinson, W. Hoodless, King, Gibson, Smith, Howson, J. Clarke, T. Richardson, and Forsyth. Sold in 1869, then used in the West Coast South America trade. Later sold again to Chileans, and re-named *Reina del Pacifico*. Re-sold again in the 1890s and re-named *Roberto Pulsford*. Abandoned June 1899.

145. *Rowland Hill* (1844)
Schooner
64 tons
Built by Thos. & Jno. Brocklebank at Bransty, Whitehaven
62 ft 1 in × 15 ft 9 ins × 8 ft 0 ins
Sold upon completion. Afloat 17 years – lost in 1861.

146. *Courier* (2) (1845)
Brig
135 tons
Built by Thos. & Jno. Brocklebank at Bransty, Whitehaven
80 ft 8 ins × 20 ft 8 ins × 12 ft 3 ins
Traded mainly to Callao, under Capts Carr, Bowes, Edmondson. Capt Francis Wise took command 7th Oct 1853. and remained with this brig until taking command of the *Rimac*, 15th Nov 1855. Vessel sold in 1856 to Robinson of Drogheda; re-sold c 1885 to Miss Annie Whitehead, Drogheda. Hulked 1895.

147. *Sir Henry Pottinger* (1845)
Barque
334 tons
Built by Thos. & Jno. Brocklebank at Bransty, Whitehaven
102 ft 4 ins × 22 ft 7 ins × 17 ft 6 ins
Traded to Calcutta 1845–50, under Capt McWean – Francis Wise 1st Mate May 1849–Dec 1850. Other commanders being Capts Conway, Cragg, Rogers and Barnes. In West Coast South America trade, mainly under Capt Barnes from 1855. Wrecked Carmarthen Bay 1859 – one man lost.

148. *Crisis* (1847)
Ship
426 tons
Built by Thos. & Jno. Brocklebank at Bransty, Whitehaven
111 ft 9 ins × 25 ft 0 ins × 18 ft 6 ins
In service and afloat 15 years, commanded by Capts Gibson, Bell, Black, and Thompson. Most voyages to China, Singapore, and Hong Kong. On her last voyage from Liverpool for Singapore she struck the Arklow Bank, Ireland, and foundered, the date of this disaster being the 16th Jan 1862. Eight men came ashore at Clogher Head – master also saved.

149. *Thomas Brocklebank* (1847)
Ship
629 tons
Built by Thos. & Jno. Brocklebank at Bransty, Whitehaven
129 ft 8 ins × 27 ft 0 ins × 21 ft 3 ins
Traded exclusively to Calcutta under Capts H. Ponsonby, Rorison, Joughan, Kelly, Jordain, Fletcher, and Graham. Sold in 1869 to Cliff & Company of Liverpool. Wrecked on Rosario Reef, Jamaica, 1878.

150. *Harold* (1849)
Ship
666 tons
Built by Thos. & Jno. Brocklebank at Bransty, Whitehaven
136 ft 4 ins × 31 ft 5 ins × 21 ft 2 ins
Traded exclusively to Calcutta; first two masters being Capts Mann and Rorison, Francis Wise taking command in 1859, remaining in command until Jan 1865. Capt Beattie then took command, the final master at Brocklebanks being Capt Steele. Sold 1869, later sold to the French, and broken up in 1889.

151. *Petchelee* (1850)
Barque
393 tons
Built by Thos. & Jno. Brocklebank at Bransty, Whitehaven
118 ft 8 ins × 22 ft 7 ins × 17 ft 6 ins
Traded to Calcutta, Callao, Valparaiso, Shanghai, Hong Kong etc., under Capts Overend, Smith, Foster, Owen, and Willis. Sold in 1871 to W. Killey and Co. Liverpool. Owner in 1884 – Hytten Tonsberg, Norway. Whilst carrying coal from Troon to Christiania wrecked at Yonderfield, nr Ardrossan, 20th Mar 1884 – crew all saved.

152. *Arachne* (1851)
Ship
654 tons
Built by Thos. & Jno. Brocklebank at Bransty, Whitehaven
139 ft 7 ins × 30 ft 2 ins × 21 ft 1 in
Traded exclusively to Calcutta, under Capts Adamson, Roddock, King, Mawson, Sharp, Fletcher, Fearon, Francis Wise, and John Kenworthy. Francis Wise took command on the 13th Jan 1865, Capt Kenworthy assuming command on 13th Jan 1866. Whilst homeward bound she had to be abandoned in a sinking condition south of the Cape Verde Islands, on the 12th Nov 1866. Capt Kenworthy and all of his crew being saved.

153. *Martaban* (1852)
Ship
852 tons
Built by Thos. & Jno. Brocklebank at Bransty, Whitehaven
171 ft 2 ins × 32 ft 0 ins × 21 ft 0 ins
Traded exclusively to Calcutta under Capts Adamson, Roddock, King, Joughan, Lowden, Brown, Williams, Selkirk, and Ainscow. In service 21 years. Sold 1873.

154. *Aracan* (1854)
Ship
864 tons
Built by Thos. & Jno. Brocklebank at Bransty, Whitehaven
186 ft 5 ins × 32 ft 0 ins × 21 ft 6 ins
Traded almost exclusively to Calcutta, but made one voyage to Bombay (1854) under Capt Adamson, and several to China. Commanders being Adamson, George Wise (Apr 1856–Sept 1857), Selkirk, T. Potts, Jones, and Harwood. Sunk in a collision in the English Channel – 9th Mar 1874.

155. *Mindanao* (1854)
Ship
482 tons
Built by R. Williamson & Sons, Harrington
130 ft 5 ins × 27 ft 5 ins × 18 ft 0 ins
Traded almost exclusively to Valparaiso and Callao, under Capt Ponsonby – 1854–65. In 1866 Capt Wm. Ray assumed command, followed by Capts Leech, Forsyth, and Wright. Foundered 1874.

156. *Florence Nightingale* (1855)
Ship
1,362 tons
Built by Jas. Nevins, St. John, New Brunswick
209 ft 7 ins × 40 ft 8 ins × 22 ft 10 ins
Traded exclusively to Calcutta, carried a crew of 40, and was commanded by Capt Mossop 1855–61, followed by Capts Fletcher, Howe, Kenworthy, and Richardson. Sold in 1869 to G. Cairns, Liverpool. Lost in the Bay of Biscay, 1872, whilst on passage from Cardiff to Rio de Janeiro.

157. *Comorin* (1855)
Ship
803 tons
Built by Thos. & Jno. Brocklebank at Bransty, Whitehaven
186 ft 5 ins × 32 ft 0 ins × 21 ft 5 ins
In service 20 years, traded exclusively to Calcutta, under Captains Roddock, Tully, Howe, Francis Wise (1865–70), Leach, Roberts, and McKenzie. Sold about 1875 to P. Sutherland, Liverpool. Re-sold to Norwegians about 1882, and abandoned in Oct 1893.

158. *Herculean* (2) (1856)
Ship
531 tons
Built by Thos. & Jno. Brocklebank at Bransty, Whitehaven
164 ft 8 ins × 28 ft 7 ins × 18 ft 9 ins
In service only four years, being traded to China under the command of Capt Bell. Advices from Batavia of 16th Jan stated that people were employed at the salvage of the cargo of the *Herculean* whilst on passage from China to Liverpool, the vessel being wrecked near the Poelo Pongo Islands, 30th Nov 1860.

159. *Eskett* (1857)
Brig
123 tons
Built by Thos. & Jno. Brocklebank at Bransty, Whitehaven
85 ft 4 ins × 20 ft 0 ins × 12 ft 0 ins
Built to the order of Capt Lowden, commander of the *Martaban* – c 1862–64. In later years Lowden became a substantial shipowner. Went missing 1877.

160. *Rajmahal* (1858)
Ship
1,302 tons
Built by Thos. & Jno. Brocklebank, Bransty, Whitehaven
224 ft 5 ins × 36 ft 9 ins × 22 ft 8 ins
Traded exclusively to Calcutta for 25 years, her masters being Capts Roddock, Mossop, Fletcher,

162

Joughan, Howe, Balderston, Campbell, Marley, Forshaw, and Bell. Sold in 1883 to H. Williams of Liverpool; whilst on passage from Birkenhead to Bombay with coal was spoken on the 20th Oct 1883, Lat. 30 S Long. 11 W. She was never seen again.

161. *Sumatra* (1858)
Ship
773 tons
Built by Thos. & Jno. Brocklebank at Bransty, Whitehaven
172 ft 4 ins × 32 ft 0 ins × 20 ft 8 ins
In service 18 years and afloat 43. Traded almost exclusively to Calcutta under Capts Rorison, Fletcher, Beattie, Roberts, and Latham. Sold about 1876 to Karron, Castletown, I.O.M. Re-sold about 1884 to A. F. Braga, Montevideo, and re-named *Clara B*. Sold again to Norwegians (1887) re-named *Clara*. Wrecked in Jan 1901.

162. *Juanapore* (1859) O.N. 27652
Barque
459 tons
Built by Thos. & Jno. Brocklebank at Bransty, Whitehaven
144 ft 4 ins × 26 ft 7 ins × 18 ft 6 ins
In service 15 years, traded to Shanghai, Nagasaki, and Hong Kong, under Capts King and Brown. Sold in 1874 to T. Davies, London. Re-sold in 1889 to R. Ferguson, Dundee. Missing 1891.

163. *Veronica* (1860) O.N. 28192
Barque
332 tons
Built by Thos. & Jno. Brocklebank at Bransty, Whitehaven
126 ft 4 ins × 23 ft 3 ins × 17 ft 0 ins
In service 13 years, being traded to China (Foo Chow Foo, Hong Kong, and Macao), under Capts Robinson, Douglas, Brown, Haldane, and Evans. Sold 1873 to Anderson and Company, London. Owned in the eighties by W. Robertson, London. Whilst on passage from Cape Town to Swansea she was sunk following a collision with the ship *Marquis of Worcester* in Port Nolloth, Namaqualand, South Africa – 8th Feb 1886.

164. *Maiden Queen* (1860) O.N. 29170
Ship
814 tons
Built by R. Williamson and Sons, Harrington
178 ft 0 ins × 32 ft 3 ins × 21 ft 1 in
In service 14 years, traded to Hong Kong, Shanghai, Manila, and Foo Chow Foo. Commanded by Capt Smith (1860–69), followed by Capt Wm. Ray, c 1870. Her last commander at Brocklebanks being Capt Forsyth. Sold about 1874 to Germany, re-named *Betty*, hulked at Santos 1892.

165. *Cambay* (1861) O.N. 29628
Ship
1,000 tons
Built by Thos. & Jno. Brocklebank at Bransty, Whitehaven
195 ft 0 ins × 35 ft 2 ins × 22 ft 6 ins
In service for 23 years, traded almost exclusively to Calcutta. Had 11 masters whilst with the firm which included Capts Loughlin, Francis Wise (1870/1), Selkirk, Russell, and Bell. Sold to the Norwegians in 1884, re-sold 1885 and re-named *Arvilla*. Broken up Mar 1909.

166. *Tenasserim* (1) O.N. 44139
Ship
1,002 tons
Built by Thos. & Jno. Brocklebank at Bransty, Whitehaven
195 ft 0 ins × 35 ft 2 ins × 22 ft 7 ins
Traded to Calcutta, under Capt Tully, then Capt J. Howson. Whilst outward bound in Dec 1865 got

163

ashore on the Arklow Bank off the Irish coast. This accident occurred during dense fog – sadly Capt Howson and three of his men were lost.

167. *Burdwan* (1862) O.N. 45394
Ship
803 tons
Built by Thos. & Jno. Brocklebank at Bransty, Whitehaven
185 ft 7 ins × 32 ft 1 in × 21 ft 6 ins
Traded to Calcutta, China, Manila, and Singapore. Circa 1873 commanded by Capt William Ray. In service 23 years. Whilst on passage from Liverpool for Manila, under the command of Capt W. Woodward, she was wrecked at Pulo Leat, Macclesfield Channel, Gaspar Straits, on the 16th Aug 1885. Capt Woodward and all his crew were saved.

168. *Ariel* (4) (1862) O.N. 44227
Brig
130 tons
Built by Thos. & Jno. Brocklebank at Bransty, Whitehaven
86 ft 6 ins × 21 ft 6 ins × 12 ft 0 ins
Built for Messrs W. R. Kelly of Whitehaven. Re-sold in the eighties to W. Tyrell of Wicklow and re-rigged as a schooner. Whilst carrying guano from Dublin to Perth she was wrecked on the North Point of Eriskay Island, Outer Hebrides – 1st May 1900.

169. *Everest* (1863) O.N. 48768
Ship
571 tons
Built by Thos. & Jno. Brocklebank at Bransty, Whitehaven
171 ft 8 ins × 30 ft 0 ins × 19 ft 2 ins
One of the Line's finest clippers – traded to Hong Kong and Shanghai for ten years, under Capts Curwen, Clarke, and T. Jones. She was wrecked in the China Seas in 1873.

170. *Alexandra* (1863) O.N. 47498
Iron ship
1,352 tons
Built by Harland & Wolff at Belfast
231 ft 5 ins × 36 ft 5 ins × 23 ft 9 ins
First iron ship owned by Brocklebanks. Traded exclusively to Calcutta under Capts Sharp, Kelly, Joughlin, Ainscow, Kenworthy, Orr, and Cochran. Sold in 1887 to Trinder Anderson. Re-sold about 1898 to Norwegians and re-named *Vigo*. Burnt Sept 1904 and condemned.

171. *Baroda* (1864) O.N. 49890
Iron ship
1,364 tons
Built by Harland & Wolff at Belfast
225 ft 0 ins × 36 ft 5 ins × 23 ft 9 ins
Traded exclusively to Calcutta for 23 years, under Capt Tully (1864–73). William Ray, 1874, followed by Kenworthy, Ellery, Brown, Russell, Peterkin, and J. Healy – 1886–87. When homeward bound in Nov 1887 she entered the Mersey in tow, and was run into and sunk by another ship; Capt Healy and his crew were all saved.

172. *Bowfell* (1864) O.N. 50496
Ship
1,002 tons
Built by Thos. & Jno. Brocklebank at Bransty, Whitehaven
196 ft 2 ins × 35 ft 2 ins × 22 ft 9 ins
Traded to Calcutta until end of 1878, then made voyages to Singapore and Manila. Her commanders being Capts Ponsonby, Balderston, and from 1870–75, Capt Wm Ellery; followed by Connell, Kershaw, Collins, Forshaw, and Graham. Whilst carrying sugar from Manila for Liverpool she was wrecked on Discovery Reef, Karimata Straits, Java Sea. The crew were all saved.

164

173. *Mahanada* (1865) O.N. 29901
Ship
1,003 tons
Built by Thos. & Jno. Brocklebank at Bransty, Whitehaven
195 ft 2 ins × 35 ft 3 ins × 22 ft 9 ins
Traded to Calcutta under Capts Mossop, Douglas, Kenworthy, and Marley. Then traded to Manila under Capts Forshaw, Wilson and Bartlett. Sold to Norwegians in 1883, re-named *Sigrid*. Owner 1904, J. Schjerig, Drontheim. Whilst in ballast and on passage from Tonsberg to Mobile foundered 8 miles N.W. by W. of Noup Head, Westray, Orkneys – crew of 14 saved.

174. *Candahar* (1866) O.N. 54983
Iron ship
1,418 tons
Built by Harland & Wolff at Belfast
239 ft 4 ins × 37 ft 2 ins × 23 ft 6 ins
Traded almost exclusively to Calcutta, from 1866–72 under command of Capt Mossop. In 1875 she made one voyage to San Francisco whilst commanded by Capt McKenzie. Then put back into Calcutta trade under Capts Brown, Marley, Russell, Peterkin, and Hughes. Sold to S. Goldberg of Swansea in 1890. Re-sold to Norwegians, re-named *Almedia* – wrecked 3rd May 1905 at Noumea (N.C.) whilst in ballast from Melbourne.

175. *Tenasserim* (2) (1866) O.N. 55026
Iron ship
419 tons
Built by Harland & Wolff at Belfast
239 ft 4 ins × 36 ft 0 ins × 23 ft 6 ins
Traded exclusively to Calcutta under Capts Ponsonby, Balderston, Potts, Campbell, Graham, Bartlett, Ellery (1887), Lindsay, and Nicholson. Sold in 1890 to Gracie Beazley & Co., and reduced to a barque. Sold to Norwegians 1900, re-named *Ryingen*. Wrecked May 1902 at Table Bay.

176. *Chinsura* (1868) O.N. 60062
Iron ship
1,266 tons
Built by G. R. Clover at Birkenhead
215 ft 5 ins × 37 ft 1 in × 22 ft 8 ins
Traded exclusively to Calcutta until 1879. Commanded by Capt Francis Wise from 25th Aug 1871–4th Mar 1874 – his last command. Sold to Hughes and Co. Liverpool in 1883. About 1893 sold to Italians, re-named *Lucco*. Next owner was Landberg & Zoon, Batavia, who named her the *Nest*. In 1920 sold to J. J. A. Van Meel of Rotterdam. About 1921 she was bought by the Polish Government and used as a training ship, named *Lwow*. Hulked 1929.

177. *Belfast* (1874) O.N. 70875
Iron ship
1,865 tons
Built by Harland & Wolff at Belfast
260 ft 5 ins × 40 ft 2 ins × 24 ft 2 ins
In service 25 years, mainly traded to Calcutta, but first and last voyages to San Francisco. Sold at that port in 1899 to Shaw Savill, and reduced to a barque. Re-sold to Chilians in 1906. Re-sold again to Peruvians in 1912, broken up 1925.

178. *Majestic* (1875) O.N. 70952
Iron ship
1,884 tons
Built by Harland & Wolff at Belfast
273 ft 4 ins × 40 ft 2 ins × 24 ft 2 ins
Mainly in Calcutta trade, under Capts Kelly, Potts, Ellery, McKenzie, Graham, Orr, Nicholson,

Campbell, Lane, and Heyburn. Made two voyages to San Francisco – 1884 Capt McKenzie, and 1885 Capt Ellery. Sold in 1898 to Chilean Government. Hulked at Iquique.

179. *Kyber* (1880) O.N. 81396
Iron ship
1,967 tons
Built by W. H. Potter & Sons at Liverpool
276 ft 6 ins × 40 ft 1 in × 24 ft 2 ins
Traded almost exclusively to Calcutta for 18 years, under Capts McKenzie, Robinson, Russell, Cochran, Peterkin, Cooke, and Saul. Sold in 1898 to J. Joyce, Liverpool. Whilst on passage from Melbourne to Channel was wrecked off the Cornish coast on the 15th Mar 1905.

180. *Bolan* (1882) O.N. 86213
Iron ship
2,003 tons
Built by Oswald Mordaunt & Company at Southampton
273 ft 2 ins × 40 ft 0 ins × 24 ft 3 ins
Traded to Calcutta for seven years under Capts Campbell, Graham, and W. P. Hughes. Homeward bound in April 1889 she was spoken on 5th July, position 33 S and 32 E, and was never seen again, Capt Hughes and his crew of 34 being lost.

181. *Bactria* (1885) O.N. 91250
Iron ship
2,112 tons
Built by Oswald Mordaunt and Co. at Southampton
279 ft 0 ins × 40 ft 2 ins × 24 ft 3 ins
Traded almost exclusively to Calcutta, under Capts Balderstone, Peterkin, Lindsay, Cornish, and Davies. Sold in 1898 to Sproat of Liverpool; re-named *Loch Finlas*. Whilst on passage from Melbourne to the United Kingdom was wrecked near Forsters Island, Sept 1908.

182. *Zemindar* (1885) O.N. 91235
Steel ship
2,053 tons
Built by Harland & Wolff at Belfast
292 ft 6 ins × 39 ft 7 ins × 23 ft 5 ins
In service 15 years, under Capts McKenzie, Campbell, Graham, Wood, Nicholson, and Frederickson. Mainly used in the Calcutta trade, but last voyage for the firm in 1899 was to Buenos Aires. Sold in 1900 to Germany, re-named *Otto Gildmeister*. Owners in 1902, Hind, Rolph of San Francisco. Re-named *Homeward Bound*. Afloat 1928 as *Star of Holland*, owned by Alaska Packers, broken up Japan in 1935.

183. *Talookdar* (1885) O.N. 91249
Steel ship
2,053 tons
Built by Harland & Wolff at Belfast
292 ft 6 ins × 39 ft 7 ins × 23 ft 5 ins
In service to Calcutta for five years, under Capts Ellery, Orr, Marley, and again Orr. When homeward bound under Capt A. J. Orr was run into and sunk by another sailing vessel in Lat 5 N. Long 25 W. off the South American coast, north of Pernambuco in Dec 1890. Eight men saved, but 27 lost, mainly due to mainsail enveloping boats already in the water.

184. *Sindia* (1887) O.N. 93757
Steel four masted barque
3,007 tons
Built by Harland & Wolff at Belfast
329 ft 3 ins × 45 ft 2 ins × 26 ft 7 ins
In Calcutta trade for 13 years, under Capts McKenzie, Peterkin, Cochran, and Heyburn. Made two voyages to New York under Capt Cochran (1894 and 1896). Sold in 1900 to Anglo American Oil Co., London. Wrecked on coast of New Jersey, 15 Dec 1901, whilst on passage from Kobe to New York.

185. *Holkar* (1888) O.N. 93772
Steel four masted barque
3,009 tons
Built by Harland & Wolff at Belfast
329 ft 3 ins × 45 ft 2 ins × 26 ft 7 ins
Last of the Brocklebank sailing ships. Traded to Calcutta for 13 years. First master was Capt Ellery (1888), followed by Capts Russell, Peterkin, Graham, Nicholson, Frederickson, and Dunning. Sold to Germany in 1901, and re-named *Adelaide*. 1913 re-named *Odessa*. Captured as prize of war in 1914. Sold to Norway Aug 1915, re-named *Souverain*. 1923 – re-named *Hippalos*. Broken up 1925.

Appendix B

Fleet List of Robert & Henry Jefferson, Lowther Street, Whitehaven

1. *Gale** (1758)[1]
   200 tons
   Snow[2]
   Built Whitehaven
   (Per Lloyds) H. Jefferson 1776–79, Capt Parker 1781
   Voyages. 1776 Virginia–London London Trans. Capt Henry Jefferson. 1778–79 Quebec–London. Capt Henry Jefferson. 1781 Antigua. Capt Parker.

2. *Doris* (1818) (4th Jly)
   133 tons
   Brigantine
   72 ft 10 in × 20 ft 7 in × 13 ft 5 in
   Built by Thos. & Jno. Brocklebank at Bransty, Whitehaven
   (PRO Transcript BT 107–122)
   Voyages. 1819, 1820, 1821 Liverpool–Brazils. Capt John White. 1822, 1823, 1824 Liverpool–Charleston. Capt John White. 1825 Liverpool–St. Domingo. Capt John White.
   The *Doris* was sold to Jefferson's some six months after her launch by Thomas & John Brocklebank at Whitehaven. *Lloyds List 24 May 1825*, '*Doris*, White, from St. Domingo for Falmouth, has been totally lost on Heneaga: crew and some of the materials saved. Report dated Nassau 15th April 1825.

3. *Thetis* (1817)
   161 Tons
   Brigantine rig
   77 ft 0 ins × 22 ft ½ in × 13 ft 10 in
   Built by William Wilson at Whitehaven
   Bought by Jefferson's from Wilson & Co. on Aug 12th 1825. At this change of ownership Henry Jefferson Snr. held 22 shares, Robert Jefferson held 21 shares, and Henry Jefferson Jnr. also held 21 shares. It must be assumed that the Brig *Thetis* was being chartered by the Jefferson's prior to her formal purchase in 1825. Henry Jefferson Jnr. going to Antigua with Capt Taylor on Company business in 1824, per his Diary for that year.
   Voyages. 1826 Whitehaven–Antigua. Capt John Taylor. 1927 Whitehaven–Montego Bay Capt J. Robinson. 1828, 1829 Whitehaven–Oporto Capt Henry Booth Hewitt. 1830, 1831, 1832, 1833 White-

---

* The *Gale* was registered E.1 at Lloyds 1776–81.

[1] Sir Henry Fletcher (of Fletcher Christian's family) was a noted M.P. and a Director of the East India Company. This branch of the Fletcher family were related to the local family of Wilson, one of whom married Lucinda Washington, cousin of the first President of the United States. The Washington family came from Warton, and were connected with the Curwen family, through the Whitehaven family of *Gale*, one of whom was the mother of Isabella Christian Curwen; another married a famous local mariner, Capt John Wordsworth, cousin of the poet. Without a doubt the Jefferson snow *Gale* would be named after this family.

[2] A snow is a brig to which has been added a supplementary trysail mast close abaft the mainmast.

168

haven–Antigua Capt Henry Booth Hewitt. 1834 Capt Benjamin Wheelwright. 1834, 1835 Whitehaven–Antigua Capt William Harper. 1836, 1837 Liverpool–Antigua Capt William Harper.

Capt J. Robinson took over command of the *Thetis* at Antigua in May 1827. Capt Hewitt took command on
the 26th Dec whilst at Montego Bay. Capt Benjamin Wheelwright only took the brigantine for one voyage,
21st March 1834–2nd Sept of that year, at which point Capt Harper took over.

The *Thetis* foundered at sea off Cape Finisterre, after striking what was thought to be a sunken wreck. Two
passengers and one of the crew being lost in this disaster which occurred in May 1837.

4. *Lady Shaw Stewart* (1827) (16th Feb)
181 tons
Brigantine
85 ft 5 in × 22 ft 1 in × 14 ft 11 in
Built by Thos. & Jno. Brocklebank at Bransty, Whitehaven
At the time of her purchase Henry Jefferson, Robert Jefferson, and Henry Jefferson Jnr. held 56 of the
vessel's 64 shares, Capt John Taylor holding the other eight. On the 30th June 1827 however the Jeffersons
sold their shares to a Mr Wilson Peny, gentleman and merchant of Whitehaven. She remained registered as
a Jefferson vessel until her sale by the company in 1846. We can assume from this that Jeffersons were either
appointed agents for the ship, or managing owners.
Voyages. 1827, 1828, 1829, 1830, 1831, 1832, 1833 Whitehaven–Antigua Capt John Taylor. Change
of Master 13th Dec 1833 (Whitehaven). 1834 Whitehaven–Antigua Capt Henry Booth Hewitt. Change of
Master 14th May 1834 (Whitehaven). 1834, 1835, 1836 Whitehaven–Antigua Capt John Taylor. Change
of Master 7th June 1836 (Whitehaven). 1836 Whitehaven–Liverpool Capt Robert Cormick. Change of
Master 29th June 1836 (Whitehaven). 1836 Liverpool–London–Whitehaven Capt William Steele. 1837
Liverpool–Demr. Antigua Capt William Steele. 1838 Liverpool–Antigua Capt William Steele. 1839
London–Whitehaven–Antigua Capt William Steele. 1840 London–Whitehaven–Antigua Capt William
Steele. 1841 Whitehaven–Antigua Capt William Steele. Change of Master 8th Feb 1842 (Whitehaven).
1842 Whitehaven–Antigua Capt Thomas James. Change of Master 5th July 1842 (Whitehaven). 1842
Whitehaven–Antigua Capt Joseph Wise. 1843, 1844, 1845, 1846 Whitehaven–Liverpool–Antigua Capt
Joseph Wise.
Registration cancelled at Whitehaven 14th June 1846. Sold to Buckingham (Capt Roper).

5. *Derwent* (1834)
221 tons
Brigantine
87 ft 6 in × 24 ft 0 ins × 16 ft 0 ins
Built by Jonathan Fell at Workington, Cumberland
Robert & Henry Jefferson – all 64 shares. At some point c 1842 ownership passed to M'Minn, in 1850 to
Messrs Walker, and 1851/2 to Messrs Wheelright. 1853–63 owned again by Jeffersons.
Voyages. 1834 Whitehaven–Antigua (Capt Wilson Harper), 2nd voyage 1834. Whitehaven–Rio. Capt
Henry Booth Hewitt. 1836 Liverpool–Canton Capt Henry Booth Hewitt. Command passed to Capt
William Steele, August 1836. 1838 Whitehaven–Antigua–London Capt Harper for Jefferson's. 1848 To
Whampoa Capt W. Steele for M'Minn. 1853 From Antigua Capt Bell for Robert & Henry Jefferson. 1855
Whitehaven–West Indies Capt J. Bell for Jefferson's. 1856 Whitehaven–West Indies Capt J. Bell for
Jefferson's. 1857 Whitehaven–London Capt J. Bell for Jefferson's. 1858 Liverpool–West Indies Capt J.
Bell for Jefferson's. 1859 Liverpool–West Indies Capt J. Bell for Jefferson's. 1860 Liverpool–West Indies
Capt Moat for Jefferson's. 1863 Whitehaven–West Indies Capt Moat, master and owner.
Listed as above per Lloyds registers till 1869 – out of registers after this date.

6. *British Queen* (1838) (20th May)
218 tons
Brigantine
84 ft 3 in × 20 ft 7 in × 14 ft 8 in
Built by Lumley Kennedy & Co, Whitehaven
All 64 shares held by Robert & Henry Jefferson, carrying on trade under the firm of Robert & Henry
Jefferson, Whitehaven.
Voyages. 1838, 1839 Whitchaven–Antigua Capt Thomas Kennedy. 1840, 1841, 1842, 1843, 1844, 1845

Whitehaven–Antigua–Liverpool Capt Thomas Kennedy. Change of Master to J. Wise 28th Feb. 1846, 1847, 1848, 1849, 1850, 1851, 1852 Whitehaven–Antigua–Liverpool Capt Joseph Wise. Change of Master to Capt Andrew Hunter 20th Aug 1883–6th Jan 1884 then back to J. Wise. 1853, 1854, 1855, 1856, 1857, 1858 Whitehaven–Antigua–Liverpool Capt Joseph Wise. Change of Master to Joseph Ledger 24th Dec. 1859, 1860 Whitehaven–Antigua–Liverpool Capt Joseph Ledger. Change of Master to Wm. Hinde 12th Jan. 1861. 1861 To W.I. and Newfoundland Capt William Hinde.

Note: Vessel lost off Newfoundland on the 6th May 1861, per form 20, 26th March 1866.

Several voyages could be made to Antigua, and or the West Indies within a twelve month period. Most of these voyages ran from Whitehaven to Antigua, and perhaps other ports of call in the West Indies, and back again to both Liverpool and Whitehaven. Capt Andrew Hunter acted as a relief master from August 1853–Jan. 6th 1854 only, whilst Joseph Wise arranged the sale of his father-in-law's ship, the *Massereene* upon Capt Glover's death at this time.

7. *Midge* (1840) (12th Nov)
   28 tons
   Sloop (later Smack)
   41 ft 1 in × 13 ft 4 in × 7 ft 5 in
   Built by Lumley Kennedy & Co. Whitehaven.
   All 64 shares held by Robert & Henry Jefferson, sold 14th December 1843 – 'Robert & Henry Jefferson have transferred by bill of sale, dated this day to George Athil of Antigua, Merchant.' – Transcript note.
   Voyages. 1840/1 To Cadiz, Whitehaven & Lancaster Capt Thomas James. 1841 To Cadiz, thence to Antigua Capt Thomas James (Joseph Wise – mate). 1842 Used at Antigua by Jeffersons. 1843 Dec. 1843 sold to George Athil at Antigua.

8. *Antigua* (O.N. 21090) (1858) (8th June)
   287.77 tons
   Barque
   107 ft 4 in × 25 ft 3 in × 15 ft 9 in
   Built by H. & George Barrick, Whitby
   14 shares held by Henry Jefferson Snr., merchant, Rothersyke, nr Whitehaven. 14 held by Robert Jefferson of Rothersyke, and 28 held by Henry Jefferson Jnr. of Springfield nr Whitehaven, Cumberland. Eight shares held by Captain Joseph Wise, Whitehaven, Cumberland.
   Voyages. 1858 Whitehaven–Antigua Capt Joseph Wise (from June). 1859 Whitehaven–Antigua–Trinidad Capt Joseph Wise. 1860, 1861, 1862 Liverpool–Antigua Capt Joseph Wise. Change of Master to J. Morgan 10th Sept. 1863 (at Liverpool). 1863, 1864 Liverpool–Antigua Capt Joseph Morgan. 1865, 1866, 1867, 1868 Liverpool–W. Indies Capt Joseph Morgan. Change of Master to John Wood 7th Dec. 1868. 1869 Liverpool–Belfast–W.I. Capt John Wood. Change of Master to Dnl. McLean 1st Sept 1869. 1870, 1871 Liverpool–Belfast–W.I. Capt Daniel McLean. Change of Master to F. T. Calf 18th April 1872 (at Liverpool). 1872 Liverpool–Hamburg Lo. Capt Francis T. Calf. 1873, 1874, 1875, 1876, 1877, 1878, 1879, 1880 London–West Indies Capt Francis T. Calf.
   Notes: The *Antigua* was sold on the 15th Oct 1880 to H. S. Van Gauten of Holland, history beyond that date not researched.
   Capt John Woof served previously in Brocklebank's *Mindanao* (1855–89), *Earl Grey* (1859–60), *Crisis* 1860–1) and *Hindoo* (1861–63). He was born in Cumberland in 1815. Ticket No. 54,247.
   Capt Daniel McLean was born in County Down Ireland in 1816. Ticket No. 48087.
   Capt Francis Trannock Calf was born in County Wicklow in 1832. Ticket No. 12,223 (Liverpool).
   Capt Joseph Morgan was born at Whitehaven in 1824, he served in the *Irt* (1858–63) on the *Antigua* as listed, and then took command of Jefferson's *Patna* purchased from Thos. & John Brocklebank. Ticket No. 17,983. Liverpool 1858.

9. *Ehen* (O.N. 47,782) (1863) (1st Dec)
   301.03 tons
   Barque
   124 ft × 24 ft 9 in × 15 ft 6 in
   Built by Lumley Kennedy & Co. Whitehaven
   Henry Jefferson & Robert Jefferson of Rothersythe both held eight shares. Henry Jefferson Jnr. of

Springfield held 16 shares. Henry Thomas Jefferson of Liverpool, Produce Merchant held eight shares. Robert Jefferson of Ambleside, Westmorland, Wine Merchant, held eight shares. George Robinson, Jnr. of Greenlane, Carlisle, Gentleman, held eight shares, and the vessel's master, Capt Joseph Wise of Whitehaven held eight shares.

Voyages. 1864 Liverpool–Lima–Callao etc. Capt Joseph Wise (1st Master). 1865 Liverpool–B. Ayres –Whitehaven Capt Joseph Wise. 1866 Whitehaven–Demr. Barbados Capt Joseph Wise. 1867 Liverpool–Antigua, Liverpool–Barbados Capt Joseph Wise. 1868 Liverpool–Antigua, Alcoa Bay Capt Joseph Wise. 1869 Liverpool–Barbados–Bahia Capt Joseph Wise. 1870 Liverpool–Rio–Barbados Capt Joseph Wise. 1871 Liverpool – ? Capt Joseph Wise. Change of Master to Albert Henry Hulme (15th Sept 1871 – at Liverpool). 1872, 1873 Liverpool – ? Capt A. H. Hulme. Change of Master to J. Morgan 28th March 1874. 1874, 1875, 1876, 1877 Liverpool – ? Capt Joseph Morgan. Change of Master to Lewis Evans 17th May 1878. 1878 (owner now Lewis Evans) Capt Lewis Evans.

In 1880 ownership of this vessel had passed to Mr L. Evans of 28 Monastery Road Liverpool, the *Ehen* then being commanded by Capt David Evans. After various changes of owners and masters the barque was finally sold to Achilles E. Pray of 110 Boulevard St. Germain, Paris, France, this being on the 14th June 1888. Capt Pray both owned and commanded the vessel at this time – owning no other ship. Not entered under the name of *Ehen* in the Registers after 1891. Capt Pray registered the barque at Havre, and, one suspects, changed the ship's name.

10. *Patna* (1842)
    362 tons
    Barque
    110 ft 0 ins × 22 ft 8 in × 17 ft 5 in
    Built by Thomas & John Brocklebank, Whitehaven
    All shares held by Robert & Henry Jefferson. Sold by Brocklebank's to Jefferson's in 1868
    Voyages. 1869 Whitehaven–W. Indies Capt Joseph Morgan (Morgan leaves *Antigua* 7th Dec 1868). 1870, 1871, 1872 Whitehaven–Cork–W. Indies Capt Joseph Morgan. 1877 Cork–W. Indies–Liverpool–Mauritius Capt Joseph Morgan till Sept 1873.
    The *Patna* was then sold to Messrs W. R. Kelly of Whitehaven, traded coastally under the command of Capt T. Evans, and broken up in 1886 – after being afloat some 44 years. For early history see Brocklebank Fleet List.

Appendix C

Continuous Fleet List, Jefferson's (Excluding the 'Gale')

No.	Vessel	1818	1819	1820	1821	1822	1823	1824	1825	1826	1827	1828	1829	1830	1831	1832	1833	1834	1835
1	Doris								(Wrecked Bahamas 1825)										
2	Thetis																		
3	Lady Shaw Stewart																		
4	Derwent																		

No.	Vessel	1836	1837	1838	1839	1840	1841	1842	1843	1844	1845	1846	1847	1848	1849	1850	1851	1852	1853
2	Thetis	(Foundered off Cape Finisterre after striking sunken Wreck May 1837)																	
3	Lady Shaw Stewart											Sold to Buckingham & Co. June 1846							
4	Derwent							Sold to M'Minn circa 1842 – bought back c 1853											
5	British Queen								Sold to George Athil, of Antigua December 1843										
6	Midge																		

No.	Vessel	1854	1855	1856	1857	1858	1859	1860	1861	1862	1863	1864	1865	1866	1867	1868	1869	1870	1871
4	Derwent																		
5	British Queen									Sold to her master, Capt Moat c 1862/3									
7	Antigua								Lost off Newfoundland May 1861										
8	Ehen																		
9	Patna																		

No.	Vessel	1872	1873	1874	1875	1876	1877	1878	1879	1880
7	Antigua									Sold to H. S. Van Gauten of Holland October 1880
8	Ehen							Sold to Capt Lewis Evans of Liverpool, May 1878		
9	Patna		Sold to W. T. Kelly of Whitehaven, September 1873							

Appendix D

With Henry Jefferson, on the brig 'Thetis', bound for Antigua 1824

11th January 1824. Sailed from Whitehaven in the brig *Thetis*, Capt John Taylor, bound for Antigua. At half-past 6 o'clock a.m. wind S.E. to 7 p.m. Day remarkably fine and clear, wind varying from S.E. Kept perfectly free from sickness all day. Read a couple of cantatas of Don Juan and two or three newspapers – saw very few sails this day. Towards 9 p.m. began to blow rather fresh, had an uncomfortable night.

January 13th. Got up at half-past 8 o'clock after having passed a restless night and found myself far from well this morning. Day fine and clear, wind now moderate at W.N.W. At 10 a.m. off the Skerries Lighthouse near Holyhead on the Welsh coast. The Skerries light is situated on a rock quite insulated by the sea and at several miles distance from the mainland. It is generally provisioned for 3 months and has a boat constantly attending its communications with the mainland and Holyhead, from which it is distant about 6 miles. Light Stationary.

The Stack Lighthouse is very near Holyhead and is also situated on a rock. The Lighthouse owing to the land overhanging the rock on which the South Stack light is placed is very high and precipitous and the communication is kept up by means of a bridge made of rope which appears suspended in the air, and must I think be a very fine sight but we are not yet quite near enough to distinguish it.

The tide is running low today, not less than 5 knots. 12 a.m. noon. We're boarded by a pilot boat from Holyhead, No. 7, by whom I wrote a few lines home. Taylor gave the crew consisting of 7 men a bottle of rum and a shilling. Had a good view of the town of Holyhead which seems to be about the same size as Maryport. The coast all along is black and hilly but there appears here and there patches of fine rich lands. At 6 p.m. wind came round to N.W. and a beautiful evening. Three lights in sight viz Skerries, Holyhead, Holyhead stationary, and Sou Stack revolving distinguished from Holyhead to the Sou Stack about 2½ miles. I.O.M. 2 revolving lights on the Calf – 1 on the point of air, + at Douglas, i at Peel ...

January 14th. This has been a delightful day, wind favourable say N.E. to E and our ship running before the wind 4 to 5 knots. Kept entirely free from sea sickness, and read or wrote three or four hours. During the forenoon in sight of the Welsh coast as far as Bardsey Island. Master Timour (Jefferson's horse) this morning underwent a regular douzing and had his ration of carrots and potatoes considerably increased as a council of war was held, and it was judged by Jack Tar that he had grown thinner since he came onboard. Shot another gull this afternoon – this is killing four out of six – almost as good as pidgeon shooting.

January 22nd. Fine warm day, ship going about six knots, saw two sail this morning which were in sight yesterday. The former one about 2 miles ahead as we lowered top gallant sails last night on account of the sky looking dirty or stormy. Sleep well at nights now and am certainly improving in

173

health. 9 p.m. very calm and little wind. We are now about the latitude of Madeira, and hope in a day or two's sail to have the trade winds. Read and arranged a file or two of newspapers and some papers in the writing desk. Taylor has been in bed about two minutes and is already snoring as loud as a pig therefore I think I had better follow his example. Must lessen Timour's feed a little as he is getting too fat. He has not laid down since a day or two after we sailed. Turned him in his stall today by way of easing his forelegs.

January 24th. Last night a fresh breeze sprang up and we had a fair run. This morning rain for about an hour after which quite a calm during the whole day. Made my first attempt in the culinary art this morning in the shape of an excellent apple tart, which with half a dozen little cakes might have rivelled any of Fanny Greaves' patisserie. During the operation of fitting the top crust to the dish a terrible uproar commenced upon deck and cries of 'Down with the boat! Down with the boat!' were sounding long and loud from the mouth of our gallant commander. On running upon deck expecting someone had fallen overboard I found after several enquiries a turtle had been seen floating past. A short time afterwards we had the pleasure of seeing the boat return with a remarkably fine one, which tho' only in a very small shell weighed 32 lbs, so that our larder at present magnificently supplied. The latitude we are now in is 34.38 being mainly that of Madeira.

February 7th. This day much the same as the one before, but not quite so hot, altho' in the morning I did not feel well from the heat, but which perhaps was caused by grooming Master Timour. Had another bath this morning. We are now very nearly in the latitude of Antigua, say 18.18. Antigua is 17.9, the difference about 132 miles, so that tomorrow we will be laying our course direct for the island.

Bugs I find are far from scarce on the brig *Thetis*, we discovered one the other day cutting its capers on our excellent Cheshire cheese, and yesterday night the Mate cracked one which was taking a nap on his bed. All this time we passed without having recourse to my little medicine chest which Stanley prepared, therefore, I think I cannot do better than give my stomach a fillip tonight with a calomile pill, and tomorrow morning have a potion of salts, as I do think I am at present a little annoyed by my old acquaintance, tho' no friend, William Bill Esquire! Salt junk to dinner, the Devil a thing else.

February 10th. Fine breeze and day rather cooler – at noon a very heavy shower of rain which completely drenched everything upon deck. At day light this morning sail in sight who had evidently expected they were near land as they had very little canvas spread. At 10 a.m. run her out of sight. Our reckoning will be out tomorrow, and I expect if the wind continues as it is we will make the land tomorrow evening. Got no observation today on account of the squall.

Have seen today and many other times on our passage across the Atlantic (and at an immense distance from the land) a bird which the sailors denominate 'an Old Wife', it is about the size and shape of a Wood Pidgeon and has a dark blue back and white belly. This morning all busy upon deck binding cables which are now all in readiness for casting anchor....

February 11th. 2 p.m. Land! Bearing W half S to our great joy and which exactly corresponds with the Mate's dead reckoning. We shortened sail last night partly expecting to see the land, or rather this morning after the moon had set. All hands are now bustling about and as the breeze is strong we will not be long making it show itself distinctly as it is at present rather hazy. Got wind into the roadstead at about sunset, after tea went on shore with John Davison who came on board and visited Mr McKie and Mr McNish to whom I delivered their letters.

Came on board again in Captain Dobson's boat with him and Capt. Taylor. Crop expected to be very good, the *Strabo* has already taken in a few casks also the *Harmony* for Rodic Shands & the *Solon* for Turners. Capt. Dobson had 7 weeks passage, the *Zephyr* about 5 weeks.

174

On the island of Antigua with Henry Jefferson, 1824

February 17th. Rode with Mr Briggs to Old Road and saw Mr Betts for whom I may reckon on 20 or 25 hlds. From thence to Mr Icks who said our account must be delivered at Mr Bradshaw in order to be settled, from thence to Body Ponds where I saw Mr Merchant who promises the usual shipment but only began to grind today therefore will be rather late. After came on to Betty's Hope (and partook of Mr Osborne's hospitality) where I am now writing and intend taking my abode till morning. Was sorry to find that instructions had come out to Mr O requesting that the same shipment only might be made this year to Whitehaven that was last, viz 20 Hlds. Mr Osborne recommends writing to England respecting it and thinks on having made such an excellent sale ought to be an inducement to their making us a larger shipment. A considerable part of their crop is ordered to go to Widderbarry House in London. There are 4 estates here at Betty's Hope belonging to Sir Charles Codrington, the produce of which some years has been nearly 800 Hlds. Sir C's property in good times, and after a good crop have produced 30,000 Stg in one year. The works are very fine and there are 2 good wine stills which will make on a good grinding day 5 or 7 Hlds of sugar....

March 25th. Breakfasted onboard the *Thetis*, afterwards we rode to the villa to see Mr Blackburn's estate which will make about 150 Hlds. Rode out to Painters and dined at home alone. Wrote part of a letter for the packet. News from Liverpool has been rec'd with a/c up to 21st February.

March 26th. Mr Briggs and Taylor breakfasted with me, read the Kings speech at home which seems a little in favour of the West Indies. Briggs, McKie and Taylor dined with me, the Jamieson's came in the evening.

March 27th. Went out to Cades Bay in the morning, afterwards to Rendezvous Bay where we dined & staid all night at Marchants.

March 29th. Came into St. John's with Captain Lough. After breakfast had a call from Osborne who offered me Betty's Hope sugar at 5 dollars a cask – 44 dollars (about 30 Hlds) Wrote home – no packet yet. Dined with Graves.

March 31st. Packet arrived from England with both the 1st & 2nd February Mails. Had only one letter from H & R's dated 2nd February. Dined at Mr Sanderson's, I met there the American Consul, Mr Harrison & a small party.

April 6th. Cleared out the *Thetis* at the Custom House. Recd from John McKie £9 0 0. paid duty on wine and porters £1 7 0. Dined at home with Taylor.

April 12th. After breakfast rode on to the valley to see Dr Osborne. Could not prevail upon him to promise sugars for the *Doris*. From thence on to Greencastle. I found Barnards intends shipping 10 Hlds to Dublin of Sir H Martin's Sugars. Got into town at 6 O'clock dined at home, and in the evening had Mrs Muir my Landlady and Miss Withers as visitors – both these ladies recollect my poor dear mother very well.

April 14th. Set off at 6 O'clock with Mr Grant to the late Mr French's Estate called Cochrams. The works and property all together is remarkably well conducted by Mr Salmon the manager. They expect to make about 120 or 125 Hlds, if they exceed 120 I will get the remainder for the *Thetis*. Breakfasted and dined there. Met Doctor Hodges who lives in the neighbourhood and came out with his sister in the *Doris*, also Mr Lloyd and a Mr Clark who lives upon a property called Makims that is likely to be sold, and is a very capital small estate. O'Connor and Mr Moor have money on it. It belongs to a Miss Masterson. Will make this year about 70 Hlds fine sugar, part of the Sugars have gone to Dublin, the remainder have yet to be shipped and it is not known as yet where they will be sent to.

May 10th.

Copy of letter P Packet

10 May 1824

Dear Father,

My last letters were by the *Mayflower* Antigua Packet since then say on the 1st Inst. the *Wilkinson* arrived bringing me your letters of the 27th March by which I regret to find that the *Doris* had not arrived at Glasgow, nor was likely to do so in time to find out how. With respect to the *Hope*, I hope you may have sent her out as I think I could load her fully, this however would deprive the *Thetis* of a load to Whitehaven, which I think if the *Doris* had been here in good time I could have managed. On reffering to my letters I see there is no chance of your getting my second letters by the *Strabo* and *Harmony* till about the 25th April, therefore you could have no idea when you wrote of sending the *Thetis* out again, this is unlucky as you would naturally suppose that a month or so in the arrival of the second ship could make no difference, however you are doing everything for the best and I must wait patiently till I hear again from you before making any further arrangements.

Barnard and his daughter are going home in the *Camden* to London to sail early next month. Briggs will have the care of Greencastle in his absence. This will not make any difference in his shipments and he intends coming out here on his return positively from Whitehaven. I think he could have waited for our second vessel had he not had his daughter with him who would have been very uncomfortable in so small a vessel as the *Doris* is. Shipping is very plentiful here now and it is thought many of the 1st London ships that intend returning will find some difficulty in getting a cargo, however, I have no doubt of being able to get the *Thetis* filled. I could have chartered her with Turners for Liverpool about a month ago but of course refused expecting to load her if not altogether at least part for Whitehaven. Since then I suppose they have written home for a vessel and even if they should not, I am not at liberty to agree with them till I hear positively from you the size of the second vessel as should it be the *Hope* she will carry within her about 80 Hlds of what both our Brigs would load, at the same time the *Hope* should she come, will be as large as I could load (unless shipments I do not expect should turn out) as many of our shippers give me a great number of Hlds if shipped at two different periods and the work divided, than they could possibly do otherwise, and this circumstance I calculate would have nearly, if not altogether completed the *Thetis*'s load for Whitehaven, more particularly so if the *Doris* had been here in good time, which not being so has caused me to lose many shipments I otherwise might have got; for instance, Dr Osborne has both his curing houses as full as they can hold and I am sure he would have shipped to Whitehaven had we a vessel laying on. He is now expecting momently a vessel from Baillies House of Bristol, by which I am afraid he will ship very largely. Barn and Briggs also each are to give her 20 Hlds.

The weather for grinding for some time past has been exceedingly good and some Estates by the end of next month will have finished crop, and after that will no doubt be anxious to ship as early as they can. I will look for the *Thetis* about the 1st July and hope she is not far from you now. With respect to the management of our business here, it struck me soon after my arrival that no one was so likely, if he would accept it as Mr Briggs, as independantly of his being much esteemed, he is a man of the strictest integrity, and on the best of terms with all our shippers, particularly Barnard, who as well as Briggs has it always in his power very much to assist us in loading our vessels and it is of great consequence to us to be as intimately as possible connected with both.

I broached the subject to Briggs the other day and was glad to find that he had not the least objection to it, on my remarking that he might consider of the terms on which he would accept it he said we would not disagree in that respect and I have no doubt I will be able to agree with him before I have to the satisfaction of us all.

There is one thing that I am sure will be the effect of it, that is in getting our first vessel away early, and in hearing through Jamieson's arrangement for the *Strabo*, particularly if the *Doris* goes out first,

176

which for the future she must always do. Mr Farquhar, in a letter just received is very much dissatisfied with the Glasgow market.

Sir H. Martin was the same in his last letter to us, and I have no doubt next year we will be able to get the first sugars from both of them. I am quite satisfied it has been the greatest disadvantge to us that we have no resident Attorney or anyone to interest himself in the past in us, except during the few months Fisher was out, who for many obvious reasons was not likely to increase our shipments much. It is very likely I think, and was observed by Mr Briggs, that from having regular advise of the markets here a few brls Herrings, Oats etc. might be sold by him for us for cash to give us a very handsome profit, but never to send anything that required retail selling, but mainly whole packages. In short I am very sanguine respecting our future business in this Island, and have no doubt with care and attention on our part and a continuance of our favourable markets we may extend it so as to be at once top and advantageous.

With respect to writing to me, you may calculate with safety on my being here till the 1st of August and give the packets about 35 days, however should they arrive after I have (left) Mr Briggs, to whom you may divert them, can return them to England for me. 5 o'clock p.m. The *Montrose* fr Liverpool sailed 5th April has just come in, no letters for me. I have directed this letter to H.J. think it may not be taken into the office.

To guard against mistakes I have to request you will not on any account accept any bills drawn on you without advise from me, except of course those drawn by my own hand or where you have funds. I believe I mentioned in a former letter that Mr Clarke would draw £1,000 on his Tcs P *Thetis* – I have just heard that Turners have taken up another vessel to sail from Liverpool – the *William Wise*. I have just agreed with Mr Clarke to pay him three or four hundred Pounds in cash as part of the £1,000 and give him Bills for the remainder as I wish to pay away what money Fisher has here in order to get him it home. He has drawn the amounts 3, 6 and 9 months as first mentioned and given them to a planter here, however he has left me to get them from him again and desires me to tell you if by any chance they may have left the Island that you do not accept them – they are drawn in his name.

With best love to you all I remain

Your affectionate son
H. Jefferson Jnr.

May 11th
The above letter with one to Fisher forwarded P Packet. Took a ride about sunset with Jno Osborne who came here to dine with us.

May 12th
Wrote a letter to my sister Mary, afterwards rode out to Five Islands to see Mrs Billinghurst who promised a – shipment, Barnes dined with me also Jno McKie.

May 13th
Strolled about the town with Jamieson, wrote a line or two home by the packet, rode to Clarks at Montero and dined at Greencastle to meet Hyndman and Jamieson.

Appendix E

Valuation of some of the Brocklebank fleet – 1842

Ship	Year Built	Age (yrs)	Tonnage	Value
Aden	1839	3	310	£5,580
Andes	1823	19	216	£1,836
Balfour	1809	33	310	£1,240
Courier	1826	16	142	£1,136
Crown	1821	21	297	£2,044
Esk	1828	14	217	£1,953
Hindoo	1831	11	266	£3,192
Jumna	1833	9	364	£5,460
Kestrel	1840	2	231	£3,860
Lanercost	1842	New	318	£5,920
Manchester	1824	18	163	£1,304
Oberon	1827	15	150	£1,200
Patna	1842	New	362	£7,100
Patriot King	1832	10	338	£4,732
Patriot Queen	1838	4	476	£8,330
Princess Charlotte	1815	27	514	£2,570
Princess Royal	1841	1	579	£10,920
Tigris	1836	6	422	£6,963
Westmorland	1814	28	195	£1,950

Appendix F

Brocklebank Family Tree

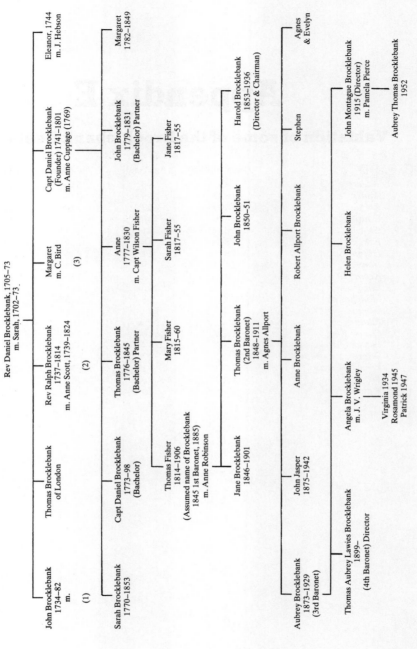

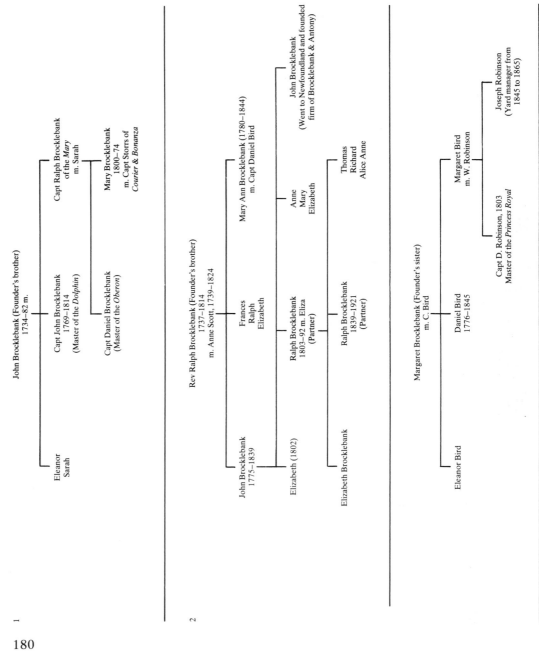

1

John Brocklebank (Founder's brother)
1734–82 m.

Eleanor
Sarah

Capt John Brocklebank
1769–1814
(Master of the *Dolphin*)

Capt Daniel Brocklebank
(Master of the *Oberon*)

Capt Ralph Brocklebank
of the *Mary*
m. Sarah

Mary Brocklebank
1800–74
m. Capt Storrs of
Courier & Bonanza

2

Rev Ralph Brocklebank (Founder's brother)
1737–1814
m. Anne Scott, 1739–1824

John Brocklebank
1775–1839

Frances
Ralph
Elizabeth

Mary Ann Brocklebank (1780–1844)
m. Capt Daniel Bird

Elizabeth (1802)

Ralph Brocklebank
1803–92 m. Eliza
(Partner)

Anne
Mary
Elizabeth

John Brocklebank
(Went to Newfoundland and founded
firm of Brocklebank & Antony)

Elizabeth Brocklebank

Ralph Brocklebank
1839–1921
(Partner)

Thomas
Richard
Alice Anne

Margaret Brocklebank (Founder's sister)
m. C. Bird

Eleanor Bird

Daniel Bird
1776–1845

Capt D. Robinson, 1803
Master of the *Princess Royal*

Margaret Bird
m. W. Robinson

Joseph Robinson
(Yard manager from
1845 to 1865)

Appendix G

The Jefferson Family of Whitehaven and Antigua

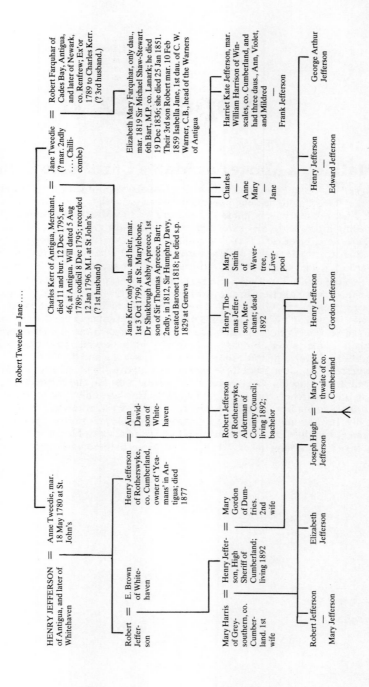

Robert Tweedie = Jane . . . .

HENRY JEFFERSON of Antigua, and later of Whitehaven = Anne Tweedie, mar. 18 May 1780 at St. John's

Charles Kerr of Antigua, Merchant, died 11 and bur. 12 Dec 1795, æt. 46, at Antigua. Will dated 5 Aug 1789; codicil 8 Dec 1795; recorded 12 Jan 1796. M.I. at St John's. (? 1st husband) = Jane Tweedie (? mar. 2ndly . . . Chillicombe) = Robert Farquhar of Cades Bay, Antigua, and later of Newark, co. Renfrew; Ex'or 1789 to Charles Kerr. (? 3rd husband.)

Robert = E. Brown Jefferson of Whitehaven

Henry Jefferson of Rotherswyke, co. Cumberland, owner of 'Yeamans' in Antigua; died 1877 = Ann Davidson of Whitehaven

Jane Kerr, only dau. and heir, mar. 1st 3 Oct 1799, at St. Marylebone, Dr Shukbrugh Ashby Apreece, 1st son of Sir Thomas Apreece, Bart; 2ndly, in 1812, Sir Humphry Davy, created Baronet 1818; he died s.p. 1829 at Geneva

Elizabeth Mary Farquhar, only dau., mar. 1819 Sir Michael Shaw-Stewart, 6th Bart, M.P. co. Lanark; he died 19 Dec 1836; she died 25 Jan 1851. Their 3rd son Robert mar. 10 Feb 1859 Isabella Jane, 1st dau. of C. W. Warner, C.B., head of the Warners of Antigua

Mary Harris of Greysouthern, co. Cumberland. 1st wife = Henry Jefferson, High Sheriff of Cumberland; living 1892 = Mary Gordon of Dumfries. 2nd wife

Robert Jefferson of Rotherswyke, Alderman of County Council; living 1892; bachelor

Henry Thomas Jefferson, Merchant; dead 1892 = Mary Smith of Wavertree, Liverpool

Charles
—
Anne
Mary
—
Jane

Harriet Kate Jefferson, mar. William Harrison of Winscales, co. Cumberland, and had three daus., Ann, Violet, and Mildred

Robert Jefferson
—
Mary Jefferson

Elizabeth Jefferson

Joseph Hugh Jefferson = Mary Cowperthwaite of co. Cumberland

Henry Jefferson
—
Gordon Jefferson

Henry Jefferson
—
Edward Jefferson

Frank Jefferson

George Arthur Jefferson

181

Appendix H

Obtaining a Master or Mates Certificate in the 1850s

By an order of 1845 the Board of Trade authorised a system of voluntary examinations of competency for men intending to become masters or mates of foreign-going British merchant ships. This system, at first voluntary, was made compulsory by the Mercantile Marine Act 1850, and the Merchant Shipping Act of 1854 extended examinations to the masters and mates of home trade vessels. There were, however, crucial exceptions to the above examination rules, e.g. those masters or mates who had served in either of these capacities prior to the above dates, could, upon application to the Board of Trade, obtain their Certificates without submitting to examination.

To obtain a Certificate without sitting an examination each applicant had to fill in what was termed a Master's (or mate's) Claim for Certificate of Service sheet, which document was about the size of an A4 sheet of typing paper. On this sheet each man had to state his full name, the number of his Register ticket, when and where he was born, and his present age. On the part of the sheet headed 'Particulars of Service' each man had to state the name of each vessel he had served in, the port the ship belonged to, the vessel's tonnage, his capacity whilst serving in the ship (whether apprentice, seaman, mate or master), the trade the vessel was engaged in, and the dates of service served in each respective vessel. Happily most of these sheets have survived, and are now in the safe keeping of the National Maritime Museum, Greenwich; they provide a useful, and surprisingly accurate, source of information for researchers today. Of the four Wise Brothers only Francis, the youngest of the four had to sit an examination, Abraham, George, and Joseph, receiving their tickets at Liverpool automatically. It was common practice for mariners' employers to correspond with both the Registrar of Seamen, and the Customs Authorities (who were responsible for transmitting Certificates to mariners), in order to obtain tickets for their men. Many of these letters have survived, including the following:–

To the Registrar of Seamen
                    London   Liverpool 28th Dec 1850
Sir,
   We will thank you to forward by *return post* Certificates of *Competency* for
Nicholas Conway   Master of the *Sir Henry Pottinger*
Francis Wise, 1st Mate 85, 393   –do–   –do–
George Scott, 2nd do   20,4386   –do–   –do–
The claim for the Certificate of the Master was sent yesterday, for the 1st and 2nd mate about a week
since.
To be forwarded to the Registrar of Seamen at this port.

                                   We remain
                                        Sir
                                   Your Obt Svts
17 Rumford St.   Thos. & Jno. Brocklebank
                                   (Signed) P. E. H. Monday.
P.S.
The vessel sails in a day or two.

Whitehaven 12th April 1851

To the Collector & Comp.
of H.M. Customs
Whitehaven

Sir
Our vessel the *British Queen*, Captain Joseph Wise, arrived at Liverpool from Porto Rico on the 10th
Inst., and as the vessel will proceed again to sea very shortly we will be much obliged by your
forwarding Capt. Wise's Certificate of servitude, in your hands, to the proper quarters by today's
post –

                        We are Sir,
                             Your Obt. Serv.
                             Robt. Hy Jefferson

Collector & Controller Liverpool

Gentlemen,
   As above requested, we enclose the Master's Certificate of Joseph Wise No. 48315 for the purpose
of being issued at your port.

                                              We are Gentlemen
                                              Your most Obt. Serv.

Custom House
Whitehaven   John Rossington
12th April 1851

The claim sheet made out by Francis Wise (for his *mate's* Certificate) was only submitted on the 12th
December 1850, and as may be noted, Capt Conway's the day before Mr Monday, at Brocklebank's,
felt obliged to press the Registrar for a prompt response! Clearly ship-owners in the 1850s expected
prompt service from Government Officials; alas, despite Mr Monday's efforts it was to be the 25th

February before Francis Wise received his Certificate. This delay meant that he never sailed in the *Sir Henry Pottinger* again, but remained ashore until the 1st March 1851. He then shipped as first mate of the *Aden*, under Capt Thomas Smith, setting sail for Hong Kong on the above date.

George Wise submitted an undated Claim Sheet, some time in 1850, and whilst residing at 18 St. James Street, Liverpool, Fletcher Hales, his brother-in-law, of 11 King Street, Whitehaven, acting as witness to his signature, whilst Abraham Vaux Wise, the elder brother submitted his sheet on the 18th Sept 1850 – some nine years after being appointed master of Brocklebank's South Pacific trader – the *Kestrel*, and whilst living at Cockermouth.

The Wise Brothers' Certificates

Abraham Vaux Wise	Master's Certificate No. 48.604 Liverpool, July 1851
George Wise	Master's Certificate No. 48.872 Liverpool, Jan. 1851
Joseph Wise	Master's Certificate No. 48.315 Liverpool, Apr. 1851
Francis Wise	Mate's Certificate No. 68.460 Liverpool, Feb. 1851
	Master's Certificate No. 85.393 Liverpool, Jan. 1852

Appendix I

The Ships of Abraham Vaux Wise and Sons, and John and James Glover

Captain Abraham Vaux Wise, Snr.
Born at Cockermouth, 1784, died Droghedra, 7th November 1827

Ship No.	Vessel's Name	Owner	Capacity	Trade	Date of Service
	Swallow	Wilson Fisher	Master	West Indies	26 Sept 1809–21 Sept 1810
	Maranham	Fisher/B'Bank	Master	West Indies	21 Sept 1810–5 Feb 1814
	Eleanor	Captain & Co.	Master	West Indies	31 Oct 1814–27 Oct 1817

Captain Abraham Vaux Wise, Jnr.
(Ticket No. 48.604 Liv. 1851)
Born at Whitehaven, 26th June 1812, died whilst in command of the 'Kestrel' 2 a.m. Wednesday 17th January 1855 – on passage to Islay

Ship No.	Vessel's Name	Owner	Capacity	Trade	Date of Service
	Bransty	Brocklebank's	Apprentice	Gulf of Mexico	Feb 1832–Aug 1834
	Tampico	Brocklebank's	Apprentice	Brazils/Nfnd'land	Aug 1834–Apr 1836
	Tigris	Brocklebank's	Seaman	Calcutta/China	May 1836–June 1837
	Oberon	Brocklebank's	Mate	Brazils/Nfnd'land	July 1837–May 1840
	Kestrel	Brocklebank's	Mate	Chile/Peru	June 1840–Nov 1841
	Kestrel	Brocklebank's	Master	Chile/Peru	Nov 1841–17 Jan 1855

Captain George Wise.
(Ticket No. 48.872 Liv. 1851)
Born at Whitehaven, 2nd July 1817, died whilst in command of the 'Aracan' 4.30 a.m. Monday 28th September 1857 – whilst off South Stack, Holyhead

Ship No.	Vessel's Name	Owner	Capacity	Trade	Date of Service
	Perseverence	Gunson & Co.	Apprentice	China	18 Jan 1832–18 June 1837
	Camerton	Hewitt & Co.	2nd Mate	West Indies	June 1837–Sept 1837
	Sarah	Tyson & Co.	1st Mate	Coasting	Nov 1837–Mar 1838
	Emma	Morris & Co.	2nd Mate	California	Apr 1838–June 1839
	Matilda	Worrall & Co.	1st Mate	Mediterranean	Aug 1839–Aug 1841
	Catherine	(At Halifax N.S.)	1st Mate	North America	Oct 1841–Nov 1843
	Princess Royal	Brocklebank's	2nd Mate	East Indies	Dec 1843–Nov 1845
	Patriot Queen	Brocklebank's	1st Mate	East Indies	Nov 1845–Dec 1847
	Esk	Brocklebank's	Master	Brazils	Dec 1847–Dec 1851
	Patriot King	Brocklebank's	Master	East Indies	1 Jan 1852–May 1855
	Tigris	Brocklebank's	Master	East Indies	5 June 1855–8 Mar 1856
	Aracan	Brocklebank's	Master	East Indies	20 April 1856–28 Sept 1857

Captain Joseph Wise.
(Ticket No. 48.315 Liv. 1851)
Born at Sandwith, near Whitehaven, 27th May 1821, died 20th October 1882

Ship No.	Vessel's Name	Owner	Capacity	Trade	Date of Service
	Lady Shaw Stewart	Jefferson/Peny	Apprentice	Antigua	21 Dec 1834–21 Dec 1839
	Lady Shaw Stewart	Jefferson/Peny	2nd Mate	Antigua	Dec 1839–Sept 1840
	Midge	Jefferson's	Mate	Cadiz/Antigua	Dec 1840–Aug 1841
	Lady Shaw Stewart	Jefferson/Peny	1st Mate	Antigua	Jan 1842–June 1842

Ship No.	Vessel's Name	Owner	Capacity	Trade	Date of Service
	Lady Shaw Stewart	Jefferson/Peny	Master	Antigua	June 1842–28 Feb 1846
	British Queen	Jefferson's	Master	Antigua	28 Feb 1846–June 1858
	Antigua	Jefferson/Wise	Master	Antigua/W. Indies	8 June 1858–10 Sept 1863
	Eben	Jefferson/Wise	Master	Lima/Antigua/W.I.	1 Dec 1863–15 Sept 1871
	William Graham	Macandrew	Master	West Indies	26 June 1872–27 Dec 1872
	Marengo	Tindall & Co.	Master	West Indies	12 Aug 1873–11 Feb 1875

Captain Francis Wise.
(Ticket No. 85.393 Liv. 1852)

Born at Sandwith, near Whitehaven, 28th January 1826, died 11th October 1875

Ship No.	Vessel's Name	Owner	Capacity	Trade	Date of Service
	Dryad	Brocklebank's	Apprentice	America/East Ind.	14 Sept 1840–20 Nov 1845
	Bonanza	Brocklebank's	2nd & 1st Mate	America/China	14 Apr 1846–20 Apr 1849
	Sir Henry Pottinger	Brocklebank's	1st Mate	Calcutta	20 Apr 1849–12 Dec 1850
	Aden	Brocklebank's	1st Mate	Hong Kong	Feb 1851–Oct 1852
	Arachne	Brocklebank's	1st Mate	Calcutta	29 Oct 1852–Oct 1853
	Courier	Brocklebank's	Master	Calcutta	5 Oct 1853–Nov 1855
	Rimac	Brocklebank's	Master	Lima	15 Nov 1855–
	Harold	Brocklebank's	Master	Lima/Callao	1859–Jan 1865
	Arachne	Brocklebank's	Master	Calcutta	13 Jan 1865–30 Oct 1865
	Cormorin	Brocklebank's	Master	Calcutta	Nov 1865–July 1870
	Cambay	Brocklebank's	Master	Calcutta	2 July 1870–April 1871
	Chinsura	Brocklebank's	Master	Calcutta	25 Aug 1871–22 Jan 1874

Captain John Glover.

Born at Whitehaven 1789, died at Liverpool 29th July 1853. (Father of Hannah Glover)

Ship No.	Vessel's Name	Owner	Capacity	Trade	Date of Service
	Kitty	B. Fisher & Co.	Master	Coastal	9 Aug 1816–15 July 1826
	Massereene	Captain & Co.	Master	Coastal	29 May 1827–29 July 1853

Captain James Glover.

Born at Whitehaven, 1815, died whilst in command of the 'Rajah Bassa' at Whampoa, China – 13th October 1848 (Brother of Hannah Glover)

Ship No.	Vessel's Name	Owner	Capacity	Trade	Date of Service
	Massereene	John Glover & Co.	Mate	Coastal	During the year 1838
	Manley	Miller's/Glover	Master	Possession/W.I.	29 Jan 1840–8 Jul 1845
	Rajah Bassa	Boadle Bros.	Master	E. Indies/China	17 Nov 1845–2 Oct 1848

Appendix J

The Wise Family – 19th Century Mariners

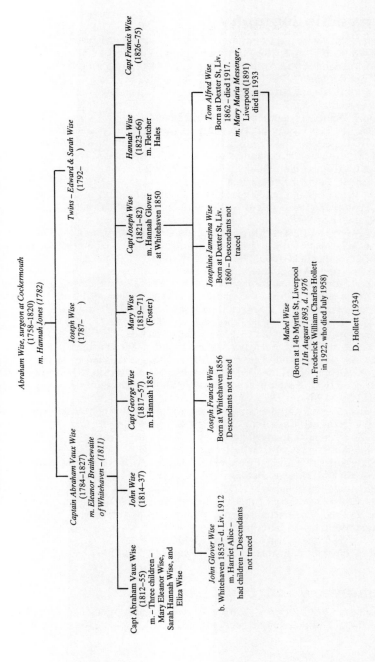

Abraham Wise, surgeon at Cockermouth
(1758–1820)
m. Hannah Jones (1782)

Captain Abraham Vaux Wise
(1784–1827)
m. Eleanor Braithewaite
of Whitehaven – (1811)

Joseph Wise
(1787–   )

Twins – Edward & Sarah Wise
(1792–   )

Capt Abraham Vaux Wise
(1812–55)
m. – Three children –
Mary Eleanor Wise,
Sarah Hannah Wise, and
Eliza Wise

John Wise
(1814–37)

Capt George Wise
(1817–57)
m. Hannah 1857

Mary Wise
(1819–71)
(Foster)

Capt Joseph Wise
(1821–82)
m. Hannah Glover
at Whitehaven 1850

Hannah Wise
(1823–66)
m. Fletcher
Hales

Capt Francis Wise
(1826–75)

John Glover Wise
b. Whitehaven 1853 – d. Liv. 1912
m. Harriet Alice –
had children – Descendants
not traced

Joseph Francis Wise
Born at Whitehaven 1856
Descendants not traced

Josephine Jamesina Wise
Born at Dexter St, Liv.
1860 – Descendants not
traced

Tom Alfred Wise
Born at Dexter St, Liv.
1862 – died 1917.
m. Mary Maria Messenger,
Liverpool (1891)
died in 1933

Mabel Wise
(Born at 14b Myrtle St, Liverpool
11th August 1893, d. 1976
m. Frederick William Charles Hollett
in 1922, who died July 1958)

D. Hollett (1934)

187

Selective Bibliography

Davy, John. The West Indies before and since slave emancipation.
Ferguson, Richard S. A History of Cumberland, published 1890.
Flannigan. Antigua & the Antiguans, published 1844.
Forward, Sir William B. Recollections of a busy life.
Gibson, John Frederick. Brocklebanks 1770–1953, published 1953.
Gores Liverpool Directories
Hay, Daniel. An illustrated history of Whitehaven.
Hutchinson, W. The history of the county of Cumberland, published in 1794.
Jackson, W. Papers and pedigrees related to Cumberland & Westmorland.
Jefferson, S. History and antiquities of Allerdale Ward above Derwent, published 1842.
Jollies. Jollies Cumberland Guide & Directory, published 1811.
Jones, Clement. Pioneer Shipowners.
Lewer, W. Report of the public meeting at Liverpool, 1829, re the East India Co.
Lloyds Captains Registers. (Held by the Guildhall Library, London.)
Lloyds Registers of Shipping.
Lonsdale, Henry, M.D. The worthies of Cumberland, published in 1874.
Mannix & Whellan. History, gazetteer and directory of Cumberland, first published in 1847, republished by Michael Moon, Beckermet Bookshop, 1974.
Martineau, Harriet. A complete guide to the English lakes.
Oliver, Vere Langford. The history of Antigua, published in 1894.
Paton, William Agnew. Down the islands, a voyage to the Caribbees, published in 1888.
Picton, J. A. Memorials of Liverpool, published in 1873.
Piele & Nicholson. Directory of Whitehaven, 1864.
Pigot. Directory of Cumberland, 1834, by Pigot & Co.
Post Office. Post Office Directory of Cumberland & Westmorland, 1856.
Runciman, Sir Walter. Collier brigs and their sailors, published in 1926.
Sawyers, William. A list of the Cumberland shipping, corrected to February 1840, by Wm Sawyers, Comptroller of H.M. Customs at the port of Whitehaven. Published by Crosthwaite & Co. 1840, republished by M Moon, 1975.
Scott, Daniel. Bygone Cumberland & Westmorland, published at Penrith, 1899.
Sea Breezes (Nautical Magazine) October 1935.
Seamans. The seaman's medical guide, published 1863.
Slaters. Slaters directory of Cumberland, 1879.
Slaters. Slaters Royal National Commercial Directory of Northern Counties, 1855.
Sturge, Joseph, and Thomas Harvey. The West Indies in 1837.
Syren. The Syren and shipping, 1942.
Victorian. Victorian history of the counties of England (Cumberland, vol 11).
Wetherill, Richard. The ancient port of Whitby and its shipping, published, Whitby 1908.
Whitehaven. Whitehaven harbour and town register, 1865.
Wise, Rev. Joseph. Miscellany of poems, published in 1775.
Young, Rev. George. A history of Whitby, published in 1817.

Documentary Sources

Cumbria County Record Office, Carlisle. Crew lists and agreements, T/RS/1 Plans of harbours and Docks, Q/RZ/2. General shipping papers, D/SEN/17. Shipping Registers. Whitehaven shipping and

harbour papers, D/Lons/W. Anglican Parish Registers (Cumbria). The Jefferson File, DB/69.
Drogheda, Co. Louth. Parish Records of St. Peters, re death of Capt Abraham Vaux Wise. See also Anfield (Liverpool) cemetery inscription, family grave.
Lancashire Record Office (Preston). Probate Records and Shipping Registers.
Liverpool Record Office. Anfield Cemetery Records (Wise family), Anglican Parish Registers (Liverpool). Brocklebank File, 387 MD. Probate Registers. Accounts of the brig *Musgrave* – Capt Samuel Wise, 387/MD/36.
Memorial University of St. John's, Newfoundland. Crew Lists and agreements.
Merseyside County Archivists Office, Liverpool. Shipping Registers (Liverpool).
Merseyside County Museums (Maritime Division). The Brocklebank Files.
National Maritime Museum, Greenwich. Crew List and Agreements. Early service records. Masters Certificates of Competence. Master/Mates record of service.
Parliamentary Papers (Slavery). General Index to accounts and papers etc. 1801–1852, Paper 215 1837–38 XIVIII 'Sums awarded by the commission of slavery compensation. Paper 160 XXIII 605 Acts resp. the treatment of slaves, Antigua, Barbados, etc.

The Public Record Office, Kew

The records of the Registrar General of Shipping and Seamen
Transcripts and Transactions Series I (BT 107) Series II (BT 108).
Index to Transcripts (BT 111) Series III (BT 109).
Agreements and crew lists Series I (BT 98) Series II (BT 99).
Register of Certificates of Competency & Service, Masters and Mates (BT 122) (BT 124) (BT 126).

Whitehaven Library, Cumbria

Index to the Cumberland Pacquet.

Newspapers

Antigua Free Press.
Antigua Herald and Gazette, 1847.
Antigua Observer.
Cumberland Pacquet.
Liverpool Courier and Commercial Advertiser.
Liverpool Journal of Commerce.
Liverpool Mercury.
Liverpool Telegraph and Naval Directory.
Liverpool Weekly Mercury.
Lloyd's List.
Myers Mercantile Advertiser (Liverpool).
Whitehaven Gazette.
Whitehaven Guardian.
Whitehaven Herald.
Whitehaven Messenger.
Whitehaven News, The.
Williamson's Liverpool Advertiser and Marine Intelligencer.

Memoirs

The rediscovered Memoirs of Capt William Ellery
Published in the 'Wallasey and Wirral Chronicle' as a series of articles, March–July 1912.

The rediscovered Memoirs of Capt William Ray
Published in the Liverpool Journal of Commerce, 22nd October 1921.

Cumbria County Council Archives Department, The Record Office, The Castle, Carlisle
Documents relating to the Brocklebank Line, Jeffersons, and the Vaux Wise family (Files No. 1–30).
Deposited at the Record Office, The Castle, Carlisle January 1983.

Key to Index

A   General Index
B   Sailing ships built or owned by Brocklebanks
C   Brocklebank Steamers
D   Brocklebank Mariners
E   Sailing Fleet of Robert & Henry Jefferson of Whitehaven
F   Jefferson Mariners
G   All other ships
H   All other Mariners

General Index

193

Sailing Ships Built or Owned by Brocklebanks

(Including two early Brocklebank-built paddle steamers)

197

Brocklebank Steamers

Brocklebank Mariners

Combes, Thomas, Appr. 66
Connell, Capt James 128, 164
Conway, Capt Nicholas 149, 160
Cooke, Capt 166
Cooke, J., 4th Mate 134
Cornish, Capt Walter 133, 166
Corran, Capt Jeremiah 150
Cowman, Capt 146, 148
Cragg, Capt (c 1820–40) 151, 154, 157, 158
Cragg Capt (c 1853) 160
Cragg, Capt of *Patriot King* 1866 156
Cragg, Capt Robert (c 1865) 107, 116
Craig, Capt 151
Crockett, Capt 151
Crowder, Capt 157
Curwen, Davey 48
Curwen, Capt E. 72, 86, 113, 157, 159, 164,

D

Davies, Capt 166
Dixon, Capt 46, 148, 151, 159
Douglas, Capt Wm 94, 107, 116, 163, 165
Dunning, Capt 135, 167

E

Edmondson, Capt 147, 154
Ellery, Capt Wm 84, 85, 90, 95, 103, 106, 108, 109, 110, 118, 123, 124, 128, 131, 132, 134, 135, 164, 165, 167
Elliot, Capt 153
Evans, Capt 163

F

Farrell, Capt 159
Fearon, Capt (c 1804) 145
Fearon, Capt (c 1863) of *Arachne* 161
Fearon, Thomas, Mate 48
Fletcher, Capt (c 1850s–60s) 107, 120, 149, 156, 157, 158, 161, 162
Fletcher, George, Appr. 39
Fletcher, Capt George 86, 116
Fletcher, Capt H. 71
Fell, Capt (c 1816) 148, 150
Fell, Capt Robert (c 1810) 30
Fell, Capt Thomas of *Constellation* 34
Fisher, Capt of *Westmorland 2* 149
Fleming, Capt 140
Folder, Capt 143
Forshaw, Capt Joseph 128, 163, 164
Forsyth, Capt William 116, 124, 160, 162, 163
Foster, Capt of *Balfour* 44
Foster, Capt George of *Maiden Queen* 113, 116, 161
Fox, Capt 144
Fraser, Capt 30
Frederickson, Capt 166, 167
Frost, James, Seaman 83
Fulton, Capt of *Westmorland* 52, 148

G

Gaitskell, Capt William 150
Gibson, Capt 51, 161
Graham, Mark, Appr. 64

Graham, Capt Wm V. 107, 116, 133, 161, 164, 165, 167
Greenlow, Capt Isaih 143
Gregg, Capt of *Caroline* – 1804 146
Greggs, Capt of *Scipio* – 1844 50
Grier, Capt 154
Grindale, Capt 44, 154
Gunston, Capt J. 146

H

Haldane, A. M., Mate of *Comorin* (later Capt Haldane) 112, 116, 163
Halliday, Capt A 71, 149
Hansen, Capt 48
Harrison, Capt (c 1787–95) 140
Harrison, Capt of *Westmorland* (c 1835) 148
Harvey, Capt 149
Harwood, Capt Charles 124, 162
Healy, Capt J. 131, 164
Herbert, Appr. 66
Heyburn, Capt 166
Hill, Christopher, Mate 66
Hodgson, Capt Jonathan 140, 145
Holliday, Capt John 146
Holmes, Henry A.B. 39
Holmes, Capt Walter S. 128
Hoodless, Capt Wm 44, 48, 80, 147, 153, 154, 158, 160
Howe, Capt Charles 83, 84, 86, 107, 116, 118, 159, 162, 163
Howson, Capt J. 86, 160, 164
Hughes, Capt W. P. 135, 165
Hunter, Capt 148
Huntress, Capt 153
Hutchinson, Capt Francis 143
Huxtable, Capt 44, 158

J

Jackson, Capt of *Lord Althorp* 44
Jackson, Capt H. of *Hercules* 30
Jenkins, Capt 95
Jenkinson, Capt John 145
Johnston, Capt John 142
Jones, Capt Henry 110, 115, 116
Jones, Capt Thomas 122, 124, 126
Jordain, Capt J. 86, 159
Joughan, Capt 161, 163
Joughlin, James Robert C. Appr. 118
Joughlin, Capt Joseph 86, 107, 114, 116, 118, 124, 128, 163, 164

K

Kelly, Hugh, Cook 39
Kelly, Capt William 86, 107, 108, 116, 118, 161, 164
Kennedy, Capt John 102
Kenworthy, Capt John 107, 116, 124, 128, 159, 161, 164
Kerr, Capt 44, 145, 148
Kershaw, Capt 164
King, Capt 44, 72, 86, 147, 151, 160, 161, 163
King, Michael Fletcher, Mate 64
Kirkpatrick, Samuel, A.B. 39
Kneale, Capt John 140, 145, 151

Sailing Fleet of Robert & Henry Jefferson of Whitehaven

Jefferson Mariners

201

Index to all other ships

Index to all other Mariners